Geoarchaeology in A

Studies in soil micromorpholo
and landscape evolution

Charles French

 Routledge
Taylor & Francis Group

LONDON AND NEW YORK

First published 2003 by Routledge
2 Park Square, Milton Park, Abingdon, Oxon OX14 4RN

Simultaneously published in the USA and Canada
by Routledge
270 Madison Ave, New York, NY 10016

Routledge is an imprint of the Taylor & Francis Group, an informa business

© 2003 Charles French

Typeset in Garamond by Exe Valley Dataset Ltd, Exeter

British Library Cataloguing in Publication Data
A catalogue record for this book is available from the British Library

Library of Congress Cataloging in Publication Data
French, C. A. I. (Charles A. I.)
  Geoarchaeology in action: studies in soil micromorphology and landscape evolution/
    Charles French.
      p. cm.
  Includes bibliographical references (p.).
  1. Archaeological geology. 2. Landscape changes. 3. Soil science in archaeology.
  4. Soil micromorphology. 5. Soil formation. 6. Excavations (Archaeology) I. Title.

CC77.5.F74 2002
930.1′028–dc21   2002068194

ISBN 10: 0-415-27309-9 (hbk)
ISBN 10: 0-415-27310-2 (pbk)

ISBN 13: 978-0-415-27309-1 (hbk)
ISBN 13: 978-0-415-27310-7 (pbk)

Geoarchaeology in Action

Geoarchaeology in Action provides fresh perspectives on what is important in conducting geoarchaeological investigations on sites and in landscapes, irrespective of date, place and environment. These are backed up by a wide range of case studies that demonstrate how to discover and decipher past landscape change from a digger's, environmentalist's or soil micromorphologist's perspective.

The first part of the book sets out the essential features of geoarchaeological practice and geomorphological processes, and is deliberately aimed at the archaeologist as practitioner in the field. It explains the basics – what can be expected, what approaches may be taken, and what outcomes might be forthcoming – and asks what we can reasonably expect a micromorphological approach to archaeological contexts, data and problems to tell us. The twelve case studies from Britain, Europe and the Near East then illustrate a range of geoarchaeological approaches to primarily buried and/or eroded landscapes.

With a distinct emphasis on landscape and micromorphology, the book weaves palaeoenvironmental histories from complex sets of data and presents them as land-use sequences that are intertwined with the interpretation of the archaeological record. It reflects the author's experience of several decades of investigation in buried and eroded landscapes in the Old World, and develops new ways of looking at conventional models of landscape change.

Charles French is Head of Department and Senior Lecturer in Archaeological Science in the Department of Archaeology, University of Cambridge. Prior to 1992, he was Assistant Director and Palaeo-environmentalist for Fenland Archaeological Trust.

To Kasia, Theo and Hugh

Contents

Illustrations

Tables

Acknowledgements

The author would like to thank a variety of colleagues and supporting organizations on a project-by-project basis for their assistance in making feasible the research that is discussed in this book, as follows:

Welland valley: Dr Francis Pryor, Dr Richard Macphail, Dr Ken Thomas, Dr Rob Scaife, Dr Mark Robinson, Dr Dave Passmore, Dr Mark Macklin, Maisie Taylor, Bob Middleton, Kasia Gdaniec, Dr Ian Kinnes, Dr Geoff Wainwright, David Hall; English Heritage, the British Museum; Fenland Archaeological Trust and Tarmac Roadstone

Nene valley/Flag Fen: Dr F. Pryor, Maisie Taylor, Dr R. Scaife, Dr M. Robinson, Dr D. Passmore, Dr M. Macklin, Rog Palmer; Don Mackreth, Royal Ontario Museum, Toronto, English Heritage, Peterborough Power, Anglian Water, Fenland Archaeological Trust

Ouse valley: Chris Evans, Mark Knight, Mat Davis, Dr Clare Ellis and Jen Heathcote; the Cambridge Archaeological Unit, Hanson Aggregates, Brian Chapman, Brian Burling and Hermitage Farms Ltd.

Allen valley: Dr Helen Lewis, Dr Mike Allen, Dr Rob Scaife, Martin Green, Roy Palmer, GSB Prospection, Philip Rymer, Paul Gosling and Claire Pinder; English Heritage, the Shaftesbury Estate (St Giles Farms Ltd), the Arts and Humanities Research Board, McDonald Institute for Archaeological Research, an anonymous private donor and the Department of Media, Culture and Sport

Aguas valley: Prof. Bob Chapman, Dr D. Passmore, Prof. Tony Stevenson, Dr Roberto Risch and Dr Rafa Mico, DGXII of the European Commission

Troina: Gianna Ayala, Prof. Diego Puglisi, Dr Caroline Malone, Dr Simon Stoddart, the Oasi Foundation and the McDonald Institute for Archaeological Research

Yemen: Tony Wilkinson, Dr Richard Macphail, Brian Pittman, the National Science Foundation (grant no. 9727355), National Geographic Society (grant no. 6040-97), the Oriental Institute, Chicago and the University of Cambridge

Syria: Tony Wilkinson, Dr Joan Oates, Prof. David Oates, Dr Wendy Matthews, the Natural Environment Research Council and the McDonald Institute for Archaeological Research

Botai: Dr Marsha Levine, Dr Victor Buchli, Dr Keith Bennett, Lucy Walker, Dr Alexander Kislenko, Professor Martin Jones, the McDonald Institute for Archaeological Research and the Board of State Scholarships Foundation of the Republic of Greece

Thin section manufacture was carried out by Julie Miller, Brendan Coyle, Karen Milek, Brian Pittman and the author, all of the McBurney Geoarchaeology Laboratory, Department of Archaeology, University of Cambridge

Figure acknowledgements

Several people have contributed to the illustrations used in this book, namely Crane Begg, Gianna Ayala, Tony Wilkinson, Helen Lewis, Chris Evans, Natasha Dodwell, Rog Palmer, Francis Pryor, Paul White, Rob Scaife, Steve Upex and Maria Kousoulakou. Of these, Crane Begg is greatly thanked for his expert input and production of many of the figures.

Preface

This book is not intended to be a textbook, as many excellent geomorphological and geoarchaeological texts already exist (Goudie 1990; Waters 1992; Rapp and Hill 1998). Rather, this book is a personal view about what is important in conducting geoarchaeological investigations on sites and in landscapes, irrespective of date and place, backed up by illustrative case studies from around Britain, Europe and the Near East. Unashamedly, most of the facts, interpretative ideas and models put forward are a direct result of a long time spent in the field on a variety of projects, looking at landscapes in detail from both a digger's and a soil micromorphologist's perspective, and with the benefit of excellent collaborating colleagues. I am also convinced it has helped to be more of a prehistorian than anything else as there is more to piece together from less evidence and one must engage with what one has at the time to tell a reasonable story, or the work is not worth doing in the first place.

I am not the only person looking at prehistoric landscapes with an eye for human and natural interactions (e.g. Richard Bradley, John Evans, Mark Edmonds, Francis Pryor, Mark Macklin, Dave Passmore and Colin Richards – to name a few), but I take a deliberately process-based look at the landscape and what fingerprints it contains. I want to know what is going on in the sealed earth below, where and what types of sequence are held within the soil and the landscape, and why, how these link up with landscape and land-use history and how they both constrain and are changed by human activities. I look at both the broad sweep of time and place, as well as the minutiae of detail held in a single horizon in a thin section slide.

As much of my micromorphological work is buried in specialist reports, published and unpublished, attached and unattached to site reports, a case study-based book such as this is the best way of making much of the information more accessible and readable. Moreover, I hope that it relates the soils and all the other environmental data to the greater archaeological picture in an understandable form, and contributes to the development of the archaeological story through time and space.

I owe a great debt to those who have acted as my mentors in the field and those who have worked for and with me subsequently. There are not many environmental specialists, let alone geoarchaeologists, who have dug and directed full-time for a living for about twenty years prior to becoming based in a university academic environment. This was a key feature of all of Francis Pryor's projects in the 1970s and 1980s, with most of which I was extremely lucky to be involved. Each team member dug every day, but in addition would contribute his or her specialist input to the interpretation of the site, as well as the full post-excavation process. This was essential for team health and decision making, as well as reasonably fast publication. Unfortunately this kind of specialist, all-encompassing team is almost impossible to field these days because of the multi-faceted aspects of any project as well as the expense and speed of contract/rescue archaeology, at least in England.

The first third of the book attempts to set out some of the basic features of geoarchaeological practice and geomorphological processes from my own perspective. This part is deliberately aimed at the archaeologist as practitioner in the field. It is intended to give some essential detail on the basics, what can be expected, some of the approaches that may be taken, and what kinds of outcome might be forthcoming. In particular, I suggest what a micro-morphological approach as applied to archaeological contexts, data and problems can and cannot be reasonably expected to say and provide to the

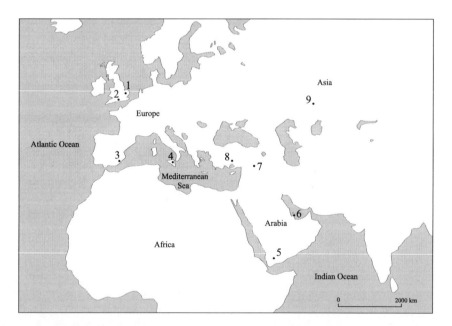

Figure 0.1 Map of Britain, Europe and the Near East illustrating the location of the main sites discussed in the text (1: East Anglian fens, and Welland, Nene and Ouse river valleys; 2: Cranborne Chase, Dorset; 3: Aguas basin, Spain; 4: Troina, Sicily; 5: Dhamar, Yemen; 6: Saar, Bahrain; 7: Tell Brak, Syria; 8: Çatalhöyük, Turkey; 9: Botai, Kazakhstan) (C. Begg).

archaeological story. The aims and approaches discussed are not intended to be an exhaustive overview, rather they are a personal view and sub-set of a vast existing literature, which are further developed in the case studies that follow. There is sufficient detail to make one aware of the processes being discussed, but without the detail to turn this into just another textbook, to which the reader is referred for the finer points of detail. Moreover, a few of what I hope are new ways of looking at conventional models of landscape development are put forward, and further elaborated upon in the twelve case studies that follow in the remaining two-thirds of the book. About one-half of these are centred in the East Anglian fens of Cambridgeshire and other parts of Britain, and the remainder from the Mediterranean fringe, the Near East and Kazakhstan (Figure 0.1).

Part 1

Some essential elements of geoarchaeology

Method and practice

1 Issues and aims in geoarchaeology

Definitions

What is geoarchaeology? Perhaps, it is best to ask what is geomorphology first, then to address the meaning of geoarchaeology second. Geomorphology is the study of the arrangement and differentiation of landforms, and the processes that shape and alter them. This includes everything from sea to river, coast to valley to hillside to mountainside. Some of the major processes responsible for shaping our environment are climate, relief and time, along with snow and ice, water and flooding, volcanic activities and earthquakes, landslides and human activities such as forest clearance and agriculture (see Goudie 1990).

Geoarchaeology is the combined study of archaeological and geomorphological records and the recognition of how natural and human-induced processes alter landscapes. The main aim of geoarchaeology is to construct integrated models of human-environmental systems and to interrogate the nature, sequence and causes of human versus natural impacts on the landscape. It is really only one major strand of environmental archaeology, which generally needs the collaborative and corroborative support of several other sets of data, but a good understanding of it is essential for reading landscapes.

The foregoing is rather a narrow definition of geoarchaeology when compared with say Rapp and Hill (1998: 1–17) who would emphasize that there is much more than the study of soils and sediments to geoarchaeology. It serves as the starting point when studying landscape and its transformations. Rapp and Hill's (1998: 1–2) definition states that 'geoarchaeology refers to any earth-science concept, technique, or knowledge base applicable to the study of artefacts and the processes involved in the creation of the archaeological record'. But they, like myself, would see geoarchaeology as part of archaeology, inextricably linked, and not just geological research. If anything, my theoretical stance is probably closer to Waters' (1992) view that field stratigraphy, site formation processes and landscape reconstruction are the most fundamental tenets of geoarchaeology, which in many respects is a further development of the approach begun by Butzer (1982).

In terms of British archaeology, geoarchaeology is a newly developing field of research that has grown rapidly over the past decade. In fact, however, geologists were applying geological principles and knowledge to archaeological problems as long ago as 1863 as can be seen from Sir Charles Lyell's *Geological Evidences of the Antiquity of Man*. From my own perspective, and I suspect that of many practising archaeologists in the United Kingdom, it would be seen as more an essential branch of landscape archaeology than anything else that uses a variety of techniques and approaches borrowed from geographers, earth and natural scientists. Indeed, these views on the potential and increasing value of scientific approaches to archaeological endeavours were stated by Mortimer Wheeler himself (Wheeler 1954: 2). In many respects, the principal development of this sub-discipline within archaeology has occurred in the United States in, for example, the work of Butzer (1982), Waters (1992), Ferring (1994) and Holliday (1997). These geomorphologists addressed specific archaeological problems, and their analyses were instrumental in shaping new interpretations of the archaeological data. Their work has greatly affected the content and workings of current research project design. But some of the major advances in certain methodological approaches – such as the use of soils in archaeology – have been made by practitioners on this side of the Atlantic such as Cornwall (1958), Limbrey (1975), Davidson (1982), Fitzpatrick (1984), Courty *et al.* (1989). It is this latter route that I will be exploring and adding to in this book.

Data acquisition

Four main types of data collection are regularly used by most geoarchaeological practitioners. Qualitative and quantitative records and measurements are taken in the field. For example, this could take the form of anything from a full-scale, multi-disciplinary field project investigating the nature and effects of early prehistoric clearance to generating modern analogue data (see Chapter 5 below). The full-scale field project could involve geomorphological drift and soil mapping, palaeobotanical and modern vegetational survey and investigations, the use and cross-correlation of deep sea core palaeo-climatic data. It would attempt to establish dated sequences of environmental change and suggest possible major influences on the environmental record of the area. The models thus generated could then be set against the archaeological record using Geographical Information System techniques (Burrough 1986) and further hypotheses of landscape development tested.

To set up a model of landscape change and to add other, more specific, interpretative layers to such a model, it might be necessary to conduct some modern field experiments. For instance, to gather information on possible erosion rates, it would be possible to set out a series of sediment traps across and down a hill-side on the chalk downlands of southern England for several periods in the year fixed in order to recover data on the ability of soil to move downslope under different environmental parameters (Small and Clark 1982; Morgan 1979, 1986). This work would provide data on the amount of sediment moved over a landform type under known conditions over time, and would be essential if one wished to begin to create an erosion model for a specified area of land.

In addition to this type of information, it is often essential to carry out experiments both in the laboratory and in the field to attempt to recreate, or at least create, situations analogous to past conditions. This might involve setting up a series of experiments in the laboratory to mimic natural processes: a wave tank could be used to simulate the effect of wind, water and shore amplitude on the movement of artefacts and animal bone on a lake margin (Morton 1995), or the behaviour of a soil of known composition and moisture content in a soil bin when ploughed with a replica Bronze Age ard could be studied in great detail (Lewis 1998a). To back up these laboratory experiments, either experimental situations in the field could be designed or possible ethnographic parallels be sought out. So, for example, Gebhardt (1992) observed ard, spade and hoe cultivation techniques in three known but different soils, and Lewis (1998a) sampled simulated ard cultivation plots under different ploughing and fertilization regimes but all on the same subsoil at Butser experimental farm in Hampshire (Reynolds 1979). In order to find greater interpretative detail about the repeated fine plastering events observed in the structures at the Neolithic tell site of Çatalhöyük, Boivin (2000) investigated a modern rural community in Rajasthan, northwestern India, who were found to repeatedly replaster different rooms in their houses according to various rules of hygiene as well as major social events in the calendar whether religious or civil (births, deaths, marriages), rather than being indicative of constructional method or necessity. This 'soil ethnographic' work is now essential in order to be much more sure of the effects on soil characteristics and to differentiate between the consequences of different processes, as well as to elucidate possible reasoning behind the activity and the time frame over which observed events may be occurring.

Third, there is laboratory analysis and quantification. To continue with the erosion model example, one might measure the particle size, bulk density, shear strength and plasticity index of the soil material (Avery and Bascomb 1974; Goudie 1990). This would provide information on how easily a particular soil type would move, given a certain set of environmental parameters, especially the degree of saturation/rainfall and slope required to cause overland flow erosion.

Fourth, there is structured manipulation of the data with the application and testing of models on the basis of the observations derived from the different sources of data retrieval. This work would create models of the probable different intensities of soil/sediment movement occurring with a soil of a certain texture, subject to a certain soil moisture content and degree of slope, and allow the construction of predictive models of how much soil could be lost over a period of years in that type of landscape. Obviously, these figures and models will only give a general idea of what might occur under a given set of circumstances, not hard and fast rules. In many respects, this type of field experimental prediction is rather like an ethnographic analogy, it only gives a possible idea of, not an absolute interpretation.

Scales of resolution

There are four scales of resolution for which environmental data may be obtained with which to address archaeological landscape contexts. The macro-environment or regional context tends to be a large chunk of landscape, say 10–20 km in length, from watershed to watershed. At this level one could be looking at the effects of climate, geology and topography as important controlling factors. The meso-environment involves the immediate region of the site, say for example an arbitrary 2 sq km block around the site. Here, land-use and position in the landscape might be major controlling factors in determining the preservation and survival of environ-mental and archaeological data. The immediate site environment is the area around the site and roughly equates with something field-sized and smaller. In this case, landscape position is crucial as is the proximity to the ground-water table, and both are major determinants for preservation. The last and finest scale of resolution is one that is not generally considered by most archaeologists but includes the within-soil micro-environment, and is essentially at the level of the soil profile. Here all potential soil forming and transformation factors come into play (pp. 36–8) and can either destroy or skew the evidence and thus affect the validity of the interpretations placed upon the data.

A good example of different scales related to an archaeological project is in the lower Welland valley (see Chapter 6) (Pryor and French 1985; Pryor 1998a) (Figures 6.2 and 6.3). Here the macro-region was the whole of the lower Welland valley from Stamford to the fen-edge over a distance of some 20 km, which was the subject of the fieldwalking transect survey. The meso-scale was represented by the *c.* 6 hectares around the Maxey great henge that was excavated at the same time (Pryor and French 1985: fig. 40). The micro-scale equates to the enclosed area within the great Maxey henge, for example, and the within-soil micro-scale relates to the buried soil and ditch sediment profiles associated with this same monument.

These scales of resolution are extremely important when related to the type of data acquired. For example, there is no point in using vegetational interpretations based on molluscan analyses alone to postulate extensive clearance, as snail data really only tells one about the feature-specific and immediately surrounding field. It would be far better to develop a series of well-dated pollen datasets taken from several positions along a transect across the region to the site, combined with archaeological survey data and the geochemical and micromorphological analyses of associated sediments and buried soils in order to suggest the timing, nature and extent of any clearance, and to relate this event to the distribution of human settlement and their living activities.

Modification processes

The type of data and the scale of resolution are subject to a variety of modification processes which are often associated with and driven by the actual forces motivating landscape change.

Landscape change can result from the influence of major climatic, relief, drainage system changes and land-use (Ward and Robinson 1990; Bell and Walker 1992; Gerrard 1992; Evans and O'Connor 1999). In particular, there are those changes associated with former glacial, periglacial and interglacial environments. Just the extremes of temperature over relatively short time periods at transition periods would have led to major landform, climatic, soil and vegetational changes. In the Holocene itself, effectively just another interglacial period, major climatic and vegetational shifts have been taking place over the past 10,000 years. For example, there is good and extensive evidence for the growth of the earlier Holocene deciduous woodland over most of northwestern Europe associated with climatic amelioration. This is followed by woodland destruction which is associated with a slow 'worsening' of climate which is still continuing. But climate change is not necessarily the sole cause of the observed woodland destruction. A whole variety of other causes may be contributing to the observed change, often as much archaeological as environmental, ranging from changes in the crops exploited over time to population growth, the development of towns and trade networks, groundwater level changes, soil erosion and type modification, to name just a few.

Site formation processes are responsible for all kinds of modification in a short to long time-frame. These involve all sedimentary processes, drainage and agriculture, both past and present (Butzer 1982; Schiffer 1987; Waters 1992). A scenario often observed in case studies is of earlier Holocene soil formation followed by erosion associated with clearance and increased water run-off. These associated events have both truncated and buried certain parts of the landscape, generally been exacerbated by human activities, and led to soil and vegetational changes, as well as differences in what type of human exploitation was feasible. A good example of this is found in the changing floodplain environment associated with the Etton causewayed enclosure in northwestern Cambridgeshire (French in Pryor 1998a) (see Chapter 6) where dry land in the earlier Neolithic soon became subject to a rising groundwater table and seasonal alluvial deposition for thousands of years until modern drainage and water abstraction for quarrying returned the landscape to dry, arable land and eventual destruction (Figures 2.1 and 5.8). Today, many of these former alluviated floodplain situations are the subject of so-called remediation in order to make them more profitable for modern agricultural use and/or tourism. The more fragile ecosystems of the fringe of the Mediterranean basin are especially affected in this way, for example in the Aguas basin of southeastern Spain and Troina area of north-central Sicily (Castro *et al.* 1998; French in press) (see Chapter 13). Agricultural disturbance, both past and present, can either provide a relatively stable and managed landscape in the longer term or act as a major destructive, distorting and altering agent of the landscape which often leads to a magnification of the effect that other 'natural' processes have on that landscape. In particular, agricultural activities tend to exacerbate erosive tendencies and to play havoc with the archaeological record (Haselgrove *et al.* 1985; Boismier 1997; Edmonds *et al.* 1999; French *et al.* 2000). In addition, sedimentary processes such as flooding and wind-blow are responsible for the removal and re-deposition of soils and sediments, often associated with major to minor alteration of the terrain, and can affect the availability of human resources and the ability of humans to exploit a landscape successfully (Goudie 1993a).

Modification of a landscape or archaeological site can be caused by a whole variety of natural and human-associated processes and activities from the largest commmercial development through to the smallest organism, and from the greatest natural de-stabilizing processes to a state of equilibrium (Butzer 1982; Gerrard 1992). Commercial development, erosion, agriculture and changes in the drainage system could be responsible for major destructive changes to an archaeological landscape or site, such as have been observed in the lower Aguas valley of Spain (Castro *et al.* 1998) (see Chapter 13). Frost heave, volcanic activity, wind-blow and flooding may cause exten-sive to localized alteration and destruction of the archaeological record (e.g. Catt 1978; French and Pryor 1993; Simpson *et al.* 1998), whereas exposure and trampling may affect the context of archaeological deposition and artefact preservation in one to many horizons (Milek and French 1996; Matthews *et al.* 1997a). Soil faunal activity may selectively destroy one type of artefact or environmental data over another, destroying and/or biasing the archaeological and environmental record that is recovered by archaeologists (Bell *et al.* 1996).

Main themes in geoarchaeology

Geoarchaeology is concerned with the identification and investigation of at least three major and interlinked themes.

First, there is recognition and decipherment of landform formation and transformation. This involves, for example, the effects of tectonics (uplift/subsidence), sea level change and glacial/periglacial processes on the actual form of the landform that we see and study today. How were the landscapes of today altered in the past, and is it possible to recognize informative palaeo-sequences within these landscapes? Are we able to relate these to other events and processes? Essentially putting all these questions together, can we determine time-dependent models of landscape evolution?

Second, is it possible to recognize the effects of humans in creating, enhancing or managing landscape change? Is it possible to differentiate the influence of climate versus humans? What are the interactions of climate, landforms, soils and humans? Can we identify the scales and intensities of changes observed? Is there any time frequency of changes and long-/short-term stability involved? Is it possible to establish chronosequences to estimate ages of surficial deposits? Ultimately, the intention is to produce long-term and detailed pictures of landscape and land-use change, and to identify inter-relationships between the land, climate and humans.

Third, what is the effect of the hydrological regime and burial regime on an environment and how has that affected archaeological and palaeoenviron-mental preservation over the longer term and when the archaeologist comes to excavate (see Chapters 2 and 11)?

To investigate these issues and themes, one must have a solid underlying knowledge of geomorphological processes and an appropriate armoury of methodological approaches. The intention of the next four chapters is to acquaint the reader with a good selection of the basic methodological techniques. This is followed by a series of case studies (Chapters 6–17) which illustrate many approaches and interweavings of palaeoenvironmental, geoarchaeological and archaeological evidence which enable the various stories of different landscapes on earth to be deciphered and written.

Essential reading

Bell, M. and Walker, M. (1992) *Late Quaternary Environmental Change*, Chapter 1, Harlow: Longman.

Evans, J. and O'Connor, T. (1999) *Environmental Archaeology: Principles and Methods*, Chapter 1, Stroud: Sutton.

Gerrard, J. (1992) *Soil Geomorphology*, Chapters 1 and 2, London: Chapman & Hall.

Rapp, G. and Hill, C. (1998) *Geoarchaeology: The Earth-Science Approach to Archaeological Interpretation,* Chapter 1, London: Yale University Press.

2 Processes of archaeological preservation

In order to understand the processes and dynamics of preservation in both naturally buried and archaeological contexts, it is essential to understand the roles of water, air, soil and groundwater chemistry, organic matter and the soil fauna. This is part soil science and relevant to Chapter 4 on buried soils, as well as Chapter 5 on lowland and upland landscape systems, with further development through case studies presented in Chapter 11. The outline presented here is of central importance in helping to determine the nature and scope of project research design, where and why one might expect to find certain classes of evidence, and what might be some of the biases in preservation potentially affecting a context.

Two of the best textbooks available from which to obtain the basic information are two of the oldest, Jenny's (1941) *Factors of Soil Formation* and Kubiena's (1953) *Soils of Europe*, which have not really been bettered. What is set out below is only the bare essentials of soil/water chemistry with respect to archaeological contexts; beyond this the reader is referred to a variety of standard and new literature (e.g. Hesse 1971; Ward and Robinson 1990).

Definitions and soil/groundwater chemistry

A series of terms are used repeatedly about preservation conditions, and so require definition.

Anaerobic or anoxic conditions refer to oxygen-excluded or reducing conditions. In contrast, aerobic or oxic conditions are oxygen-rich or oxidizing conditions. The best way of measuring the presence of oxidizing or reducing conditions is to measure the redox potential. It is a measure of electrical activity (Ward and Robinson 1990). Oxidation involves the addition of oxygen and the loss of hydrogen, whereas reduction involves the loss of oxygen and the addition of hydrogen. High and positive redox values signify oxidizing conditions, and low or negative values indicate reducing conditions are present. The amount of dissolved oxygen in the groundwater, or the level of oxygen in solution in the soil-water complex is also a very good indicator of whether oxidation/reduction conditions pertain.

A classic example of reducing conditions is the greenish-grey infills often present in the primary fills of an archaeological feature. This, for example, was evident in the upper primary and lower secondary fills of the western arc of the Neolithic ditches at the Etton Woodgate enclosure ditch and adjacent Etton causewayed enclosure ditch segments (Figure 2.1) (French 1988a; Pryor 1998a). Oxidizing conditions are marked by reddish to orangey brown soil colour, and are regularly seen in the upper parts of ditch fills, again such as found in the secondary and tertiary fills of the Etton/Etton Woodgate enclosure ditches. The halfway state is an irregular mottled, grey to orangey brown in colour, which is indicative of alternating wetter and drier ground/soil-water conditions.

The pH scale is a measure of acidity (pH <6) or basicity (or alkaline pH >7) of a soil/sediment. The pH is determined by the ratio of hydrogen and hydroxide ions in soils, and is particularly affected by the concentration or activity of hydrogen ions. Acids are substances which produce hydrogen ions, whereas bases donate hydrogen ions and produce hydroxides.

The process of hydrolysis, which is the reaction of ions of water and ions in other solutes, is important here. It is measured by electrical conductivity and correlates the total solute content of aqueous environments (Jackson 1958). For example, the fen wetlands of East Anglia and the Somerset Levels tend to exhibit high conductivity values as they are fed by groundwater

Figure 2.1 Section through the Etton Neolithic enclosure ditch with the primary, waterlogged infilling at the base of the section grading upwards into now oxidized, alluvially derived, silt and clay-rich upper fills.

containing many solutes. The conductivity values can therefore be a measure of introduced groundwater.

pH, hydrolysis and reduction/oxidation are responsible for most processes that go on in the soil/water complex. Consequently, they have an enormous effect on the preservation of organic remains in soils and archaeological contexts. For example, basic or calcareous soil conditions favour the preservation of molluscs, bone and carbonized remains, and without the addition of water to exclude air are detrimental to most other forms of organic environmental evidence. Acidic soil conditions usually destroy the molluscan and animal/human bone remains, but do allow the preservation of plant remains and pollen, although again the addition of water and the exclusion of air is the only way to ensure the preservation of organic remains in these circumstances.

Some examples of preservation monitoring

Various monitoring programmes in fen-edge locations of East Anglia have indicated the sensitivity of fen and riverine drift deposits as well as the archaeological record to hydrological change caused by external factors (and see Chapter 11). There is the famous examples of some 4 m of peat shrinkage since about 1850 in Holme Fen as seen at the Holme Fen post (Figure 2.2), just south of Peterborough, as a result of drainage (Godwin 1978). This order of magnitude of peat shrinkage is believed to have occurred in the past three centuries or so across the whole East Anglian fenland area where there are peat deposits, less where there are marine and freshwater sequences overlapping (Hutchinson 1980; Purseglove 1988; R. Evans 1992) (see Chapter 11). This process has undoubtedly been responsible for the emergence of the prehistoric archaeological record so that it may be recovered, but at the same time has been destructive through wind-blow, deflation, dewatering and associated oxidation, and mechanical destruction by intensive arable agriculture.

Monitoring of individual sites such as the Etton causewayed enclosure in north Cambridgeshire (French and Taylor 1985), the Over quarry in the lower Ouse valley of southwest Cambridgeshire (French *et al.* 1999), and Market Deeping in south Lincolnshire (Corfield 1993, 1996) has produced short- to long-term trends detrimental to the preservation of the organic record (see Chapter 11). In each case, gravel extraction has been the destructive force. Water abstraction accompanying extraction can lower the groundwater table by 5 m or more over about one month, and the draw-down effect can be seen to be affecting everything within at least a 500 m 'halo' from the quarry face and causing the beginnings of destruction of organic remains within a few months. Once there is that much water removed from the system, the soil fauna can really get to work, and it is then too late to reverse the destructive trend.

Other types of long-term experiments concerning the preservation of archaeological and environmental data are on-going at the Overton Down

Figure 2.2 The Holme Fen Post near Peterborough, illustrating the substantial amount of peat shrinkage through drainage since 1848.

and Wareham experimental earthworks (Bell *et al.* 1996). In the alkaline, oxidizing and bioturbated environment on the chalk downland at Overton, uncarbonized organic remains have perished within less than the thirty-two years over which the project has been running. More importantly there is differential preservation/destruction depending on the material and where it is buried in the earthwork. For example, organic preservation is much shorter term in the buried soil beneath the chalk rubble part of the bank, but better beneath the turf core of the bank, and better still in the primary fill of the associated ditch. In the acidic but well-aerated environment on sand at Wareham, some materials such as pollen grains survive much better than at Overton, but others much worse, such as the animal bone. There is also considerable differential preservation introducing potential biases in interpretation.

Roles of water and air

Water in the soil and groundwater system acts as a transporting agent, especially for salts and secondary minerals. For example, a common occurrence is the formation of secondary calcium carbonate crystals in soils, which are often called micrite in the micromorphological literature, that are subject to drying out. This is particularly common in semi-arid regions of the world such as southeastern Spain (Figure 2.3), but could just as easily occur in a brown earth on a river terrace or in a rendsina on chalk downland in temperate lowland England.

Water is generally held in the pore space of a soil or sediment as well as in the groundwater. Both the soil and groundwater may hold a greater or lesser degree of oxygen. It is a factor in reduction, but can introduce as well as exclude oxygen. In addition, it partly controls the pH of a soil or sediment and hydrolysis.

Air is found both in soil and introduced. It is a crucial factor in burial context, just as is the amount of dissolved oxygen in the soil water complex. It is essential for oxidation and the activities of the soil mixing fauna (Figure 2.4).

Role of the soil fauna

Micro-organisms have a great effect on the soil complex and soil faunal activity is dependent upon oxygen (Odum 1963). In general terms, they are responsible for the comminution and mixing of organic matter in soils. Most soil micro-organisms prefer neutral soils (pH 6–7). In basic soils, earthworms are predominant, whereas in acidic soils fungi are present.

The soil fauna are responsible for some basic components and processes in soils. Bacteria and fungi are both essential for humus production as they split proteins and cellulose, liberate nitrogenous and carbon compounds and subsequently combine with modified lignins to create the 'skeleton' of

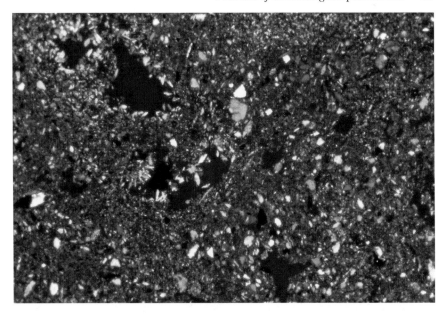

Figure 2.3 Photomicrograph of the formation of calcium carbonate crystals (or micrite) and gypsum in a dried-out soil on marl in southern Spain (in crossed polarized light; frame width=4 mm).

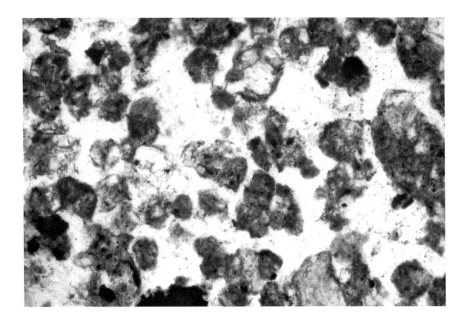

Figure 2.4 Photomicrograph of the soil faunal, or excremental/pellety fabric in a former organic topsoil (in plane polarized light; frame width=2.25 mm).

humus (Odum 1963). They are also essential for nitrification, combined with a weakly alkaline environment and free oxygen (Fitzpatrick 1986). Conversely, nitrification is low in acidic soils such as podzols that characterize heathlands in Britain, and therefore significantly contributes to their low potential for growing and sustaining arable food crops.

So, what happens under different soil conditions in terms of soil faunal activities? In dry conditions, aerobic bacteria are most common, and both organic and mineral substances are affected by oxidation. Thus, in dry, oxygen-rich conditions preservation will be poor except where conditions are so dry that desiccation occurs. The soil in thin section takes on a pellety appearance called an excremental fabric (Figure 2.4), because the soil has all been through the gut of earthworms. Under more moist and neutral conditions, the role of fungi increases but anaeorobic bacteria are especially at work (Bunting 1967; Steila 1976). Importantly, the organic and mineral complexes are not subject to much change, and the potential for evidence reflecting archaeological and environmental circumstances is much better. In moist but acidic conditions, the number of micro-organisms decreases. Fungi are predominant, and play a major role in the decomposition of plant residues and have a high capacity for acid formation (Bunting 1967; Steila 1976). In particular, iron becomes very mobile under these reducing conditions. The preservation of organic remains under these circumstances is usually very good (Caple and Dungworth 1997; Caple *et al.* 1997). When there is excessive moisture present or permanent waterlogging, anaerobic bacteria predominate, and there is much reduction of ferric iron and the sulphur compounds reducing to form hydrogen sulphide. In this case, organic preservation is excellent.

Role of organic matter

The presence of organic matter is responsible for humus formation, either mor in a basic soil, mull in an acidic soil or moder in inbetween conditions (Limbrey 1975). Organic matter is an important factor in soil formation as it enhances biological activities and the water transpiration cycle, and produces humic and fulvic acids formed by the rotting of organic matter which leads to soil acidification and translocation of iron. Organic matter modifies soil properties such as structure, texture, porosity, carbon dioxide content, infiltration capacity and available water capacity (Curtis *et al.* 1976).

Very importantly, it is responsible for the protection of the soil surface from run-off and soil erosion, and effectively acts as a 'binding' agent within the soil. Surface vegetation and the organic component within a soil act to intercept rainfall, decrease the velocity and erosive action of run-off water, influence soil porosity, contribute to biological activity and have a role in water transpiration. The ability of the organic matter to help stabilize a soil and its surface is a major sustaining factor in creating stable soils and landscapes. Its removal or destruction could lead to the disruption of previous equilibrium, and cause extensive and intensive erosion and soil change and soil/sediment aggradation.

The accumulation of acidic leaf litter on a poorly drained substrate subject to high rainfall can lead to the creation of podzols, heaths and eventually blanket peat formation (Limbrey 1975: fig. 16; Bell and Walker 1992: 174–82 with references) (see Chapter 5) (Figure 5.9). When rainfall exceeds evaporation and transpiration losses, leaching occurs and the soil's soluble constituents are lost. The soil becomes acidic and the supported vegetation more acid-tolerant. Thus podzol formation occurs, often associated with a heathland vegetation of poor grasses, bracken and heather. The soil-mixing fauna also tend to disappear and surface litter begins to accumulate. The surface mat absorbs water and maintains a wet upper surface to the soil. This further inhibits decomposition and encourages the growth of heather, bracken, rushes and sedges, leading eventually to the development of acidic blanket peat. This type of scenario is witnessed repeatedly in the palaeoenvironmental record both on and off archaeological sites in Britain. For example, podzol and heath formation have been documented at Iping Common in Sussex associated with Mesolithic activity (Keef *et al.* 1965) and at Sutton Hoo in Suffolk from later prehistoric times (Dimbleby 1972; French forthcoming; Scaife forthcoming). Elsewhere, good examples of blanket peat formation have been observed prior to the construction of the later Bronze Age reaves on Dartmoor in southwestern England (Balaam *et al.* 1982; Fleming 1988), and on Islay, off western Scotland, it is associated with Mesolithic activity (Mithen *et al.* 1992; Mithen 2000).

On the other hand, organic material accumulating in a basin with poor drainage outfall can lead to fen or basin peat formation (Figure 5.4). In this case, soils previously formed under dryland conditions become gradually waterlogged as the groundwater table rises. As the organic matter no longer decomposes as it would in a well-drained and aerated soil, it accumulates on the ground surface and grows/accumulates upwards over time. The vegetation changes to those species tolerant of having drowned roots such as alder, willow, sedges and reeds, leading to the formation of fen carr and reed peats with pools of standing water. Good examples of this type of soil and vegetation change have been recorded at the Fengate fen-edge and Flag Fen basin in eastern England (Pryor 1992; 2001) occurring from later Bronze Age times onwards (see Chapter 7).

Examples of soil/sediment type and preservation conditions

In order to put the detail summarized above into a live and relevant context for the field practitioner, what can be expected in terms of preservation survival of environmental data in some major types of environments?

Typical dryland soil or ploughsoil

The typical circum-neutral to basic (pH 6–8) and well-drained dryland soil may be found on river gravel terraces and on chalk downland in southern England. There would be abundant biological activity leading to the break-down of organic matter and its incorporation in a stable, well-mixed soil exhibiting few horizons. It would have a high redox potential and contain many solutes. The removal of the solute component over time as a result of disturbance, oxidation and drainage would need addressing in time by the addition of fertilizers. The aerated and bioturbated conditions would lead to poor organic preservation in the soil, and the 'scrambling' of any micro-stratigraphy. Whether ploughed in the past and/or the present, this would only serve to exacerbate the mixing processes at work. This type of environ-ment is further discussed in Chapter 5 and the case studies in Chapters 6, 10 and 12.

A lowland fen basin

This type of environment would be alkaline, fed by calcareous groundwater, waterlogged and anaerobic or air-excluded. Good examples would be the East Anglian fens and the Somerset Levels of eastern and southwestern England, respectively. The groundwater would bring many solutes into the system that are highly mobile, much hydrolysis would occur and anaerobic bacteria would be present, but there would be oxygenated water in the system. There would be abundant organo-mineral complexes and nitrates present, so it should be very fertile. Organic preservation should be quite good, but if air was introduced through drainage, there would be increased bacterial decay and the concomitant destruction of the organic component. Unfortunately this has been a feature of the most low-lying basins with fen peats in England since the advent of drainage and modern mechanized farm-ing, especially since the Second World War. This type of environment is further discussed in Chapter 5 and the case studies in Chapters 9 and 10.

Upland moor or blanket bog

This environment would be acidic, wet and waterlogged. Examples include Dartmoor, the north Yorkshire Moors and the Pennines in England, and much of northwestern Scotland (Pearsall 1950). The role of the soil fauna and micro-organisms would decrease, although there would be active fungi in the soil and the iron component would be highly mobile. Organic matter would accumulate under these reducing or anaerobic conditions, leading to the formation of blanket peat and associated good organic preservation. Drainage or physical disruption of this kind of landscape can lead to acidic and non-waterlogged conditions, causing the destruction of much of the organic component. This type of environment is further discussed in Chapter 5.

Urban context

A typical deeply stratified archaeological site beneath a modern agglomeration could contain the best and worst of all types of preservation. The combination of the proximity to the groundwater table plus burial by later buildings has often led to air exclusion and excellent conditions for the accumulation and preservation of organic material, whether acidic or basic conditions pertain, such as Roman London or early medieval York. But more modern industrial pollution or construction impact could have had a severely detrimental effect on preservation (Davis *et al*. 1998).

Essential reading

Fitzpatrick, E.A. (1986) *An Introduction to Soil Science*, 2nd edn, pp. 56–73, Harlow: Longman.

Jenny, H. (1941) *Factors of Soil Formation*, London: McGraw-Hill.

Kubiena, W.L. (1953) *Soils of Europe*, London: Thomas Murphy and Sons.

Limbrey, S. (1975) *Soil Science and Archaeology*, pp. 50–66, London: Academic Press.

Pearsall, W.H. (1950) *Mountains and Moorlands*, London: Collins.

Ward, R.C. and Robinson, M. (1990) *Principles in Hydrology*, London: McGraw-Hill.

3 Geomorphological processes

Recognition of geomorphological processes is essential in order to be able to interpret the mechanisms and processes at work in any landscape. Getting to grips with the timescales and rates of change involved in these processes is also necessary if one is interpreting landscape change over archaeological timescales, but this is the much harder part of any landscape study.

There are some excellent existing textbooks on this subject, such as Waters' *Principles of Geoarchaeology* (1992), Goudie's *Geomorphological Techniques* (1990) and Brown's *Alluvial Geoarchaeology* (1997), so I do not propose to give more than the bare essentials here. Most processes mentioned are also brought out in examples that are amplified in the case studies that are set out in Part 2 of this book.

Slope processes and soil erosion

Slope processes are one of the most important to recognize and understand as they are regularly involved in both the destruction and the preservation of archaeological sites and landscapes.

There are three main types of movement involved on slopes. First, there is flow or rapid mass movement (Statham 1979, 1990). This generally involves the downslope movement of rock and soil debris from a rupture surface and/or shear plane, which is usually controlled by the intact strength of the soil and/or subsoil. It is a fast movement, with stability quickly returning. A rock fall after a thaw or slab failure on a rock face are typical examples. For example, in the Sierra Cabrera mountains of southeastern Spain, rock debris regularly shears off the upper slopes above the Barranco de Gatas and is deposited on the first agricultural terraces below (see Chapter 13) (Figure 3.1).

Heave or slow and seasonal slope processes produce slow downslope translocations of soil debris (Statham 1979, 1990). These are often near-continuous to seasonal to random, affect small to large areas of slope, and can occur anywhere. This type of movement can result from frost heave in soils, periglacial conditions and solifluction, and seasonal waterlogging. Examples include soil creep and colluviation or hillwash (Figure 3.2). Soil movements involving splash creep may result from rainsplash impact or frost creep. There is also

Figure 3.1 Debris fall in the Barranco de Gatas, southeastern Spain.

Figure 3.2 Colluvial creep or slumping in the valley south of Troina, north-central Sicily.

the direct downslope displacement of soil as a result of ploughing (see Chapter 12; Figure 12.12).

Colluvium can be of any size grade from clay to coarse sand plus rock rubble; the heterogeneity that it exhibits is its most diagnostic feature. It may also occur where there is more than two degrees of slope, even beneath woodland (Imeson *et al.* 1980). For example, a mixture of soil and rock debris as thick deposits of colluvium has been observed to aggrade in dry valleys in Sussex in southeastern England from at least the Beaker period (Allen 1992; Bell 1992).

Third, slide or water flow processes such as overland flow and alluviation produce variable rates of deposition. It is particularly influenced by the slope angle, soil and vegetation type, and in turn by the amount of rainwater splash impact. During flow, the sediment load tends to decrease with time. Overland flow occurs when the infiltration capacity of the soil is exceeded during either high intensity rainfall or during the rapid melting of snow.

Alluvium tends to be homogeneous and well sorted in size grades. Characteristically there is a lobate and fining down- and outwards aspect to the zone of deposition, such as seen in alluvial fans. For example, the lower reaches of the river valleys that drain into the East Anglian fens of eastern England are often dominated by extensive zones of alluvial sediments aggrading on and smoothing former floodplain and lower first terrace areas (Figure 3.3).

Rates of flow, heave and slide can vary enormously over time. For example, debris flow in southern Spain can produce up to several metres of accumulation in one event, that is even after just one thunderstorm (see Chapter 13). This is because of almost no moisture infiltration into the soil/substrate system, a high erodability index and lack of vegetative cover, all leading to very high rates of run-off. Colluvial soil creep can be continuous, seasonal or random, but is typically in the order of less than 10 mm per year. On the other hand, experimental work has indicated that just three cycles of freeze/thaw action on a soil can destroy the soil's structure (T.L. White, pers. comm.).

Rates of colluviation have been observed such as 6 cm per 100 years under woods on loessic (or wind-blown) soils in Luxembourg (Imeson *et al.* 1980; Kwaad and Mucher 1979), whereas rates varying from 45 g per square metre per year on stable, well-vegetated land to 4.5 kg per square metre on agricultural land could be expected (Young 1969). A major controlling factor is the angle of slope. For example, the total transport caused by sheet erosion has been observed to increase six-fold as the slope angle increased from flat to 25 degrees (Moseley 1973).

Rates of alluviation vary depending on what is being moved and where it is being deposited in the valley system. For example, 12 mm per year upstream to 61 mm per year in the middle of the basin could be expected in a lowland English river context (Brookes *et al.* 1982), but at Etton in the lower Welland valley a maximum 1.25 m thickness of alluvial silty clay deposition over the last 1,500–2,000 years gives an annual average increment of <1 mm per year (French 1983). Obviously, in some years there may have been much

Figure 3.3 Silty clay alluvial overburden on a sandy loam palaeosol at Fengate in the lower Nene valley, Peterborough, Cambridgeshire, England.

more accumulation than this, and in other years little or no deposition, but at either end of this scale, the actual deposition of sediment would have been virtually unnoticeable at an annual scale, and only sometimes really registered as noticeable over a lifetime.

Factors which influence soil erosion and its severity are rainfall, run-off, wind, soil type, slope angle and the amount of vegetative cover, both on localized and regional scales. Erosion tends to reach a maximum in temperate areas with a mean annual rainfall of *c*. 250–350 mm per year (Langbein and Schumm 1958). In more humid areas and as one moves from drier to wetter areas, rates of erosion initially decrease rapidly to the point (at *c*. 600 mm per year) at which total vegetation cover is established and changes little thereafter. For example, in the northern Cambridgeshire region where the annual rainfall varies between 500 and 600 mm (Burton 1981), the greater vegetative cover may tend to counteract the erosive effect of greater rainfall.

Rainsplash is probably the most important detaching agent and contributes considerably to run-off. Medium-sized (silt) and coarse (sand) particles are most easily detached from the soil mass, whereas clay resists detachment (Farmer 1973). Splash-back following raindrop impact on a level surface has been observed to move stones 4 mm in diameter by up to 20 cm, 2 mm sized stones up to 40 cm and smaller stones up to 150 cm away (Kirkby 1969a). Short-lived, intense and prolonged storms of low intensity have the greatest erosive effect (Morgan 1979).

Surface run-off or overland flow occurs on slopes when the soil's infiltration capacity is exceeded (Kirkby 1969a). Overland flow transports soil particles detached by rainsplash, and may erode distinct channels. It has been suggested that overland flow covers two-thirds or more of hillsides in a drainage basin during the peak period of a storm (Horton 1945). Grains of *c*. 0.5 mm in diameter (or medium-sized sand) are most easily moved, whereas both smaller and larger grains require a much higher threshold velocity. But grains are not redeposited until very low flow velocities are reached (Morgan 1979). On the other hand, sub-surface soil water flow only erodes possibly 1 per cent of the total material from a hillside (Roose 1970).

The resistance of soil to detachment and transport depends on the steepness of slope, vegetative cover and disturbance by humans. It also varies with soil texture, aggregate stability, shear strength, infiltration capacity, and the organic and chemical components. The least resistant particles are silts and fine sands. Soils with a low shear strength or low cohesiveness are susceptible to mass movement, as are those with a low infiltration rate and a low organic matter content (Morgan 1979).

The effect of slope is to increase erosion with increasing slope angle (Kirkby 1969b). Numerous forces such as gravity, frost heave, rainsplash, soil texture and the type and absence of vegetative cover produce erosion on slopes. This results in slope wash, or all types of transport by water downslope, and mass movements such as mudflows and solifluction (Small and Clark 1982).

The amount of vegetative cover has a considerable effect on the suscept-ibility of a soil to erosion. Its effectiveness in reducing erosion depends on the height and continuity of the canopy, and the density of ground and root cover. Both forest and dense grass are more or less equally efficient at reducing erosion. Vegetation intercepts rainfall and reduces the impact of rainsplash, the velocity of run-off and of wind. For example, the mean annual soil loss on bare ground equals 4.63kg per sq m as compared to 0.04 kg per 2 sq m from dense grass-covered ground (Morgan 1979). Horton's (1945) figure for overland flow is reduced to 10–30 per cent where slopes are well vegetated (Kirkby 1969a). The conversion of forest to arable land may drastically increase the erosion from almost none to *c*. 200 kg per 2 sq m per year (Wolman 1967) (Table 3.1). Thus vegetation is a very critical factor, and the removal of plant cover especially on slopes may considerably enhance the potential for erosion by overland flow or some other mode of transport.

Table 3.1 Measured rates of soil erosion from experimental plots in the southeastern United States (after Kirkby 1969a)

Vegetation cover	% run-off	Soil loss (mm per year)
Oak forest	0.8	0.008
Grass pasture	3.8	0.03
Scrub oak woodland	7.9	0.10
Barren abandoned land	48.7	24.4
Cultivated :		
with rows along contour	47.0	10.6
Cultivated :		
with rows downslope	58.2	29.8

Riverine processes

River systems are ubiquitous throughout the world, and their study and understanding is crucial to understanding the development of any valley system and floodplain, and their human use and exploitation over time. Features in the floodplain provide a record of past river history and often human activity as well (Brown 1997: 63–103).

The morphology of a river system determines flow characteristics and governs the properties and quantities of bed and transported sediments (Lewin 1990; Brown 1997). It is essential to understand the fundamental processes, mechanics of the movement of water and grains, and products of floodplain evolution. First, it is important to distinguish between internal or autogenic change and externally forced or allogenic channel change. Auto-genic change involves the infilling of storage sites or sudden channel modific-ation, whereas allogenic change involves climatically induced changes and alterations in catchment characteristics and tectonic activity. Consequently, both channel and floodplain change may occur concurrently. Soil/sediment transport may vary systematically and non-systematically dependent upon changes in sediment availability and flood history, and therefore floodplains display significant lateral variation. Most commonly, soil/sediment is moved in rivers by rolling along the bed or in suspension in water. In particular, the fine sediment that often comprises alluvial material in an overbank flood situation is carried in suspension until still water conditions pertain and the silt and clay gradually settle out of suspension on the old ground surface. This is generally the case for example in the lower reaches of river valleys in lowland England. Thus threshold velocities are crucial to the movement of different size grades of material, and these are controlled by flow rate and depth/volume of flow.

The hydraulic geometry and dynamics of the river system tend to govern channel form characteristics (Lewin 1990; Brown 1997). Slow flow and shallow, gradual outfalls tend to go together with braided, meandering systems. Extreme flood events and greater run-off often associated with significant changes in land use lead to channel avulsion and the cutting of new channels and the cutting-off of previous channel courses, and even the destruction and/or burial of archaeological sites. Cut-off channels soon become stagnant backwaters and become repositories of vegetational and sedimentological history as sediments accumulate in them and gradually infill the former channel. These small zones of accumulation within the valley bottom are an excellent source of local and sub-regional environmental records of great use to the archaeologist. There are numerous meandering channel belt systems in most river valley systems in Britain, for example that mapped in the lower Welland valley exhibits at least four channel belt systems in existence from the late Mesolithic period (7350 BP) to the present day (see Chapter 6) (French *et al.* 1992; Brown 1995; Howard and Macklin 1999) (Figure 3.4). Anastomosing or ladder-like pattern channel systems tend to be associated with colder climatic, often periglacial, conditions and are characterized by low sinuosity, low outfall slope, varied sedimentary sequences with levee development, crevasse splays, shallow and localized wetland environments, infilled channels and peat development. These are a regular occurrence in present day northern Canada, but in England are associated with very late glacial times. For example, there is an anastomizing system present between Maxey and Etton villages some 5 km to the south of the present River Welland in northern Cambridgeshire with a set of radiocarbon determinations of between about 10 900 and 10 000 BP (see Chapter 6) (French *et al.* 1992) (Figure 3.4).

Glacial processes

Glacial erosion, debris entrainment and transport and deposition all depend on the behaviour of ice, sediment and rock materials on/within/beneath/ around glaciers (Collins 1990). Much can be observed *in situ*/in reality today.

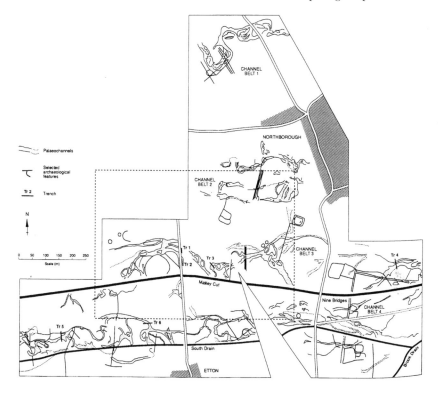

Figure 3.4 Map of relict channel belts in the lower Welland valley area between Etton and Northborough (after French *et al.* 1992: fig. 16.2).

Glaciers can change surface morphology, drainage, vegetation and local climate. I have only stood at the foot of a glacier once, and that was in the Rocky Mountains of Alberta on a hot summer's day. Great chunks of ice were periodically crashing to the ground with melting rivulets emanating from beneath, the bare rock surface was glistening wet, changing to moss and lichen covered rock a few metres away from the glacier face, with a mist rising off the face of the glacier creating a very damp and cool micro-environment. Here was primary weathering and the beginnings of soil formation going on right before one's eyes.

Glacial processes result in a variety of deposits which affect the archaeological record and preservation. Solifluction debris can partially infill valley systems and bury late glacial soils (Evans *et al.* 1978; French *et al.* 2000) (Figure 12.5). The dumping of ice-collected debris on bedrock can create drumlin and moraine dominated landscapes, and 'head' or 'till' drift deposits left behind by glacial ice and meltwater can sometimes contain reworked Palaeolithic artefacts. It can scour and leave behind bare rock surfaces. It creates its own micro-environment with a high local humidity, which often leads to very localized peat formation. This forms small reservoirs of past vegetational history in the least likely places. Glacial and periglacial conditions often lead to the creation of various features in subsoils such as ice-wedging, convolutions and polygons, which can often fool and confuse archaeologists when they are amongst real cut archaeological features.

Aeolian processes

Wind erosion of soils is a function of soil type, vegetation cover, climate and moisture content (Cooke *et al.* 1993). The critical wind velocities required to move soil particles vary, but are least for particles with a diameter of 0.1 to 0.15 mm (or fine sand-sized material), and increase with increasing and decreasing grain size. Transport by wind occurs in suspension in air over long distances, especially fines of less than 0.2 mm in diameter, by surface creep (very fine sand and coarse silt) or rolling of grains along the ground (i.e. gravel and coarse sand); and by saltation or grain movement in a series of jumps (i.e. very fine sand, silt and clay) (Morgan 1979).

Studies have suggested that the most extensive sources of wind-blown material are areas of extensive fluvial sediments which are deposited after infrequent but intense storms (Statham 1979), and glacial deposits under periglacial conditions which are a source of loess (Catt 1978). Loessic or windblown silt deposits have been observed in many parts of southern England, but specifically in Kent and south Wales (Weir *et al.* 1971), and in a great band from central Europe across to China where they contain lengthy climatic records of great importance.

Coastal processes

There is much high-energy input through waves and wind on any coastline (Dugdale 1990). The surf zone witnesses oscillating movements and currents associated with shoaling and breaking waves. The actual morphology of the beach involves the effects of slope, wave approach and tidal range over time. Shifting dunes, the formation of groins on the beach, wave and tidal amplitude can lead to massive coastal erosion. For example, it is estimated that the northeastern coast of Yorkshire witnesses erosion of some 0.04 mm of coastline every tide depending on the wave energy and depth of overlying beach material, or just less than 2 m per annum for the long-term erosion rate (van de Noort and Davies 1993: 114–15).

One characteristic indicator of past beach morphology is the assemblage of marine shells present. An excellent example of this type of work has been done in the Outer Hebridean island of Harris where Evans (1971) showed the oscillation between sandy and rocky shores exposed at the inter-tidal zone through the presence of limpets indicative of rocky shores versus winkles as indicative of an exposed sandy shore. Foraminifera can also be used to indicate the tidal level represented by a particular deposit. For example, foraminifera analysis of the ditch deposits on a series of Iron Age and later salt-making or saltern sites excavated recently in the East Anglian fenlands has indicated what level the tide reached at many now inland and non-marine sites (Lane *et al.* 2000).

A related environment but without tidal influence is inland lake margins. A study by Morton (1995) of lake margin processes and morphology and how they might affect the archaeological artefact record indicated that most of the same processes relevant to coastlines were similarly important controlling factors. In particular, the angle of the beach, wind direction and speed and wave amplitude were significant, and could disperse artefacts both laterally up and down the beach, and vertically through the shore deposits, making a single event in death look as if a series of events had been involved over time. This salutary warning, confirmed by both field and laboratory experiments in a wave tank with controlled parameters, could just as easily apply to archaeological sites found in any shore or near-shore environment.

Neotectonic processes

Present day, historical and deep-sea core records are used to infer the rates and distribution of tectonic change. Long-term changes in emergence and submergence of land can also be conducted using archaeological remains of known age (Bell and Walker 1992: 51–65 with references).

For example, an extensive study of Greece, its islands and the Turkish coast has indicated that there was at least a one-third greater land mass available in Upper Palaeolithic times than today, and that this coastal zone is now 1–5 m below the present day sea level (van Andel and Shackelton 1982: figs 2 and 3). Major changes such as this over extensive areas go some way to explaining the dearth of earlier prehistoric sites in the region. Isostatic uplift of the land on either side of the North Sea basin between eastern England and northern Germany/Holland combined with the earlier post-glacial rise in sea level led to the disappearance of the land bridge by about 7500 BP (Shennan 1986a and b). Ironically, and more recently, the continuing subsidence of eastern England may mean much of the Cambridgeshire and south Lincolnshire fens becoming re-inundated by the sea within our lifetime as no flood defences are being built to combat the inevitable.

Volcanic eruptions and the resulting lava and ash flows are also useful time markers in combination with the archaeological record. For example, the eruption of Thera or Santorini of *c.* 1645–1625 BC was responsible for burying the Bronze Age town of Akrotiri as well as the valley in which it sits (Figure 3.5). Indeed, lenses of ash from this eruption have been observed in excavations in Crete to overlie late Minoan sites, with confirmation through deep-sea records in the Mediterranean (Aitken *et al.* 1988).

Figure 3.5 The Bronze Age town site of Akrotiri on Thera, Greece, buried by
volcanic ash about 1450–1425 BC.

Nine-unit land-surface erosion model

Although it is an 'old' principle now, the use of Dalrymple *et al.*'s (1968)
nine-unit land-surface erosion model (Figure 3.6) is probably one of the best
ways of envisaging erosion and landscape change both in section and in plan
over a landscape. It forces one to visualize what is going on in each part of a
landscape at whatever scale of investigation is being used. The model is an
idealized cross-section through one-half of a valley, from watershed at the top
to the river in the valley below. If this model is then combined with the
catena concept, geomorphological processes and soil formation and change
can be seen in combination. When archaeological distributions by time
period are laid over and related to these geomorphological contours, there are
the beginnings of a two-dimensional model of landscape development.
When extended and viewed in plan, this technique allows the use of digital
terrain and geographical information system models to analyse landscape
change in three dimensions.

A catena is based on the observation that particular slope forms are
associated with particular soil sequences, usually on one parent soil material
(Milne 1935; Limbrey 1975: 83). The differences between the group of soils
of a catena are generally related to their different position on the slope and
their drainage characteristics, which produce a series of changes in soil
properties from the upper to lower members of the catena (Figure 4.1). Thus
there is a sequence of soil profiles which appear in regular succession with

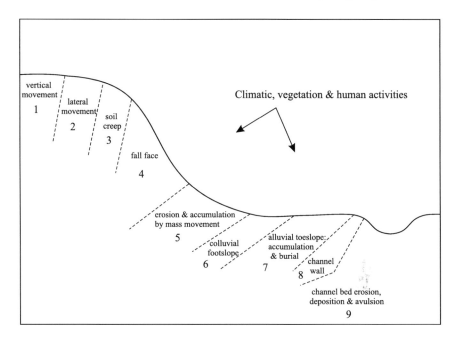

Figure 3.6 The nine-unit land surface model (C. Begg after Dalyrmple *et al.* 1968).

similar and differing morphological features on uniform lithology (ibid.). This concept will be further discussed to in the following chapter (4) on palaeosols.

The nine-unit land-surface model combines slope aspect and degree, erosion and soil forming processes (Dalrymple *et al.* 1968) (Figure 3.6). The uppermost unit (1) exhibits less than 1 degree of slope and is characterized by pedogenic processses with vertical subsurface movement and is often associated with waterlogging or severe denudation. Unit 2 (below) exhibits 2–4 degrees of slope, with both chemical and mechanical eluviation (or removal) by lateral subsurface water movement. Unit 3 (below) is the upper part of the fall face with 35–45 degrees of slope and is characterized by bare rock surfaces, sheet erosion and soil creep and terracette formation. Unit 4 (below) is the lower and steeper part of the fall face with 45–64+ degrees of slope, which is characterized by much physical and chemical erosion leading to much bare rock, rock falls and slides. Unit 5 (below) is the mid-slope zone with 26–35 degrees of slope, surface and subsurface water action, transport by mass movement, terracette formation, and both the removal and accumulation of soil and sediment material. Unit 6 (below) is effectively the colluvial footslope zone where there is subsurface water action and redeposition of material by mass movement and some surface wash as colluvium, as well as transport further downslope and down valley. Unit 7 in the flood-plain is characterized by alluvial deposition as well as downstream water movement containing colluvially derived material as alluvium. Unit 8 is the active floodplain which exhibits channel avulsion and erosion, bank slump and fall. Unit 9 is the active channel itself with bed transport down valley, as well as periodic aggradation and erosion. Obviously not all units and slope angles apply to every landscape that one might encounter during fieldwork, but many elements will and the most appropriate may be sub-selected. Moreover, it gives potential foreknowledge of where there may be good and poor archaeological and palaeoenvironmental preservation of sites and deposits.

In addition to applying the nine-unit land-surface model and catena concept, a variety of other standard methods can be used to create a geomorphological map of a study area. Aerial photographic mapping from vertical stereo pairs of photographs is an excellent starting point in combination with the drift geology and soil maps of the study area as it allows mapping of relict channels, alluviated and colluviated areas, as well as locating a good proportion of the archaeological record. This should then be backed up by systematic augering in transects across the soil/geological zones to establish soil types, depths and survival, the presence/absence of palaeosols, and the nature and thickness of colluvial and alluvial deposits. On the basis of the mapping and augering surveys, test pits should be excavated in representative soils, deposits and parts of the valley system to confirm stratigraphy, and to take of a combination of samples for physical, geochemical, palaeoenvironmental and micromorphological analyses. In an ideal world, it would be preferable also to examine buried soils/deposits associated with known archaeological sites/monuments for comparison and corroboration, and to carry out detailed palynological studies from any available small basins in the area to establish the nature of vegetation change over time in the study area. In addition to the relative dating provided by the archaeological record, a programme of radiocarbon and optically stimulated luminescence dating of the fine grained colluvial/alluvial deposits would be required to provide time control on the erosion phases. This type of approach is more fully amplified in the Allen valley, Cranborne Chase, case study (see Chapter 12). Ultimately, the various levels of geomorphological, vegetational and archaeological data can be superimposed in digital terrain models (Figures 12.3 and 12.14), or used to create geographical information system models of landscape change.

Rates of change

Rates of change in geomorphology for denudation or removal and degradation, and weathering or alteration by physical and chemical processes are extremely difficult to measure, as is deciding what parameters to measure (see various papers in Cullingford *et al.* 1980). There is considerable local variability in terms of spatial scale and location. The variation may be due to a whole range of factors from the micro- to local to regional climatic and environmental changes or fluctuations. Is the variation uniform, continuous, periodic, sporadic, seasonal or chaotic, and does the periodicity and frequency vary? Consequently the reliability and utility of short-term monitoring and experiments may be questionable, and therefore there is a need to use both historical and archaeological data to extend the time frame. In particular, consideration must be given to longer-term environmental change (Bell and Walker 1992: 50–65). Also, present day conditions are probably not exactly analogous to those in the past, and how much impact has modification by humans affected rates of change? Consequently, every potential and available dating technique needs to be employed, none of which may be especially precise.

How does one go about trying to measure physical (disintegration) and chemical (decomposition) weathering? This involves the investigation of archaeological monuments and landscapes which may provide sealed horizons with good relative dating, geomorphological phenomena such as volcanic eruptions, dune and lake formation, as well as experiments, field measurements and personal and anecdotal observations. For example, this could entail setting up a series of sediment traps at various positions on the slope of a Wessex down to measure soil erosion on the chalk over the whole agricultural cycle, comparing those results with the colluvial and buried soil sequences associated with archaeological sites in the same locale and conducting some shear and plasticity tests on the present day ploughsoil to see how easily erodable the soils may be in the area. Then it should be possible to generate some models of possible scenarios of erosion on the basis of the field and laboratory results, possibly using geographical information system mapping techniques to layer-stack the data in different combinations.

Examples of rates of weathering and soil formation

Examples of rates of weathering, soil formation and environmental change are found above as well as in the case study chapters, but a few are given here and expanded upon in subsequent chapters.

For surface weathering and soil formation, long time scales are the norm. The surface weathering of granite takes at least 100,000 years, whereas soils forming on glacial till need an estimated 7–13,000 years, and soils forming on chalk subsoils probably only require one-third to half that time (Goudie 1993a). Soil change can occur much more quickly, as has happened in the enclosure at the Overton Down (Wiltshire, England) earthwork where a well-drained downland rendsina soil has become a stagno-gley soil in about a thirty-year period due to the absence of any management or grazing (Macphail and Cruise 1996). In even greater contrast, a new gully several metres deep and wide may appear almost overnight from a few thunderstorms of several hours duration in the marl of southeastern Spain, generating tonnes of colluvial marl deposits downslope for a distance of several kilometres (personal observation) (e.g. Figure 13.7).

In semi-arid southern Spain (see Chapter 13) there is a highly eroded and easily erodable landscape. The marl subsoils have a low shear strength and plastic limit, thus making them highly erodable off slopes when devegetated, and/or they become half-saturated. Personal observation during fieldwork suggests that when erosion occurs it is fast and is reflecting episodic change or punctuated equilibrium. But concerted geoarchaeological fieldwork indicates rare periods of tectonic unconformity, and several earlier prehistoric and more recent periods of colluvial aggradation, channel incision and avulsion, gullying, soil formation, shearing, soil creep and terrace collapse within an otherwise quite stable system (French *et al.* 1998).

Essential reading

Brown, A.G. (1997) *Alluvial Geoarchaeology*, Cambridge: Cambridge University Press.

Bell, M. and Boardman, J. (eds) (1992) *Past and Present Soil Erosion*, Oxford: Oxbow Monograph 22.

Goudie, A. (ed.) (1990) *Geomorphological Techniques*, London: Unwin Hyman.

Goudie, A. (1993) *The Landforms of England and Wales*, Oxford: Blackwell Scientific.

Waters, M. (1992) *Principles of Geoarchaeology*, Tuscon: University of Arizona Press.

4   Soils, sediments and buried soils

Introduction

A reasonable understanding of soils, sediments and buried soils is central and crucial to being a good archaeologist and indispensable if one is doing any kind of fieldwork. Soils and sediments are the matrix in which artefacts, features and structures are found, and the processes going on in them can be associated with any combination of past and present natural and human events, and their interpretation aids the interpretation placed on the archaeological record itself. It has been said that to study artefacts without regard to their sedimentary matrix, their spatial arrangement, subsequent movement and alterations induced by post-depositional processes, is to study only a fraction of the archaeological record (Schiffer 1976, 1983, 1987; Clarke 1977; Binford 1981). The evidence contained within soils and sediments is essential in helping to reconstruct both past environmental events and changes, as well as to elucidate the nature of human influence on the environment and landscape (Goudie 1993b).

It goes without saying that soils are a difficult subject to read about and understand. There is a massive literature available (e.g. Limbrey 1975; Fitzpatrick 1986; with references in each), much of which is highly technical, obscure and not very user-friendly. As it is impossible to cover everything on this subject without writing a separate and lengthy textbook, the aim is to present some of the basics, and in particular, what an archaeologist should know about soil and mainstream soil science applications to archaeological problems. This will be by no means exhaustive either, but should present a good idea of the possibilities available. Throughout there will be an emphasis on the use of geomorphological and micromorphological techniques applied to archaeological problems. These approaches are further exemplified in the case study chapters set out in Part 2 of this book.

Definitions and components of soils

So, what is a soil? It is the organic/inorganic material developing through the weathering of the subsoil or geological substrate by physical and chemical processes through time. A soil usually exhibits horizonation. In contrast, a sediment is any inorganic/organic material from a fine clay to a coarse rock which has undergone weathering, transport and redeposition by various geographic agencies.

Soil is comprised of an inorganic and an organic fraction. The inorganic fraction comprises the sand, silt and clay components, and a soil is defined on the basis of their proportions (Bullock *et al.* 1985: fig. 22). Although there are several classification systems based on size classes available and used in the world (Fitzpatrick 1971; Smith and Atkinson 1975; Soil Survey Staff 1975), they exhibit only slight variations between them. I use the British system devised by the Soil Survey of England and Wales (Hodgson 1974; Bullock *et al.* 1985: fig. 22).

Sand measures from 2 to 0.063 mm in size, and is usually mainly quartz but may also include other various minerals like felspars. The silt fraction, or 0.063 to 0.002 mm (or 63–2 μm), is fine textured and is important in wind- and waterlain deposits. The clay component (or <2 μm) is composed mainly of crystalline clay minerals and amorphous material and is defined in terms of the organization of the structural units, or sheet or layer silicates (Fitzpatrick 1986: 17–24 and 87). Clay minerals are called sheet or layer silicates which are the result of the alteration and re-synthesis of aluminium silicate sheets by weathering. There are two major structural units for clays, either a silica tetrahedron (or a silica atom at the centre equidistant from four oxygen and hydroxide atoms) or octahedron (two sheets of hydroxide and oxygen atoms attached to a plane with magnesium, iron and aluminium in an octahedral formation). These three-dimensional units can be stacked in a variety of different ways, and these determine the clay type (i.e. montmoril-lonite, kaolinite).

The organic fraction or humus component is mainly composed of carbon, hydrogen and oxygen, made up of dead and decaying plant and animal matter (Bunting 1967). Vegetation acts as a reservoir of water and nutrients. Humus can combine with a variety of other constituents, move down profile and reform in different forms (see Chapter 2). It is essential for soil development, fertility and stability.

Factors of soil formation

Traditionally, the main factors in soil formation are the parent material, climate, relief or topography, living organisms and time (see for example Jenny 1941; Bunting 1967; Fitzpatrick 1986), to which I would add the effects of human activities. The parent material or the type of rock or substrate provides the basic constituents of any soil developing on it through physical and chemical weathering processes. For example, acidic igneous-type rocks produce quartz-rich and acidic soils, whereas basic igneous rocks produce less quartz and sand, but more clay and minerals with iron and magnesium. Limestones on the other hand produce base-rich or calcareous, fine loamy soils with a high nutrient status. At the other extreme, sandstones produce mainly quartzitic, low base status and permeable soils. The rate of both physical and chemical weathering affects the rate of soil formation and accumulation. The parent material affects the relief pattern and drainage characteristics of the landscape, as well as the micro-climate. Thus, the nature of the parent material is one of the important agents responsible for spatial variability of soil characteristics within a given soil type.

Climate, world-wide, locally and seasonally, all affect temperature and rainfall, which in turn influences soil development and therefore the soil type (Bunting 1967). Temperature determines humidity, evaporation, micro-climates, length and intensity of the growing season and the type of vegetation able to grow. Rainfall affects most other factors, such as the amount and type of vegetation and the amount of leaching and removal of nutrients or bases from the soil. For example, the Barranco de Gatas in the Sierra Cabrera of southeastern Spain is a very arid part of the country with an average temperature ranging between about 12 and 30 degrees Celsius, and an average of 254 mm of rainfall per year over the past 30 years (see Chapter 13). This obscures a much greater variation in rainfall as it can be both highly irregular and unpredictable. In practice, this means that the northern side of the valley is parched, brown, virtually without vegetation and prone to gullying and sheetwash erosion for most of the year as it is in the full glare and heat of the sun all year round. In contrast, the southern side of the valley is greener, more humid, the soil more moist, receiving eroded material from above, and thus able to support vegetation, both natural and cultivated. The valley bottom is a 'halfway house' between these two sets of conditions, but is, in particular, is prone to wetting and drying episodes, incision, soil/sediment removal and aggradation. It can support crops but generally only with some form of irrigation, but it is debatable whether the tributary valleys of this system ever supported dense woodland cover (Castro *et al.* 1998: 33–7).

Relief and topography affect many soil properties such as the depth or loss of soil on slopes and in valleys, as well as the moisture gradient, amount and variety of vegetation, altitude and aspect, soil water run-off and filtration (Bunting 1967). For example, the tree-line is determined by a combination of altitude, relief and climatic factors, and for most of Britain in the present day, trees rarely grow much above 1,000 m. On slopes of greater than 45 degrees of gradient, little of anything is expected to remain *in situ* for long, whereas accumulation zones such as occur at the base of slopes or in river valleys could be expected to have greater soil depths and be more moist, as well as being better at retaining moisture and easily supporting vegetation.

Living organisms affect the physical structure of the soil (Bunting 1967; Curtis *et al.* 1976). They are responsible for mixing, comminution, aeration and the formation of humus-clay complexes which tend to give a soil stability. Different types of organism are found in different soil conditions, for example earthworms in basic conditions and fungi in acidic conditions (see Chapter 2).

All of the above factors are ever-changing, so that one is not dealing with a steady state concept, but rather a situation developing and changing through time (Birkeland 1974). The magnitude of each soil property is related to the time factor. Generally, the rate of soil development decreases with great age, but the differentiation of soil horizons depends on the sum of all applicable factors.

Obviously, human activities can affect any part of the soil development process at any time and over brief to long periods. Some of the most significant processes which human activities have enhanced are deforestation and erosion of landscapes leading to dramatic soil, vegetation and drainage changes. Most of the case studies chapters set out in Part 2 below discuss these impacts in one way or another.

Soil as an ecosystem

Soil acts as a complete ecosystem. It is a dynamic and open system comprising the living and non-living parts of the soil environment acting as a unit (Odum 1963; Sheals 1969). There are four main constituents of soil as an ecosystem – non-living abiotic substances such as nitrogen, oxygen, water, protein and carbohydrates, producers such as green plants and organisms which fix energy and manufacture food, consumers such as animals and ourselves at the top of the food chain, and decomposers such as bacteria and fungi which break down compounds and release mineral nutrients. Essentially these four constituents are involved in a series of bio-/geo-chemical cycles for carbon, nitrogen, phosphorus, sulphur and a whole variety of trace elements. Soil acts as a reservoir and medium of action and exchange, and the interaction of the ecosystem components play a role in soil development, soil and plant nutrition, the maintenance of the atmosphere and the regulation of ecosystems.

To explain some of these cycling/recycling processes briefly, let us look at the carbon, nitrogen, phosphorus and sulphur cycles. In the carbon cycle, plants obtain carbon from atmospheric carbon dioxide, and fix and convert it to glucose by photosynthesis. Most carbon is incorporated in the plant body, with some returned to the atmosphere by respiration as carbon dioxide. Organic carbon is an agent of intensive alteration of soil minerals, and their breakdown creates weak acids such as humic and fulvic acids. They also form compounds with chelating abilities, that is they combine with iron, aluminium and magnesium which move down profile under leaching conditions and are responsible for acidification processes. Both of these transformations relate to soil change, acidification and the development of nutrient-poor and acidic soils such as podzols. The release of carbon dioxide into the air can combine with rain to form carbonic acid which is a factor in increasing soil acidity.

The nitrogen cycle consists of two main processes, ammonification and nitrification. Ammonification changes organic nitrogen compounds of dead organic matter to inorganic form as ammonium salts. During nitrification, bacteria converts ammonium salts to nitrates. These are then reduced to nitrogen and nitrogen oxides by denitrifying bacteria, and then are made available again to the atmosphere and plants. Nitrogen is essential for building amino acids and ultimately proteins in plants. If nitrogen is not retained in the system, rapid leaching is the result. One of the best ways of insuring the retention of nitrogen in an arable system is through periods of fallow and the growing of clover. Thus, this cycle is integrally responsible for longer-term soil stability and sustainability of use by humans for food crops.

Phosphorus is an essential component of nucleic acids and is indispensable to plant and animal life. Iron, aluminium and calcium all strongly absorb phosphorus, and together enhance soil fertility. In this case, the plant community acts a regulator of the phosphorus supply.

Sulphur is found mainly in dead organic matter in soil, but is unavailable to plants until oxidized to sulphate by soil micro-organisms. It is also needed by all living things as it has a central role in building amino acids and forming proteins (like nitrogen).

There are various trace elements which are also essential to soil and vegetation development. Sodium and potassium form hydroxides and act as dispersing agents for clay and humus. Magnesium and calcium help to assure soil stability. Aluminium forms hydroxides in tropical areas and is characteristic of very weathered, acidic soils. Ferrous iron is found in wet and poorly drained soils and gives grey to green soil colours; ferric iron is found in well-drained soils and gives red and black colours. Like iron oxides, manganese can function as a plant-limiting nutrient.

Producers, decomposers and the root environment are essential to the good functioning of soil as an ecosystem. The soil fauna act as decomposers of organic matter, and play a major role in the accumulation of nitrogen in the soil and its conversion to a usable form. It also has a central role in maintaining soil stability. Roots play a strong role in nutrient cycling, removing soil water and creating an oxidizing environment around them. In the ecosystem model, the rate of nutrient cycling and energy flow may control the functioning of the soil-water system and the nature of soil development. Thus, soil is the main component and medium of a self-regulating system of exchange of energy and substances.

Soil genesis

What are the processes going on in the soil material itself that are responsible for soil genesis? There are two main types of weathering processes involved, as well as a whole series of specific pedogenic processes (Bunting 1967; Limbrey 1975). Physical weathering involves mechanical effects and transformations such as transport, redeposition of soil by erosion agencies such as frost shattering, and wind and water abrasion, as well as the disruptive effects of plant, animal and human activities such as rooting, burrowing and ploughing. Chemical weathering involves processes which cause alteration of soil composition, and some of the main processes include oxidation, reduction and hydrolysis (see Chapter 2). For example, oxidation may cause the formation of iron pans which in turn lead to drainage impedence. On the other hand, reduction causes iron to become soluble and easily removed, especially under waterlogged conditions, causing leaching. Hydrolysis is the reaction of disassociated hydrogen and hydroxide atoms of water with ions of mineral elements, and this process can lead to a loss of soil stability through the expansion and decomposition of silicate structures (which are the building blocks of clay) in the soil (Ward and Robinson 1990: 314).

Specific pedogenic processes that are involved in soil genesis can occur on a grand and/or micro-scale. For example, surface erosion and accumulation elsewhere as occurs in colluvial and alluvial transport and deposition, can lead to additions and removals of soil material, as well as changes in soil composition and drainage characteristics. At a more micro-scale, eluviation and illuviation processes lead to the washing out and in, respectively, as well as the transport of fine material and nutrients from one part of the soil profile to the other, but generally down-profile. Leaching is essentially analogous to eluviation but acts on a greater scale and generally causes the loss of soluble materials from the soil into the water system, and is consequently responsible for both soil degradation and associated instability. This latter process is associated with podzolization where concomitant leaching and acidification associated with vegetation change and/or rainfall increases lead to the movement and removal of iron and/or humus down-profile, and the formation of iron/humus pans, with associated gleying and soil deterioration. Enrichment on the other hand involves the addition of soil material and/or nutrients in solution. For example, the process of lessivage leads to the removal of clay from the upper horizons of a soil (or clay eluviation) and its redeposition towards the base of the profile (or illuviation) forming a clay-enriched or argillic horizon. Similarly, bioturbation of the soil by the soil fauna can lead to decalcification, or the removal of lime and carbonates. Or, a calcium carbonate groundwater system or severe evapo-transpiration can lead to calcification and the accumulation of lime and carbonates anywhere in the soil profile as well as the formation of pans or crusts. There are also many transformations occurring of soil constituents from one form to another by physical and chemical weathering, decomposition of organic matter to form humus and of rock-forming minerals to clays, and the synthesis of new compounds such as clay-humus complexes. These are the briefest possible explanations of many processes (for fuller explanations see Limbrey 1975; Fitzpatrick 1986, 1993; Courty *et al.* 1989), most of which are very important in the study of archaeological soils and associated major trends in post-glacial soil formation.

Palaeosols and buried soils

Palaeosols are soils with features representing conditions which no longer exist today. There are three main types. Relict palaeosols occur on exposed surfaces with some of their features derived from former environments; buried soils or palaeosols are found on land covered by younger sediments and which continue to undergo soil-forming processes; and exhumed palaeosols are once buried and now exposed through erosive processes. In archaeology, the term buried soil is generally used to refer to former soils preserved beneath upstanding monuments and/or more recent erosion deposits such as colluvium and alluvium. As mentioned above, one of the best ways of envisaging a cross-sectional slice through a landscape containing palaeosols is through the palaeocatena concept (Dalrymple *et al*. 1968; Valentine and Dalrymple 1975). This refers to a group of palaeosols developed on the same buried land surface and geology whose original soil properties differ owing to their different original landscape position and soil-water regimes (Figure 4.1).

How does one go about identifying palaeosols and buried soils? It is often extremely difficult in the field alone because horizons are either missing because of erosion or homogenized by later processes and therefore now invisible. So, a suite of characteristics is used to identify buried soils. These include the nature of burial, characteristic features in the field and in thin section which suggest soil formation or pedogenesis is taking place such as structure, horizon development and clay coatings, and the use of biological indicators such as pollen, beetles and molluscs which can give an idea as to development in past environments and in different periods.

Buried soils contain much evidence about the evolution of past landscapes and in particular the processes that have occurred and are going on today (Gerrard 1992). It is possible to gain ideas about past land-use, ecology and the associated vegetation complex, as well as geomorphological and some-times even climatic changes. The presence of soils can indicate periods of stability as well as change over time, and past environmental conditions. Soils that are buried by later/younger deposits such as an earthwork monu-ment or flood-deposited alluvium have had many of their features preserved. Of course they are not strictly 'fossilized' as they continue to undergo pedo-genic processses since burial. For example, the seasonal deposition of silty clay alluvium will gradually result in the apparent disappearance of the organic A horizon. Instead, it will be gradually modified over time by the seasonal aggradation of silt/clay sediment which creates a 'new', thicker, more minerogeneic and more fines-rich (silt and clay) A horizon above (see Chapter 6). The boundary or upper surface of the old land surface becomes very blurred, both in the field and in thin section, and the structural aspect becomes columnar blocky from crumb, and the textural make-up of the soil changes from a sandy loam to sandy/silty clay loam. Soils buried by earthworks are often affected by compaction (Macphail and Cruise 1996), increases and decreases in soil faunal activity (Hunter and Carrie 1956; Abdul-Kareem and McRae 1984; Crowther *et al*. 1996), changes in structure and density (Abdul-Kareem and McRae 1984), the formation of iron pans at their upper surface and/or at their base (French 1994; Breunig-Madsen and

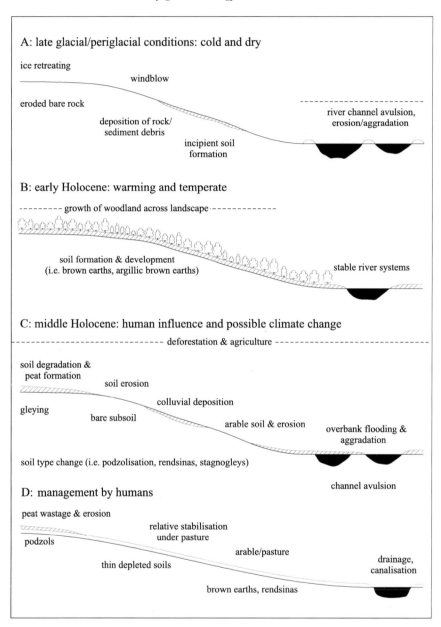

Figure 4.1 Hypothetical catena sequences for the late glacial and Holocene periods in northwestern Europe (C. Begg after C. French).

Holst 1996, 1998), and/or the illuviation/movement and redeposition of fine material in the former A horizons as a result of the act of burial with disturbed soil (Wilson 2000).

The investigation of buried soils can provide evidence for major trends in post-glacial soil formation (Figure 4.1). These include post-glacial amelioration and development of woodland associated with the growth of argillic brown forest soils, deforestation, colluviation and alluviation (see Chapters 6–8), as well as soil degradation processes such as acidification, gleying and podzolization, decalcification (see Chapter 8), the formation of various pans and crusts, and desiccation associated with dewatering (see Chapter 11).

The whys, wherefores and techniques of analysis

The best-case scenario is to investigate buried soils on a wide spatial scale in the field, associated with a variety of experimental analogue sites both in the field and in the laboratory to gain ideas about specific processes and time-scales involved. Excellent examples of this type of experimental study are Helen Lewis' (1998a) work on the recognition of ancient tillage practices from the soil and Richard Macphail's work with Gill Cruise and John Crowther at the experimental earthwork site of Overton Down (Crowther *et al.* 1996; Macphail and Cruise 1996).

What techniques are best and most informative to use? Several good papers have been written on the holistic approach that is necessary to carry out good archaeological soil investigations (Barham and Macphail 1995; Canti 1995), and obviously one must 'cut the cloth' to some degree to suit the questions, time and money available. Ideally as many techniques as possible should be used, including soil-analytical techniques and other palaeoenvironmental techniques such as palynology and molluscan analysis, as well as an array of dating techniques.

How does one start? Good field description and assessment is the first and most crucial step. This entails first walking around the whole site or survey area with the archaeologist in charge of the digging, looking at all available exposures/sections, as well as wandering off-site if at all possible to look at profile change away from the direct influence of human occupation. In an ideal world one can take up to several weeks to become really familiar with the landscape that one is dealing with. 'Breezing in' for a few hours as the specialist can work on a small excavation site, but is often unsatisfactory and certainly would not do if one were trying to get to grips with a landscape. Once one has decided on which zones to sample, which are the most representative sections on- and off-site to sample, and at what intervals one is going to describe and sample the site's profiles, it then becomes a question of the level of description, the relevant techniques to use, and the sample intervals necessary. No one can tell you the absolute 'right' answer to this, it is a matter of individual judgement in consultation with the archaeologist's aims and questions. Effectively here, the more you see, the better you get at this part of the process. There is no substitute for time in the field. Thus initial assessment work should be done by the most able and qualified person who can be persuaded to come out to the site, not by the novice. Initially, I would rather look at an uncleaned section or one that has seen a month's weathering than one that has just been cleaned for photography, as it gives a much better idea of structure and boundaries. After photographing and drawing a section to scale with appropriate layer/horizon descriptions, then it is best to clean it. Also, examine the section opposite if there is one. This is now the time and place to describe colour and the exact nature of the contacts/boundaries between horizons. Sometimes there is little need to do more than this at this stage of the assessment and description process, especially when a site is heavily damaged or truncated by ploughing, or it is the first preliminary evaluation stage. Of utmost importance is that one must know why and what samples one wants to take, and set out a timetable for processing them, or they will fester in a heap somewhere for some eventual but unlikely analysis.

There are no absolute rules for soil sampling. Intact blocks are required for micromorphology (Figure 4.2), x-radiography, energy dispersive x-ray analysis, bulk density, plasticity and shear strength. Small bulk but loose samples (i.e. <0.5 kg) are suitable for most other soil analytical techniques (Hesse 1971). Large (1–25 kg) bulk samples are only needed for macro-botanical, molluscan and insect samples. Every sample must be measured in/related to a datum point on the site, and marked on a section and/or plan.

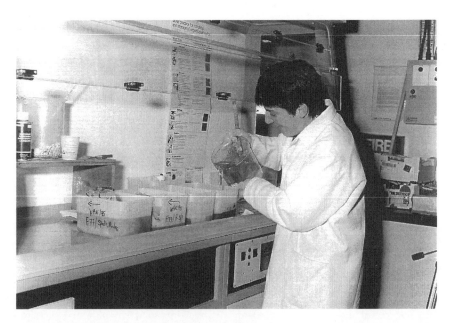

Figure 4.2 Julie Miller impregnating soil blocks to make thin sections.

Also, it is best if you are sampling for other sets of analyses at the same time such as pollen and molluscs and that the sample sets are taken side by side in relation to the stratigraphy. Close interval or contiguous sampling is necessary for old land surfaces/buried soils and primary feature fills. But if there are only a few thick horizons present, samples either taken across and/or above and below boundaries are usually sufficient, and/or in combination with a series of spot samples taken from the main layers/horizons. Samples should also be taken across the upper and lower zones of feature cuts to gather ideas about the implements used and infilling factors.

How many profiles should one sample ? Again this can largely depend on research questions/priorities, money and time, but the aim should be to take a representative series of samples across and off a site to gain an idea of lateral and spatial variation. For example, in a best-case scenario in the later Neolithic houses at Saar in Bahrain (Figure 4.3), block samples for micromorphology were taken from every face of every metre square in an alternate checkerboard fashion so that no sample was more than 50 cm apart, with the intervening metre square then bulk-sampled and dry-sieved for artefactual, faunal and botanical remains (Matthews *et al.* 1997a and b). In another case, the buried soil beneath a Bronze Age barrow mound could be sampled at three different loci about 10 m apart for micromorphology, particle size analysis and a suite of geo-chemical analyses, and one or two profiles taken from outside the mound for comparative purposes, with bulk samples taken from alternate metre squares from the old land surface beneath the mound and from the primary ditch/pit feature fills for sieving for macro-botanical and artefactual remains (e.g. French 1994). At the other extreme, there is often a thin, probably truncated, buried soil surviving on an enigmatic prehistoric site on the fen-edge of East Anglia where it was hard to justify taking more than one profile for micromorphology and particle size analysis given the post-depositional disturbance and destruction of the horizon and site (e.g. French 2000a), but the whole surviving thickness of the buried soil would be excavated by hand to recover the archaeological remains.

What techniques are best to use? There is no one single best type of method, rather it is a question of deciding which suite of methods is appropriate to the site, the nature of preservation of soils, the questions being asked and, unfortunately, the funds available for analysis. Usually a combination of techniques is the best approach, with some type of sampling strategy being employed. Also, the approach depends on the type of archaeological deposit being sampled – is it feature fill, floor or occupation sequence, midden deposit, old land surface and/or buried soil? Typically, soils on archaeological sites are often poorly preserved in terms of burial conditions and only feature fills are available for sampling. Consequently a series of representative small bulk samples could be taken on a systematic basis from the fills of a suite of features of different types and ages across the site for particle size and organic matter content. If one was dealing with a well buried/sealed site with buried soils and *in situ* floors or archaeological

Figure 4.3 The interior room of a late Neolithic house being sample excavated
(with permission of R. Killick, J. Moon and H. Crawford).

surfaces available, a combination of micromorphology with small bulk
samples for magnetic susceptibility and phosphates could be appropriate on
a systematic grid basis (Allen and Macphail 1987; Courty *et al.* 1989; Canti
1995). If there were certain features in the micromorphological analysis that
required quantification such as the degree of compaction of a surface, image
analysis and/or x-ray techniques would be appropriate to employ to examine
the changes in void space frequency and organization (Adderley *et al.* in
press).

Other types of landscape often present a combination of eroded and
aggraded sediments, truncated surfaces and surviving fragments of buried
soils. In this case, a combination of field recording with sampling for
micromorphological (Murphy 1986), particle size analysis, pH and organic
content (Hesse 1971; Avery and Bascomb 1974) could be the first line of
sampling, with the possibility of taking further samples for a selection of
other purposes such as x-ray fluorescence, heavy mineral analysis, bulk
density, plasticity, shear strength, phosphate, iron and calcium carbonate
analyses as appropriate (Avery and Bascomb 1974; Limbrey 1975; Shackley
1975; Smith and Atkinson 1975; Goudie 1990; Butler 1992). At a later
stage it might be necessary to examine a sub-set of samples by multi-element
analysis (i.e. ICP-AES) or scanning electron microscope and microprobe
(Mackereth 1965; Canti 1995) to gain a better idea of the elemental composition of some of the sediment sources, in combination with a programme

of targeted radiocarbon and optically stimulated luminescence dating (Aitken 1985; Rees-Jones and Tite 1997; Lang and Wagner 1998) to gain an idea of the major periods of movement and stabilization in the system. Variations on the theme of this kind of approach can be seen in the case studies set out in Chapters 13–15.

Soils and micromorphology

Many doubt the ability of the micromorphological analysis of soils ever to provide sufficiently concrete information related to a time-frame to be of any great use in the analysis of landscapes and cultural deposits. There are just too many variables present in terms of composition, structure and pedo-feature development, plus the effects of human activities and conditions of burial that can skew the picture and therefore make any conclusions speculative and consequently unreliable.

Obviously I am not one of those doubters. I believe that the methodology has 'come of age' in the past decade and is an extremely useful and all-encompassing technique to use. Since Cornwall (1958) first used the technique in relation to buried soils associated with archaeological sites in southern England, the technique has become much more widely used and researched. It is now often stipulated as part of the design specifications of a contract archaeological project. Moreover, a whole variety of research projects have been and are being carried out on how various human activities show up in the archaeological record, as well as ethno-archaeological studies which examine the physical processes and activities as well as the socio-economic aspects that produce various constructs evident in the archaeological and soil/sediment record. For example, Gebhardt (1992) and Lewis (1998a) have shown in experiments both in the field and in the laboratory, how different tillage implements affect soil structure and produce various pedogenic features in some ploughsoils, both modern and ancient. There is also excellent experimental work on soil changes occurring over set time periods under controlled conditions such as Crowther *et al.*'s (1996) work on post-burial humic rendsinas at the Overton Down experimental earthwork (Bell *et al.* 1996) and Breunig-Madsen and Holst's (1996, 1998) studies of the effects of barrow mound building on the burials within and under the mound and on the buried soils beneath. These types of work strongly suggest that the doubters are much too pessimistic about the capabilities of the method across the board. For the preservation and observation of features produced by ploughing for example, it depends, as with most things in archaeology, on conditions of burial and preservation factors as well as subsoil type, drainage, subsequent human activities and any number of soil formation factors at work. Such analysis depends on a complex 'cocktail' of factors and events – sometimes conditions are suitable and the 'fingerprints' are there, sometimes these have just vanished, but occasionally they leave tantalizing hints behind. For this reason alone, on occasion it is possible to create a great and reliable story of events going on at a site that is excellent for the archaeologist and archaeological interpretation, and at other times little can be said that is reliable. Moreover, no one is suggesting that this technique should be used on its own and not in conjunction with a whole array of other available environmental techniques (Canti 1995; Evans and O'Connor 1999).

On the other hand, the detailed microstratigraphic analysis of archaeological contexts, sediments, occupation sequences and floor and walling material can provide concrete answers about the types of constructional material used, and the sequences of use during and after the life of the structure, and the nature of post-depositional effects and distortions on the soil/sediment matrix (e.g. Davidson *et al.* 1992; Courty *et al.* 1994a; Matthews 1995; Matthews *et al.* 1997a and b, 1998). For example, at the tell site of Çatalhöyük in central Turkey a typical set of observations might include multiple fine layers of plaster that are found in certain rooms and not in others, and that when in use the room was kept completely clean and then became used for the deposition of hearth and stable-derived debris at a later stage (Matthews *et al.* 1996). Other recent good examples of this type of work have been carried out on occupation sites for example at Saar in Bahrain (Figure 4.3) (Matthews 1997b), Tell Brak in Syria (Matthews *et al.* 1998) and Hofstaðir in Iceland (Simpson and Milek 1999). In addition, the investigation of ethnographic analogues and explanations of various constructional features can provide a rich overlay of beliefs and social actions which control the processes and materials that are observed in an archaeological context, as for example Boivin's (2000) study of house floors in present day Rajasthan, India. Here the almost daily replastering of the kitchen floor in a modern rural house is carried out because of strict beliefs of cleanliness, whilst other rooms in the house are replastered in response to major events in the life cycle such as births and marriages in the family. This type of work is building up a vast bank of reference data and situations which will go some way to extending the viability and reliability of using the micromorphological approach on archaeological sites.

As both a contract and research practitioner of micromorphology and an archaeologist involved with digging and directing my own sites for many years, believe it is important to state what micromorphology can reliably do for archaeology and the refinement of the archaeological record. This topic cannot be considered in great detail, but field archaeologists should have some idea of what is possible when this technique is employed.

At the most basic level, a series of thin sections made of either a buried soil profile, an occupation sequence and/or feature fills can tell one what it is in soil descriptive terms and what, if any, is the anthropogenic content of that soil, sediment or fill. Micromorphology is much the best way of doing this task as it presents and preserves an intact replica of the soil/sediment as it was in the ground, plus the internal arrangement and relationships of the component parts in a way that particle size analysis, for example, cannot.

Both the impregnated soil block and the thin section slide also form part of the site archive, and are relatively indestructible.

At the next level of description, there should be suites of observable characteristics which indicate the different horizons present in the soil profile. Their identification features, number and thicknesses should be sufficient to tell one what soil type one is dealing with on a certain subsoil at that point in the landscape. For example, is it a thin, poorly developed, rendsina soil with a bioturbated turf developed on a calcium carbonate-rich silt loam developed on a chalk subsoil or is it a brown earth with several horizons, illuvial clay formations and good soil structure developed under forested conditions, or is it an acidic but thick, bleached and fines depleted, podzol with iron/humic pans at its base? In England and Wales we are very fortunate that the Soil Survey systematically sampled and analysed the horizons of all its major soil types using an array of physical, chemical and micromorpholgical techniques as part of the mapping process. This inform-ation is accessible in published and unpublished soil memoirs, maps and at the Soil Survey head office. Similar information is also available for a wide variety of world soils at the International Soil Museum at Wagingen in the Netherlands. This is how we can be sure when we find the clay-enriched or argillic horizon at the base of a brown earth soil profile, it can be reliably called an argillic horizon and there are a number of features and vertical developments that can be expected to be associated, which in combination will give that soil a name, such as a brown forest or argillic brown earth.

At the first level of interpretation, there is generally a series of features that are normally recognizable in thin section that indicate past and present processes going on in the soil/sediment. For example, these could range from grey/orange mottling suggestive of oxidation/reduction and secondary iron formation associated with alternate wetting/drying to the movement of clay down profile associated with disturbance of the soil surface and/or the upper horizons and an increase in rainsplash impact and greater percolation of water containing dislodged fines through the soil. These easily visible and common processes can give clues as to past transformations from one soil type to another, plus leave relict features which indicate past conditions which no longer exist, or suggest more recent processes. But it is impossible to add a specific time dimension to these observations. Nonetheless, it is possible through the careful observation of the order of occurrence of the imprint left by different processes to tell what order certain events occurred in, thus building up a hierarchy of events from the soil. This is where it is crucial for the soil data either to be associated with archaeological material or levels for dating, or to have an associated but independent programme of radiocarbon and/or luminescence dating to give an idea of the relative time parameters involved during the life of the soil profile.

At a second level of interpretation it may be possible through the observed set of features to suggest the influence of a particular activity or form of land-use in the past. One of the most debated types of land-use has been the recognition of arable agriculture or tillage in buried soils from micro-morphological evidence alone (Jongerius 1979, 1983; Macphail 1986, 1998; Gebhardt 1990, 1992; Macphail *et al.* 1990; Carter and Davidson 1998, 2000; Lewis 1998a). In my view and for many other practitioners, despite some reasonable sceptisicm and caution in interpreting/ascribing certain features to tillage alone, there is now a sufficient body of well-corroborated experimental and field data to be able to say, sometimes, this soil has been ploughed in the past, whether ploughmarks are visible or not. Some of the most important features include organizational pedofeatures such as alternating very fine sand, silty clay laminae on the edges of the ard mark, dirty and strongly oriented clay coatings in a similar position, slight changes in porosity or compaction (i.e. greater) immediately beneath the base of the plough zone, the mixing of fabrics from different horizons, and small aggregated fabrics within the furrow (see Lewis 1998a: tables 4.3, 4.4, 4.5 and 8.1). In further corroboration of this seminal work, many of the diagnostic tillage feature types observed experimentally by Lewis (1998a) were recently and repeatedly observed in a micromorphological study of a buried Late Bronze Age archaeological context at Welland Bank Quarry in south Lincolnshire (French and Marsh 1999) (Figures 4.4–4.8 and 10.6–10.9). Moreover, the subtle cut-line of an ard mark even showed up in thin section

Figure 4.4 A series of photomicrographs (Figs 4.4–4.10) exhibiting characteristic features in thin section of the plough zone of a buried soil at Welland Bank Quarry, south Lincolnshire, England: the base of an ard cut (in crossed polarized light; frame width=4 mm).

Figure 4.5 The edge of the ard cut marked by micro-laminated, fine dusty to pure clay (in crossed polarized light; frame width=4 mm), Welland Bank Quarry.

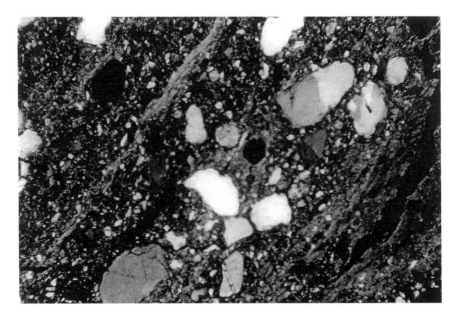

Figure 4.6 Alternate coarse/fine fabric striae within an aggregate in the ard mark (in crossed polarized light; frame width=4 mm), Welland Bank Quarry.

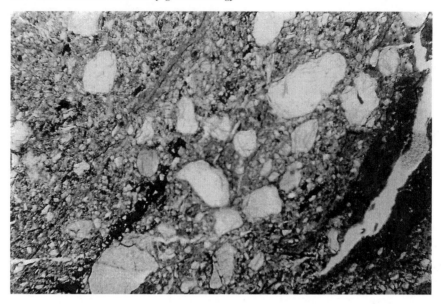

Figure 4.7 Alternate coarse/fine fabric striae within an aggregate in the ard cut (in
plane polarized light; frame width=4 mm), Welland Bank Quarry.

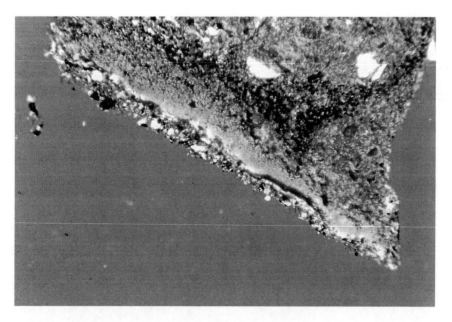

Figure 4.8 Part of an aggregate in the ard mark turned through 45 degrees with a
coarse/fine fabric coatings aspect to the lower edge (in crossed polarized
light; frame width=2 mm), Welland Bank Quarry.

without being seen at the sampling stage. This is not to say that at every site the evidence for tillage will be so clear-cut and unambiguous; it is fair to say that at most sites the evidence will be more enigmatic. Although I have no direct proof, I am convinced that the survival of indicators of past ploughing is undoubtedly to do with how fast and effective was the burial of the soil after the last ploughing episode.

Other major events that are usually recognizable in thin section include the development of woodland on brown earths, leaching, acidification and podzolization, turf grassland, alluvial and colluvial additions and aggradation, and the onset of waterlogging conditions. For example, if woodland development occurs on stable, well-drained soils with good pore structure, the lower half of the soil will be characterized by successive, well-oriented, pure (or limpid) clay coatings occurring in an illuvial zone (or Bt/argillic horizon) beneath a zone depleted of fines (or an eluvial A or Eb horizon) (Figures 4.9 and 4.10) (Fedoroff 1968; Limbrey 1975; Fisher 1982). In rather simplistic terms, the gentle rainsplash off the tree leaves percolates through the upper part of the soil, dislodging very small quantities of the finest clay in an otherwise well-structured and stable soil, and moves it down profile where it is deposited against the walls of the voids just above the weathering zone of the substrate. This can result in beautiful crescentic-shaped infills of successive laminae of pure clay (Figure 4.10), as well as the

Figure 4.9 An argillic or clay-enriched and well-organized lower B or Bt horizon in thin section from the pre-Iron Age buried soil at Welland Bank Quarry, Lincolnshire (in cross polarized light; frame width=2 mm).

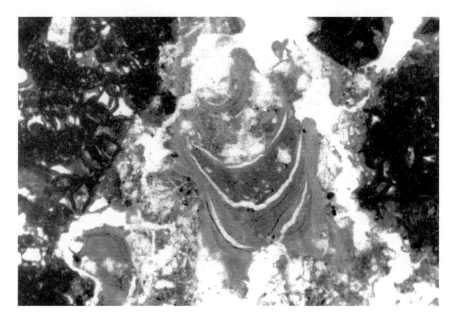

Figure 4.10 Well-organized, crescentic shaped clay coatings at the base of a former
    woodland soil in thin section from beneath the long barrow at
    Haddenham, Cambridgeshire, England (in plane polarized light; frame
    width=2 mm).

whole of the lower B horizon being dominated by pure clays, laminated and
non-laminated, throughout the groundmass (Figure 4.10). Subsequent
disturbance of this woodland soil results in the formation of impure clay
coatings containing micro-contrasted very fine organic matter, charcoal and
silt material throughout the profile but generally increasing in frequency in
the lower part of the B horizon. These may be laminated or non-laminated,
and range from slightly to very dusty/dirty in composition (Slager and van
de Wetering 1977; Macphail 1987) (Figure 4.11). The more numerous and
varied, very fine sand to silt size additions to the clay of silt and organic
matter derive from the disturbed and opened-up soil, increased rainsplash
impact and percolation of surface and soil water down profile. Obviously the
nature of the disturbance of the upper part of the soil profile is not always
easy to pin-point to a single cause or event. If it is ploughing or perhaps tree
throw, or these plus some later truncation through erosion, there may be
sufficient other features present in thin section to lead to one of these
conclusions, but this is not always the case. It is the observation of a hierarchy and order of features in thin section that leads one to an interpretation
or putting forward several possibilities. It is not an absolute rule book, and is
open to reinterpretation in the light of future developments. In particular,
further experiments need to be devised, set up and monitored under both

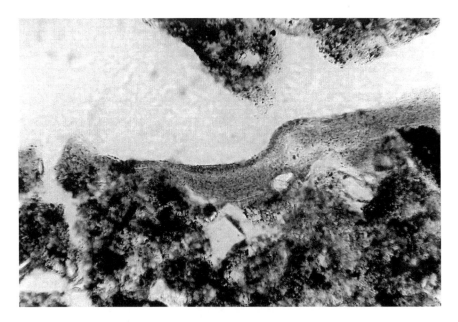

Figure 4.11 Photomicrograph of dusty/dirty clay coatings in the pore space in thin
section in the pre-Neolithic buried soil at Ribat Amran, Dhamar
survey, Yemen (in plane polarized light; frame width=2 mm).

laboratory and field conditions for a variety of archaeological scenarios,
constructs and processes.

The processes of leaching leading to acidification and podzolization are
also quite evident in thin section, both in terms of characteristic horizon
development and within-soil processes. The bleaching and removal of fine
material from the upper eluvial horizon of a podzol (or Ea horizon) is easily
visible both in the field and in thin section, generally leaving a fabric
dominated by single sand grains often with thin 'halos' of amorphous iron
oxides surrounding and occasionally linking them (Figure 4.12). Towards
the base of the profile, which may be extremely thick (i.e. several metres), in
thin section there are usually zones of accumulation of amorphous humic (or
a Bh horizon) and/or amorphous iron oxides (or a Bs or spodic horizon)
material which are often visible in the field as pans (Figure 4.13). In
addition, the fabric may be polymorphic, or have a porous, small, irregular
aggregated aspect (Figure 4.12). These features result from leaching and the
removal of fines and either their redeposition down profile or removal
altogether, and the soil-mixing action of fungi, respectively (de Coninck and
Righi 1983). It is sometimes possible to find fragments of various relict
features which act as clues towards the pre-podzol soil type and indicate
transformations in soil type over time. For example, fragments of argillic

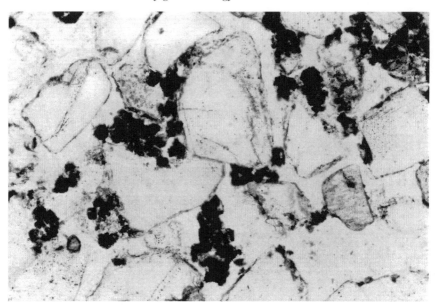

Figure 4.12 Photomicrograph of the polymorphic fabric characteristic of the upper part of a podzol in thin section at Sutton Hoo, Suffolk, England (in plane polarized light; frame width=2 mm).

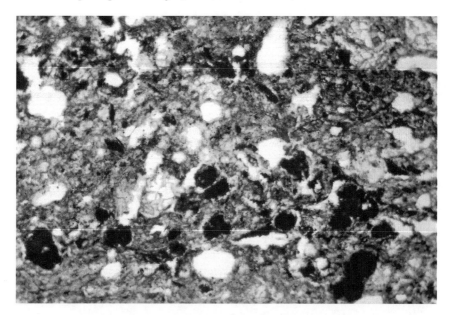

Figure 4.13 Photomicrograph of the spodic Bs (below) and amorphous humic pan (above) or Bh horizon found in thin section at the base of a podzol at Sutton Hoo, Suffolk, England (in plane polarized light; frame width=2mm).

clay features are sometimes found in the podzol and are suggestive of major soil changes that have already occurred in the Holocene, with deforestation ascribed as initiating the process (Dimbleby 1962; Limbrey 1975; Balaam *et al.* 1982). In fact, whole areas of landscape may have been transformed from former forest soils to acidic podzols in later prehistoric periods which now support either heath, moorland or peat bogs, resulting mainly from human disruption of these more marginal landscapes (Keeley 1982). This is an example of the third level of interpretation that is possible concerning the archaeological record on a landscape scale. Good examples of this in Britain are found in the sandy heaths of Suffolk and Norfolk and upland blanket bogs in Wales, Dartmoor, the Pennines and many parts of Scotland.

Colluvial additions to soils are usually visible as an heterogeneous and poorly sorted set of additions to a soil matrix, whereas alluvial material tends to clog the whole fine groundmass and pore space with fine, homogeneous material. In thin section, colluvium can be recognized by the disoriented juxtaposition of partially mixed but different fabrics (Figure 4.14), and alluvium by very abundant intercalations of silty clay throughout the whole fabric (Figure 4.15).

Waterlogging is usually easily visible in the field through a combination of colour and matrix type. Greens, greys, greenish greys and black colours,

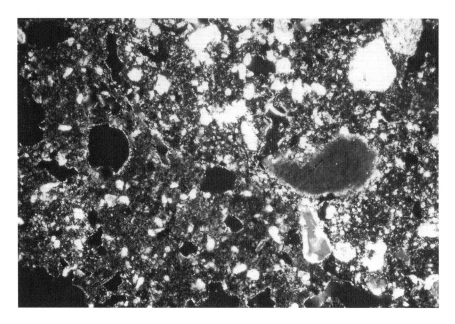

Figure 4.14 Photomicrograph of an example of intermixed, poorly sorted colluvial fabrics in thin section in the upper fill of a late Neolithic ditch at Etton Woodgate, Cambridgeshire, England (in crossed polarized light; frame width = 4 mm).

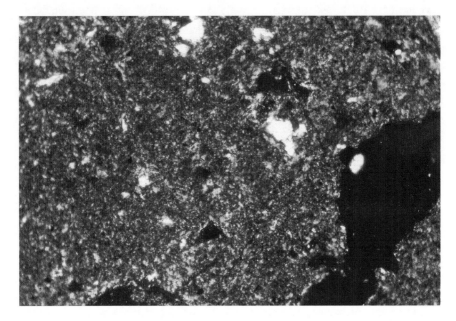

Figure 4.15 Photomicrograph of an example of silty clay intercalated alluvial fabric in thin section at Etton, Cambridgeshire, England (in crossed polarized light; frame width = 4 mm).

and fine silts, silty clays, organic muds and peats are common giveaways to waterlogging. Mottled greys and oranges in section suggest alternate wetting and drying of the profile, and reddish browns to orange colours suggest strong oxidation. Oxidation features in thin section may be orange to reddish orange to red/black depending on the light source; waterlogging features tend to be black to dark to pale grey.

Essential reading

Boivin, N. (2000) 'Life rhythms and floor sequences: excavating time in rural Rajasthan and Neolithic Catalhoyuk', *World Archaeology* 31: 367–88.

Canti, M.G. (1995) 'A mixed-method approach to geoarchaeological analysis', in A.J. Barham and R.I. Macphail (eds) *Archaeological sediments and soils: their analysis, interpretation and management*, pp. 183–90, London: Archetype Books.

Courty, M.-A., Goldberg, P. and Macphail, R.I. (1989) *Soils and micromorphology in archaeology*, Cambridge: Cambridge University Press.

Gerrard, J. (1992) *Soil Geomorphology*, Chapters 3 and 12, London: Chapman & Hall.

Macphail R. I. (1986) 'Paleosols in archaeology', in V.P. Wright (ed.) *Paleosols*, pp. 263–90, Oxford: Blackwell Scientific.

Matthews, W., French, C., Lawrence, T., Cutler, D.F. and Jones, M.K. (1997) 'Microstratigraphic traces of site formation processes and human activities', *World Archaeology* 29: 281–308.

5 Lowland and upland landscape systems

Introduction and concepts

Although valleys come in a variety of forms and topographies, they are particularly useful study units for the investigation of landscape history and development. They have distinctive climates, often with considerable range and micro-variability, which support different vegetational regimes. Also, they are subject to erosion and aggradational factors. All systems like valleys have boundaries with pathways for energy inputs and outputs. Thus, it is necessary to think of an open system with physical/chemical transformations of matter going on within the system over time. As geoarchaeologists, we need to be able to chart these changes and the reasons why they occurred as accurately as possible.

In studying valley landscapes, what are geoarchaeological and geomorphological studies trying to achieve? First, it is essential to understand the interaction of soil development, rainfall, run-off rates and erosion, vegetational change and temperature variation and their roles in shaping the valley system that is observed today. Second, one is attempting to develop chronosequences and palaeocatenas that can be used to estimate the age of surficial deposits and can be related to human prehistory and history of that region, and how it has been exploited and utilized in the past. It is essential to know how long it has taken to form key properties in different environments. Third, can soils and vegetation types be used as indicators of long- and/or short-term stability? Fourth, is it possible to determine the evidence for and indicators of climatic and/or human impact on land-use change? Finally, from these datasets and interpretations is it possible to understand environmental–human interactions?

Major types of lowland systems

There are three major types of lowland system which occur repeatedly within the geographical and archaeological spheres of reference in England. These are basin mires such as the East Anglian fenland, river valleys and flood-plains, both alluviated and unalluviated, such as the Welland, Nene, Great

Ouse and Thames valleys (Figures 5.1 and 5.2), and the chalk downlands of southern England, in particular the Wessex region (Figure 5.3). Most of these environments are investigated further and elaborated on in the case study chapters in the second part of this book.

Basin mires or fenland or lowland bogs are usually calcareous and formed as a result of the accumulation of freshwater in a natural depression (Figure 5.4). They support a vegetation of reeds, sedges and grasses, with large zones of open water, and are often fringed with fen carr woodland composed of alder, willow and hazel (Figure 5.5). Unfortunately, as a result of drainage and modern arable farming there are almost no surviving, untouched environments of this type that I know of, there are only re-creations through conservation management schemes such as Wicken Fen in Cambridgeshire and West Sedgemoor in the Somerset Levels (Coles 1995: 66–9) (Figures 5.5 and 5.6).

This type of fen is both ground- and flood-water fed, with the lack of outfall to the sea leading to ponding and the creation of a permanently waterlogged environment, although it is subject to seasonal variations. Despite recent dewatering on an ever-increasing scale, and especially since the Second World War in Britain (Coles 1995), both palaeoenvironmental and archaeological records of the Holocene period often survive within the mires and on their margins. In particular, it is common to recover good

Figure 5.1 A waterlogged, relict stream channel at Orton Meadows, Peterborough, Cambridgeshire, both cutting and overlapping with a Bronze Age barrow ring-ditch.

Figure 5.2 Typical view of the floodplain entering the fenland basin, here in the lower Ouse valley, with a Bronze Age barrow mound emerging in the centre ground.

Figure 5.3 Typical view of chalk downland in the Cranborne Chase area of Wessex, here looking north across Wyke Down.

Figure 5.4 Deep peat section in a basin fenland environment at Holme Fen, Cambridgeshire, England.

Figure 5.5 Typical view of fen carr woodland in the Somerset Levels, England.

Figure 5.6 Recreated basin bog environment at Wicken Fen in Cambridgeshire, England.

pollen sequences representative of both the regional and immediate environments, as well as evidence for periods of sedimentary influx. In addition, these mires often contain palaeochannel systems which are excellent repositories of wood, plant macro-fossil, pollen and molluscan evidence, as well as containing the geochemical fingerprints of where the minerogenic component in them may have originated. Good examples include the East Anglian fenland and the lower river valley systems which empty into it (Figures 5.1 and 6.1) (see Chapters 6–10) (Hall 1987; French and Pryor 1993; Waller 1994). In a completely different environment in Hungary and Slovenia, small lakes adjacent to archaeological sites that have become infilled with peat and minerogenic deposits have produced detailed palynological and geochemical sequences of change which are believed to be indicative of widespread and long-lived, but minor forest disturbance, throughout the Neolithic period (Willis *et al.* 1997, 1998; Gardner 1999).

There are different scales of preservation in the river valleys and chalk downland systems. In both cases, soils may be either truncated through erosion and/or buried by accumulations of colluvium and/or alluvium. Colluvium or hillwash is a loose, non-stratified, non- or ill-sorted, heterogeneous mixture of various size grades found on the lower part and base of slopes (Figures 12.12 and 13.2). Alluvium is well-sorted, homogeneous, generally fine (silt and clay) sediment deposited in a floodplain of shifting river and stream meanders on a seasonal or intermittent basis (Figures 2.1, 5.1, 7.2 and 10.8). The areas of burial by alluvium may be very extensive in former and active floodplains, whereas the zones of burial in the chalk downland system are more confined to the tributary and main valley bottoms. Also, most of the slopes and higher areas of the chalk downs tend to be seriously denuded of soil (Allen 1992; Bell 1992; Boardman 1992).

These types of disruption to the system are discussed previously (in Chapter 3), but it is important to point out that the zones of burial are rarely associated with permanent waterlogging such as is found in basin mire environments. It is more probable that the act of burial itself was accompanied by some exclusion of oxygen that can lead to better preservation of the organic record than might be thought possible (Figure 5.7). Moreover, colluvium and alluvium often bury old land surfaces and former topsoils, and their investigation through archaeological and micromorphological methods can provide good evidence of past land-use. Sometimes one can be lucky and recover a wide range of additional palaeoenvironmental data from these buried soils, and despite attendant problems of bias, mixing and the interpretation placed on these forms of proxy evidence (e.g. Dimbleby and Evans 1974; Carter 1990), this can aid in the interpretation of former landscapes (Bell and Walker 1992: 23–9). Nonetheless, one often encounters completely oxidized, circum-neutral preservation environments which are just about good enough for the preservation of bone, molluscs and carbonized seed remains, but little else (see Chapter 2).

(Frame width 40 mm)

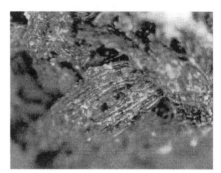

(Frame width 5 mm)   (Frame width 2.5 mm)

Above: overall view and images of twisted fibres within the larger fragment.

Below: overall view and detail of the smaller textile fragment.

(Frame width 20 mm)   (Frame width 10 mm)

Figure 5.7 Fragment of cloth in a Bronze Age cremation pit beneath a turf mound at Over, Cambridgeshire, England (N. Dodwell).

Models of associated soil types and change

On the margins of a lowland basin mire, soil types ranging from buried/drowned argillic brown earths to raw or immature soils could be expected to be found. In a river valley system, the soil types could range from argillic to brown earths, both buried and plough-damaged, and on chalk downland, soil types could range from argillic to brown earths to thin rendsinas. Various models of soil change throughout the Holocene have been suggested, for example by Limbrey (1975), Fisher (1982) and Macphail *et al.* (1987). What is presented here is an amalgam of their views plus some new ideas. Many of the details in relation to the research conducted in the Welland, Nene, Great Ouse and Allen valleys may be found in the case studies in Chapters 6–8 and 12 (below).

The conventional model states that with the rapid warming in the Holocene and the growth of tree cover, slightly acidic brown forest earths characterized by a clay-enriched or argillic horizon towards the base of the profile were formed throughout the earlier Holocene (Figure 4.1). By the early Neolithic period or fifth millennium BC, there were well-drained and well-developed brown soils associated with deciduous woodland found over most of lowland Britain. Various types and degrees of disruption, ostensibly caused by human activities of one kind or another, led to the gradual deterioration of these soils, either continuously, episodically or catastrophically. The speed of change very much depended on the intensity and severity of change. It could be set in motion by either human activities or natural events or some combination of the two, but the propensity for change already existed in the system. Some practitioners would support the view that the main driving force behind these changes as the subtly changing climatic regime over the long term (M. Macklin pers. comm.). 'Climatically driven, human-induced' is a phrase often heard at a geoarchaeological conference. Others (such as myself) would see the main factor as being human activities in landscapes that had a series of inherent characteristics, in some of which where the threshold for change was reached and crossed, and where climate change could be one of a combination of several essential factors that led to the observed change.

Forest soils, once disturbed, could certainly become rapidly depleted of much of their organic and soil moisture status. In addition, there would undoubtedly be some leaching down and through the profile of nutrients essential for plant growth, some 'flushing out' of the organized clay component, and many secondary formations, often involving the formation of iron oxides and hydroxides and various forms of calcium carbonate. These secondary formations could lead to other processes occurring, such as panning, seasonal waterlogging and increased biological activity, thus leading to further degradation of the soil profile. More than likely this did occur in many instances, and particularly if the soil was not managed or replenished with nutrients through the use of fertilizers or long periods of fallow.

Certainly recent research has aided our ability to identify the use of fertilizers in soils in the past (Simpson *et al.* 1998, 1999), but concrete evidence of this on archaeological sites is rarely found. But what if a much greater mosaic of different soil types already existed in the landscape of the earlier Holocene, so that many more different types and variants of soils were already present in the system. The soil type was controlled by the main factors of soil formation, and in particular the subsoil type and the vegetation it supported. The key in the past to 'reading' these soil types would have been the nature of the vegetation cover itself. Consequently, it would have been possible for different soil types to be exploited differently and deliberately for their individual properties by humans from the outset. This is the scenario that is discussed for the Cranborne Chase area of southern England (see Chapter 12). Obviously, this new suggestion does not mean that the conventional sequence of soil change from brown forest earth to brown earth to rendsina or some other variant did not occur in many instances, and indeed I have found sequences in thin section which suggest that this was the frequently the case (and see for example Chapters 6–8). It is rather that different stages of development occurred in different parts of the landscape, and not all areas necessarily had in effect the 'climax' soil type present that one might have expected to have formed.

Fieldwork strategies

For example, in the lower Welland valley between Stamford on the edge of the Lincolnshire limestone to the northern Cambridgeshire fen-edge at Borough Fen over a distance of some 20 km (Figure 6.2), what were some of the fieldwork strategies that were used to investigate the valley system? This landscape archaeology study was published in four volumes (Pryor and French 1985; French and Pryor 1993; Simpson *et al.* 1993; Pryor 1998a) and used a combination of existing data and targeted new field survey, excavations and analysis. Even though the project was not conceived as a unitary whole from the outset, and is really the product of at least five different projects, it has served to investigate the whole lower part of the valley system, and put forward ideas on land-use change over time with respect to deforestation, agriculture intensification and gradual waterlogging of some parts of the system followed by more recent dewatering and desiccation (see Chapters 6, 10 and 11).

The methodological approaches used fell into four major categories. First, a series of non-intrusive surveys and desk-top studies were made using existing sources of information. This involved compiling all the known archaeological, drift geological and soil data and putting it together as overlays on the Ordnance Survey map of the area at one scale (Pryor and French 1985: figs 1–5). Effectively, this defined various characteristics of the study region, and in particular showed immediately where the apparent blanks were in the archaeological record (ibid.: fig. 3). Second, this was followed by a series of evaluation and assessment investigations. This mainly involved transect field walking survey using 100 m sample swathes every kilometre from one watershed to the other across the valley floor (ibid.: fig. 9), and dyke surveys of any cleaned drainage ditch sections with the stratigraphy recorded, described and levelled at least every 150 m (French and Pryor 1993). Then, third, there was selective intervention on the ground for a variety of reasons and involving several different scales of fieldwork and subsequent analysis. These included small test excavations of natural features such as palaeo-channels for sedimentological, ecological and land-use evidence (French *et al.* 1992; Passmore and Macklin 1993), and mainly selected, large-scale excavation of waterlogged and/or buried sites and non-waterlogged and plough-damaged sites (Pryor and French 1985; Pryor 1998a).

Some sites were excavated on an extensive scale in advance of destruction, mainly by gravel extraction and road building, and some sites were purely research excavation projects involving either full or sample excavation. At the pre-excavation stage, as many non-instrusive techniques as possible were utilized such as hand augering, geophysical, magnetic susceptibility and phosphate surveys. With the buried sites, such as the Etton Neolithic cause-wayed enclosure (Pryor 1998a), the first stage of excavation was to remove the alluvial overburden and address the upper surface of the buried soil (Figure 5.8). Because of the excellent preservation of this old ground surface, non-intrusive survey techniques were re-employed at this stage such as intensive gridded fieldwalking for artefacts, magnetic susceptibility survey and phosphate analyses (Pryor and French 1985: 34–58; Pryor 1998a: 71–80). This is of critical importance because on a plough-damaged site one is very unlikely to recover the more enigmatic types of evidence which may suggest human activities on the contemporary land surface. The second stage of excavation involved the removal of the buried soil to reveal the earth-fast features at the base of the soil and cut into the top of the subsoil, as one would find on any normal plough-damaged site. As such large areas were investigated on many of the excavations and many of the features covered many hectares of land, this meant that it was impossible to dig all of the linear and non-structural features, so a 10 or 20 per cent sample strategy was regularly employed for excavating these (Pryor and French 1985: fig. 40). On the other hand, structural, buried and waterlogged features tended to be dug in their entirety where time and funding allowed. This leads into the fourth category of approach, establishing sampling strategies at the feature and context level, as well as the greater site level.

During the excavation of extensive, linear and non-structural features, one approach was to sample every layer in every section of each feature fills for artefactual and palaeobotanical remains. Another approach was to be more selective and only sub-sample the primary fills, or to take only representative sets of samples from all major fill or context levels. Ultimately, the approach to be taken is very much a matter of the questions being asked of the site, the level of data and detail sought, and the time and funding available. This

Figure 5.8 Aerial view of the interior of the Etton causewayed enclosure with the alluvial overburden removed and the buried soil surface revealed (S. Upex).

choice is never easy, and often with hind-sight one wishes one had done it another way at the time.

Sites or possible sites that were found by various survey techniques also required investigation by some form of evaluation. This could involve more detailed and site-specific surveys, and/or some sample excavation. Random, systematic or judgemental sampling excavation strategies could be employed, or some combination of all three approaches. It is perhaps best to illustrate this by way of an hypothetical example. If there was a small lithic scatter on an small gravel island in the fens which had been discovered by fieldwalking survey to be emerging from the peat fen, where there was no other physical threat to the site other than drainage and arable farming, one could justify cutting say three 2×2 m squares, one in the densest part of the flint scatter, one on the edge of the island and the margin of the flint scatter and one off-site to investigate the deeper, associated stratigraphic sequence. In all three judgemental sample trenches, one would be aiming to sample every possible feature, context and horizon for as many different analytical techniques as possible in order to maximize the information return. For instance, this could mean dry or wet sieving all of the buried soil in arbitrary spits for artefactual, faunal and charred plant macro-fossil remains, taking adjacent sample columns for molluscs, soil micromorphology and geo-chemical analyses, pollen and diatoms, and bulk samples for uncharred plant macro-fossil and insect remains. This type of sampling and the information return from this sort of work can be seen at sites such as Crowtree Farm in the northern Cambridgeshire fens of East Anglia (French and Pryor 1993: 33–51).

From this work, where have the best environmental and archaeological deposits tended to come from? Almost without fail, the best preservation occurs at the margins, where the landscape gradually changes from one type to another. This process may be controlled by a variety of factors such as elevation, degree of burial, proximity to the groundwater table and the underlying geology. For example, in the floodplain and fen-edge zones of eastern England, the best position for good preservation regularly involves the subsoil dipping gradually downhill over a long distance with a well-preserved buried soil sealed by overburden deposits which are generally air-excluding, with a groundwater table at the level of the top of the subsoil but which remains more or less steady at this level year-round. In addition, deep features such as buried soils under monuments and palaeochannels provide good to excellent contexts for *in situ* archaeological and palaeoenvironmental preservation. Each of these types of context is potentially prone to various taphonomic agencies that may skew the sanctity of the context or feature or type of evidence, especially truncating flood events. But, as long as one is aware of these and openly tests the data for the signs and mechanisms responsible for various distortions, I see no reason why these types of context cannot be relied upon to offer good archaeological and palaeoenvironmental data.

On the chalk downlands of Cranborne Chase (see Chapter 12), the environs of Stonehenge (Richards 1990; Cleal *et al.* 1995) and the Maiden Castle area (Sharples 1991) in southern England, for example, fieldwork strategies were employed that are broadly similar to those discussed above. But the techniques were often deployed over a much wider geographical range or more often with a particular monument or time period focus. Unfortunately, however, the survival of buried landscapes under either air-excluding or waterlogged deposits is much more uncommon in these well-drained areas. Here also there is often no overall conception by one project team over a lengthy period of study from site to site, landscape to landscape. As a complicating factor, many of the sites are protected, which makes archaeological field research much more burdensome to instigate and often curtails what may be attempted in terms of the scale of operations. Similarly, there are not so many extensive and large-scale destructive developments such as gravel quarries which allow extensive rescue excavation projects in advance of destruction, with a few notable exceptions such as Durrington Walls (Wainwright and Longworth 1971) and the A35 Bypass (Hearne and Birbeck 1999). For example, the strategy for investigating a series of scheduled prehistoric monuments in their landscape context in the upper

Allen valley of Cranborne Chase involves aerial and terrain mapping, off-site auger transects, prospection for colluvial/alluvial and river valley peat deposits, sampling of palaeochannel systems for their vegetational record, extensive geophysical survey and augering of individual sites with targeted sample excavation for structural and palaeoenvironmental evidence (Allen 1992, 1997a and b, 1998; French *et al*. 2000) (see Chapter 12). In many instances, large research projects have been set up to deal with one monument, for example Maiden Castle (Sharples 1991) and Stonehenge (Cleal *et al*. 1995), or a whole landscape such as the Stonehenge environs (Richards 1990) and Cranborne Chase (Barrett *et al*. 1991 a and b). The latter project in particular attempted to combine survey and selected excavation, extensive off-site and detailed on-site studies in combination with pre-existing and new environmental data.

Nonetheless, the situation in the chalk downland zone of southern Britain has not been conducive to looking elsewhere in the region for new sets of data in different parts of the landscape. First, existing theories on landscape change and development need to be tested with good sets of palaeoenvironmental data. Obviously, this means finding new repositories of reliable and well-preserved data. My hunch is that most of the river valleys draining this region such as the Avon, Allen, Kennet and Stour will contain sequences of palaeochannels and associated waterlogged, organic deposits which make detailed Holocene landscape reconstruction possible. This potential has now already been hinted at by work done in the upper Avon valley just to the east of Durrington Walls (Scaife in Cleal *et al*. 1994), and in the upper Allen valley by my own research team (French *et al*. 2000). In both cases, peat-filled palaeochannels have been discovered which still contain reliable Holocene pollen sequences for the immediate region (Figure 12.13). Despite the presence of calcareous groundwater conditions, this makes one wonder about the types of deposits that may be contained, as yet undiscovered, in say the Kennet valley in the vicinity of Silbury Hill and Avebury, the dry valley named Stonehenge Bottom which runs from the Stonehenge to the alluviated floodplain of the Avon just west of Amesbury, and the winterborne stream valleys to the north of Maiden Castle, to name just a few. These landscape zones require systematic investigation for the discovery of capture zones of palaeoenvironmental data. Only then by looking and testing new parts of the landscape will it be possible to examine how this most important area of Britain became so extensively exploited in prehistoric times.

Essential reading

Allen, M.J. (1992) 'Products of erosion and the prehistoric land-use of the Wessex chalk', in M. Bell and J. Boardman (eds) *Past and Present Soil Erosion*, pp. 37–52, Oxford: Oxbow Monograph 22.

Allen, M.J. (1997) 'Environment and land-use', in B. Cunliffe and A.C. Renfrew (eds) *Science and Stonehenge*, pp. 115–44, London: *Proceedings of the British Academy 92*.

Allen, M.J. (1998) 'A note on reconstructing the prehistoric landscape and environment in Cranborne Chase; the Allen valley', *Proceedings of the Dorset Natural History and Archaeological Society* 120: 39–44.

Brown, A.G. (1997) *Alluvial Geoarchaeology*, Cambridge: Cambridge University Press.

Cleal, R. *et al*. (1995) *Stonehenge in its Landscape*, Archaeological Report 10, London: English Heritage.

French, C. and Pryor, F. (1993) *The South-West Fen Dyke Survey, 1982–86*, Cambridge: East Anglian Archaeology 59.

Pryor, F. and French, C. (1985) *Archaeology and Environment in the Lower Welland Valley*, Cambridge: East Anglian Archaeology 27.

Sharples, N. (1991) *Maiden Castle*, Archaeological Report 19, London: English Heritage.

Major types of upland systems

Turning to upland systems, the same types of research criteria apply, with most of the same aims in mind also. Here, some of the physical constraints are different, but one is still trying to understand the nature of landscape change, develop accurate and detailed sequences of landscape development and identify both human and climatic inputs into the system as well as interactions between them.

The main landscape types that are typical of upland zones at least in the British Isles are blanket peat or upland bog, glaciated valleys containing lakes and eroded, bare rock slopes. Blanket bogs are characterized by high rainfall combined with poor drainage, and are found in a number of topographical situations including slopes up to 45 degrees. These areas tend to have acidic and impermeable bedrocks beneath, the peat bogs themselves are generally acidic, with the vegetation dominated by heather, *Eriophorum* (or cotton grass) and *Sphagnum* (or moss) vegetation (Figure 5.9). Well-known examples include Dartmoor, the Pennines, much of western Scotland, large parts of Orkney and Shetland, and central and southwestern Eire, and they are also found in large parts of northern Europe and Scandinavia. Unlike basin peats, blanket peat has a greater tendency to suffer decomposition as the peat may dry out for a small part of each year, especially at its surface. Glaciated valleys, such as in the Black Mountains of Wales (Figure 5.10), the English lake district in Cumbria and the Dingle Peninsula of Ireland, often contain lakes (Figure 5.11) which in turn preserve excellent sedimentological records of great depth and age range. Bare rock slopes may be frequently found in any of these regions.

Despite the greater erosive activity and more common bare rock surfaces in upland regions, in many respects it is much easier to find appropriate sampling locations for palaeoenvironmental data in these upland bog and lake contexts than in any lowland situation. Also, they tend to have suffered less destruction through drainage, arable agriculture and construction projects, and are often still actively forming, aggrading and infilling.

Obviously between the two extremes there are several other types of landscape which are characterized by peat deposits and/or poor, acidic soils, namely raised bogs and heaths. Raised bogs may occur in upland and/or lowland types of terrain, but heath tends to be found in lowland areas. Heath may take the form of heather moor in upland areas and is effectively a transitional type of environment to blanket peat bogs. The former form as a result of the impedence of groundwater in any situation and the growth of peat characterized by an acid-loving flora mainly of *Sphagnum* moss (Pearsall 1950; Pennington 1974). Examples occur throughout the western side of Britain, in particular the mosses of Cumbria and Lancashire (Middleton *et al.* 1995) and in the Somerset levels, such as Street Heath and Westhay Moor (Coles 1995: 69–70). Heathland is characteristically found on podzolic sandy soils which are dominated by ling (*Calluna vulgaris*), bracken and sparse grasses. Large parts of Norfolk and Suffolk are characterized by these heathlands, and they certainly seem to be a landscape type which has developed since the Mesolithic period as a result of human over-exploitation, at least in Britain (Dimbleby 1965; Scaife and Macphail 1983). There is also high montane grassland which colonizes bare mountain top rock detritus and thin, skeletal soils. It is characterized by moss, lichens, sheep's fescue (*Festuca ovina*) and bent (*Agrostis tenuis*), and may well be the only natural grassland to be found in Britain (Pearsall 1950).

Figure 5.9 Typical surface of a blanket bog showing heather, cotton sedge and *Sphagnum* vegetation, in this case in Islay, Inner Hebrides.

Figure 5.10 Valley in the Black Mountains of South Wales with the characteristic bracken-dominated valley sides, cultivated and pastoral lower sides and valley base, with blanket peat on the upper slopes and crests.

Figure 5.11 Small glacial lakes surrounded by blanket bog in the mountains of the Dingle Peninsula, southwest Ireland.

Models of landscape, vegetation and soil change

The conventional models for the formation of blanket peat tend to follow either climatic or pedogenic pathways (Figure 4.1). In northwestern Europe, it has been repeatedly observed that a major phase of upland blanket peat formation began about 7,500 years ago, that is from the Mesolithic period onwards, with a major intensification in peat formation in upland areas during the Bronze Age or second millennium BC. Peat growth is occurring at different times and in different places and not always in association with proven human disturbance. Nonetheless, this process was probably associated with relatively slight changes in climate as much as anything else, that is increased rainfall and slightly lower annual air temperatures (see Bell and Walker 1992: 69–73, with references). These blanket bogs rest on former dryland soils that developed during the early post-glacial and that once supported woodland. Opinion is divided as to what initiated these associated major changes in soil and vegetation type. Was it a result of increased wetness with associated natural pedogenic processes leading to soil degradation and blanket peat formation? Or was it purely human-induced through deforestation, land exploitation and poor management causing a critical threshold to be reached and passed, causing soil degradation to begin which culminated in the formation of podzols and blanket peats (see Bell and Walker 1992: 174–82, with references)?

The associated, typical sequence of soil formation for the earlier part of the Holocene in these upland, acidic and more poorly drained parts of the British Isles tends to follow a different route than in more low-lying and calcareous regions (Figure 4.1). The model suggests that acidic brown earths formed in the earlier part of the Holocene, in most cases associated with woodland development which may have been more sparse than in lowland areas and affected by the frost/snow line. With deforestation and increased rainfall and poor land management, rapid leaching and acidification (or podzolization) occurred. The resulting podzols are characterized by acidic leaf litter or a mor horizon overlying a leached eluvial (or Ea) horizon, which is more or less depleted of fine soil and organic material and can be very thick (up to *c.* 1.5 m), beneath which may be one and/or two horizons of accumulation of either amorphous humic material (or a Bh) and/or redeposited iron (the spodic or Bs horizon) (Figure 4.13) (Limbrey 1975: 137–45). The development of a podzol goes hand in hand with the development of a heath-like acidic vegetation dominated by ling and bracken (Pearsall 1950; Scaife and Macphail 1983).

In many areas and often within lowland systems also, the soil/vegetation complex stabilized at this stage to give a heathland landscape such as found in parts of Suffolk (e.g. around Sutton Hoo) (Carver 1998), Norfolk (e.g. Breckland) (Scaife in Wymer 1996) and Sussex (e.g. Iping Common) (Keef *et al.* 1965), all in England. In many other areas, especially on higher ground, these soils and vegetation types set in train a cycle of increasing acidity and the growth of acidic-tolerant plants. The spodic horizon of the developing podzol in particular often caused impermeable iron pans to form at the base of the profile, leading to drainage becoming poorer and eventual saturation, which then led to the accumulation of standing groundwater. This in turn led to more accumulation of acidic-loving plant material on the upper surface of the podzol and saturation of the soil profile, and often peat formation had been initiated. This soil/vegetation system was now dominated by a tussocky landscape of heather, cotton sedge and *Sphagnum* moss with small shallow pools of water inbetween.

Perhaps it is best to look at a few examples where climatic and anthropogenic influences appear to have combined in causing major landscape change. One of the most commonly used archeological examples in Britain is the Dartmoor region of southwestern England. Here, there are massive areas covered by a system of land division and enclosure known as the Dartmoor reaves (Figure 5.12) dating to the later Bronze Age which Fleming (1988) investigated extensively, with more targeted fieldwork carried out by the Central Excavation Unit (Balaam *et al.* 1982). How was this system established and sustained in such an impoverished, blanket peat landscape that was open to the effects of increased rainfall? One of the most informative published sections is from Saddlesborough reave which shows the stone rubble of the reave burying a sequence comprising an earlier reave bank and a thin peat horizon developed on a podzol (ibid.). Immediately this tells one that there was a precursor system to the later Bronze Age system, at least in some parts of the moor, and that this earlier field boundary bank was already established on thin blanket peat, with an already developed podzol present. Soil pollen and micromorphological work on podzols such as this have suggested that this area had once supported mixed deciduous woodland and this woodland had probably been associated with brown earth soils which were much better drained, well developed and nutrient-rich (Keeley and Macphail 1982). Obviously putting a secure date on this other than saying it was pre-second millennium BC is almost impossible, but it makes the point that major landscape, soil and vegetation change had occurred by the earlier Bronze Age on Dartmoor.

What was/were the prime cause(s) initiating this change in soil/vegetation complex in Dartmoor? By the later Neolithic and earlier Bronze periods, several large stone circles and probably some linear embanked boundaries on the higher/upper parts of Dartmoor such as Grims Pound had already been constructed. These areas could have been cleared ostensibly, either through natural causes such as forest fires, or human-encouraged fires to provide food for and control game such as deer. Or, perhaps the woodland was never very well developed in these higher zones at all, it was sparse and scrubby, and this was why it was exploited first. Once open and subject to the elements, there was a natural propensity for pedogenic processes to occur which began the process of deterioration. Perhaps, this scenario could have been hastened along somewhat by human-induced activities such as the setting of fires to

Figure 5.12 Typical view of a transverse reave on Dartmoor.

aid in the hunting of game and in an attempt to control bracken and heather growth, scrub clearance and grazing of pigs, sheep and cattle. Once into that cycle of increased exposure, increased wetness and some disturbance associated with human activities, however infrequent, a threshold had been reached and gradual change in the soil/vegetation system had begun. Without significant regrowth of woodland occurring or rigorous land management, this natural but human and climatically exacerbated process was probably unstoppable. This led to significant blanket peat development over large areas of land but concentrated on the higher parts of the moor, probably in the later Neolithic period. Peat encroachment would have increased almost imperceptibly outwards and downslope with clearance and grazing activities. This process of an ever-widening sphere of soil change or deterioration to podzol type may well have become significantly enhanced by increasing rainfall throughout the Bronze Age, ultimately leading to widespread peat encroachment in the valleys and mid-lower valley slopes.

I suspect that the great explosion of land enclosure and reave construction on Dartmoor in the later Bronze Age occurred on the margins of podzol/peat development. This made it possible to exploit the best remaining land on the lower-mid slopes for enclosed winter grazing and the occasional summer hay crop, with the unenclosed bog and moor beyond utilized in the drier summer months for grazing. It is not just the layout of the Dartmoor reave system that took a lot of thought, but how it would be utilized to its best advantage. Perhaps also, this imposed system of land management was never entirely successful, and would have required input from farming communities in the neighbouring river valleys to provide sufficient cereal stocks and vegetable foodstuffs that could not be easily grown in this increasingly marginal landscape. Ultimately, the combined natural processes of increasing rainfall, podzolization and peat encroachment made the reave and enclosure system untenable, probably within a few hundred years or so. More than likely, human use of the slopes helped to speed up a process that was already underway, but was not the prime cause of the demise of this system.

Fieldwork strategies

How does one approach this kind of system from an intertwined landscape and archaeological perspective? The fieldwork strategies that are viable are very much as stated for the lowland examples set out above, but there has to be a much greater emphasis on extensive earthwork survey and palynological studies. I do not propose to go into how to conduct good field surveys as there are several good texts and examples of how to do it in the literature (Hogg 1980; Bowden 1999), but the palaeobotanical aspect deserves some further development.

The combination of relatively impermeable bedrock, perched water tables, and acidic podzols and blanket peats is obviously conducive to good pollen preservation, with the Dartmoor area being a clear example. Although the soil/peat system is acidic today, it may not always have been so. The soil analytical work done by Helen Keeley and Richard Macphail at Shaugh Moor (1982: 219–20) has indicated that the podzolization may have occurred from the later Neolithic period onwards, with even some peat development prior to reave construction. Although these soils were already weakly acidic initially, they would nonetheless have been subject to some soil faunal mixing, and therefore the pollen sequence in the soil would have also undergone some differential mixing. Although this mixing may have been relatively minor and is nowhere near the same disruptive influence that is encountered in basic or calcareous soils (Dimbleby and Evans 1974), I would be more cautious about the interpretation of the pollen sequences that Balaam (1982: 204–15) illustrated for the buried soils from Saddlesborough Reave and Wotter Common, particularly from the lower two-thirds of the soil profile downwards. Only the pollen sequence derived from the peat developed on the podzols and the mor horizon of the podzol should really be trusted. Even with these thin blanket peats in upland situations, there are potential provisos as they are prone to truncation and their upper surfaces often suffer seasonal drying out. The pollen sequence derived from the eluvial and illuvial horizons below should be treated more as a mosaic amalgam of all previous environments, rather than distinctive pollen zones by soil horizon and depth.

Thus what would be the best approach to getting good detail from the palynological record in the Dartmoor area to formulate ideas of land-use exploitation on a specific and sub-regional scale? The reaves and the enclosure boundaries act as forms of linear preservation of old land surfaces, potentially at different times and over different parts of the Dartmoor landscape. In effect they provide ready-made transects for excavation and sampling on an extensive or intensive scale. They also provide ready made palaeo-catenas for the examination of buried soils over large areas of the landscape. In addition, the many small stream systems within the valleys dissecting Dartmoor have not been investigated to my knowledge, and would undoubtedly repay prospection for small peat infilled and waterlogged basins and small lakes. These repositories would provide much safer pollen records with both an immediate, valley, sub-regional and regional catchment. This is probably the only real way to get at the impact, if any, of Mesolithic and earlier Neolithic influence on the woodland, provide reliable dating and detailed vegetational sequences, as well as to examine the impact of climatic changes and possibility of arable agriculture ever occurring at any time during the Neolithic to Iron Ages. The potential is undoubtedly there, it only requires new projects with a slightly different way of looking at the landscape to retrieve new sets of data which may shed light on the landscape development of the area.

Essential reading

Balaam, N. Smith, K. and Wainwright, G.J. (1982) 'The Shaugh Moor Project – the fourth report', *Proceedings of the Prehistoric Society* 48: 203–78.

Bell, M. and Walker, M. (1992) *Late Quaternary Environmental Change*, pp. 69–73 and 174–82, London: Longman.

Goudie, A. (1990) *The Landforms of England and Wales*, Oxford: Blackwell Scientific.

Pearsall, W.H. (1950) *Mountains and Moorlands,* London: Collins.

Part 2

Geoarchaeology in action

Case studies and syntheses

Introduction

The series of twelve case studies which follow attempt to illustrate many of the concepts, techniques and approaches that were briefly set out in Chapters 1–5. In addition, they discuss possible models of land-use through time, and point out where further research needs to be done.

The work is based on published and unpublished sources on projects with which I have been involved over the past twenty-five years or so. All those who have provided hard 'graft' and information are gratefully acknowledged at the outset. Without so many holes in the ground and other analytical studies to draw on as well as my own, this book would be a thin shadow of what is presented. It goes without saying that what follows is my view, with my own preconceptions and conceptions of the evidence. Ultimately, I hope that these studies draw the available evidence together in an holistic way and present a series of narratives in which some new things have been added. The text also has an emphasis on soils and within-soil and landscape processes, which are integrally related to the greater archaeological and environmental picture being discussed.

About half of the case studies which follow deal with my involvement in the archaeology of East Anglia in eastern England (Chapters 6–11) before moving further afield in England, Europe, the Near East and beyond (Chapters 12–17). The first six case studies discussing the palaeoenvironments of East Anglia are all related in the sense that they all deal with the lower parts of three major river valleys and the adjoining fen basins of Cambridgeshire into which those rivers flow. The other landscape essays that follow in Chapters 12–17 address different types of terrain and climate, and range geographically from southern England to Spain, Sicily, Yemen, Syria and Kazakhstan. These are all associated with drier climatic regimes and landscapes that are often prone to widespread erosion problems. The specific locations of these projects were driven as much by funding parameters and collaborators' interests as anything else, but do indeed address some common issues. These issues include the identification of natural versus climatic causes of erosion, and the nature of human influence and its role in causing, shaping and altering these events and processes. I hope that these case studies aim to be as much palaeoenvironmental and archaeological histories of landscapes as strictly geoarchaeological studies, and that they serve to illustrate and inform on the first five chapters of this book that deal with some aspects of methodology and approaches in geoarchaeology today.

6   The lower Welland valley, Cambridgeshire, England

Introduction

Between 1979 and 1990, a whole series of prehistoric sites as well as the landscape inbetween, ranging in date from the fourth to first millennia BC, were investigated, often in advance of gravel extraction and road construction. The principal sites excavated were Barnack/Bainton, Maxey, Etton Woodgate, Etton and Etton Landscape, covering the earlier Neolithic to the Romano-British periods (Figures 6.1 and 6.2) (Pryor and French 1985; Pryor *et al*. 1985; French 1990, 1992a; French *et al*. 1992; Simpson *et al*. 1993; Pryor 1998a; French and Pryor forthcoming). This lowland river gravel landscape was seen as potentially rivalling the upper Thames valley in terms of the quality and range of prehistoric sites present (RCHM 1960), as well as providing the links between the fen-edge and river's edge hinterland that in the adjacent Nene valley to the south were largely obscured by the establishment of modern Peterborough (see Chapter 7). In addition, many sites were either affected by subsequent alluviation leading to the creation of buried and sometimes still waterlogged landscapes, and/or the presence of upstanding monuments enabled the survival of pockets of old land surface on the higher terrace gravels. Thus there was great, mainly prehistoric, archaeological potential in the lower Welland valley which was ostensibly under-explored and relatively undisturbed by recent disturbances.

The archaeological and palaeoenvironmental work in this area, once started, grew organically rather than systematically. When the Welland Valley Project was set up in 1979, there was a concerted effort to place the large-scale excavations on the south side of Maxey village undertaken in advance of gravel extraction in their sub-regional context (Pryor and French 1985). This involved aerial mapping, systematic fieldwalking transects across the valley and selected augering transects, as well as bringing all the existing published and unpublished work together in one body of research. The seven hectares of land investigated at Maxey using a barrage of geo-prospection, archaeological and environmental sampling techniques revealed a length of the Maxey cursus, half of the Maxey great henge, a small oval Neolithic barrow, one round barrow within the henge, two Iron Age square barrows, an exten-

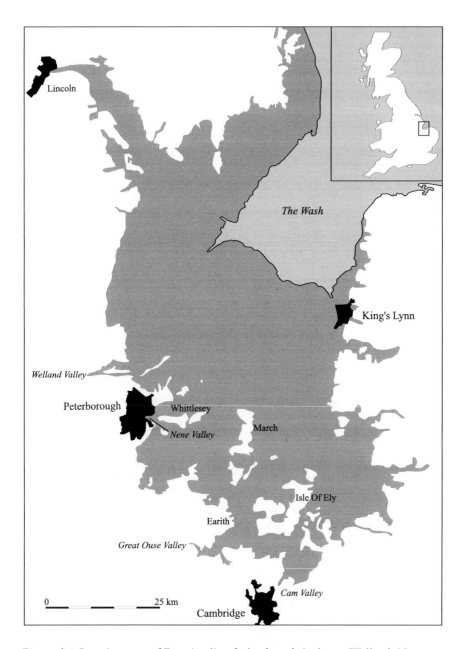

Figure 6.1 Location map of East Anglian fenlands and the lower Welland, Nene and Great Ouse valleys of Cambridgeshire (C. Begg).

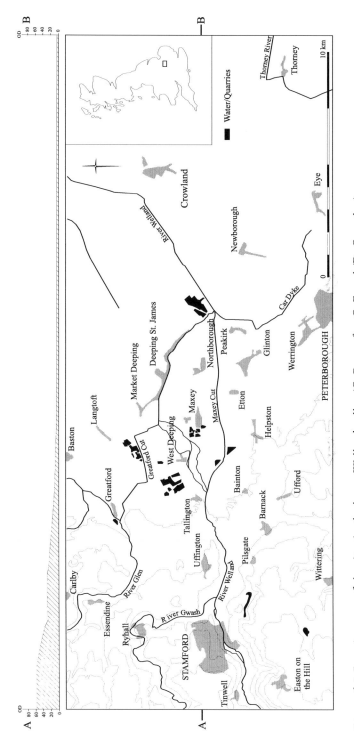

Figure 6.2 Location map of the sites in the lower Welland valley (C. Begg after C. French/D. Crowther).

sive area of dispersed Iron Age and Romano-British occupation and small field systems. Quarry expansion eastwards between 1983 and 1987 allowed the discovery and excavation of the waterlogged Etton Neolithic causewayed enclosure and a whole series of henge and barrow sites called Etton Landscape sites 1–8 (Figure 6.3). Finally the construction of the A15 Bypass about 400 m to the east in 1987 (Figure 6.3) enabled the excavation of a 30 m wide transect across a *c.* 2 km length of the alluviated valley floor through a series of prehistoric domestic, field system and burial sites, and a pipeline route across the valley about 5 km upstream between Bainton and Barnack enabled a series of glimpses of parts of prehistoric fields and settlement to be made (Pryor and French 1985: Vol. 2). For the first time in this area these projects allowed the examination of large tracts of buried gravel terrace landscape, and the discovery of new and different types of site for the region, combined with a range of new palaeoenvironmental analyses. It should not be forgotten that all of this work was done pre-Policy Planning Guidance 16 (D.o.E. 1990) and was paid for by the public purse on a project-by-project basis, either from English Heritage (and its various predecessors), the British Museum, the Fitzwilliam Estate, British Gas and Cambridgeshire County Council.

Except for the Barnack/Bainton site, the sites are found in relatively close proximity to each other on the southeastern edge of Maxey 'island', an area of slightly higher First Welland Terrace gravels surrounded by a slightly lower zone of first terrace gravels and relict floodplain with numerous palaeochannel systems (Figures 3.4 and 6.3). The two earliest sites are of the earlier fourth–third millennia BC: the large 'boundary' ditch of Etton Woodgate (Pryor *et al.* 1985) effectively defines the southeastern tip of Maxey 'island' with the causewayed enclosure at Etton (Pryor 1998a) situated more or less opposite some 100 m to the southeast on the other side of the contemporary palaeochannel and within a meander loop (French *et al.* 1992). Towards the end of the third millennium BC, the causewayed enclosure may have witnessed some occupation within its interior (Pryor 1998a), and there is evidence of the dumping of contemporary domestic rubbish on the northern edge of the stream system about 400 m downstream at the Etton Landscape/A15 Bypass (French and Pryor forthcoming). At about the same time, a series of small henges were built just inland and uphill from these sites, namely the Etton Landscape sites 2, 4 and 7, as well as the Maxey 'great' henge less than 1 km to the northwest (Pryor and French 1985), the C-shaped ditch or Etton Landscape site 3 and a separate length of cursus ditches aligned northwest to southeast that begins within the Etton causewayed enclosure (Figures 5.8 and 6.3). The Bronze Age landscape is mainly dominated by barrows situated entirely on the first terrace gravels on the northern margins of the furthest extent of alluvial deposition, for example Etton Landscape sites 1 and 8 and another two barrows on the A15 Bypass route, with elements of field systems and enclosures built around them as well as pit alignments and the occasional shallow midden deposit of domestic

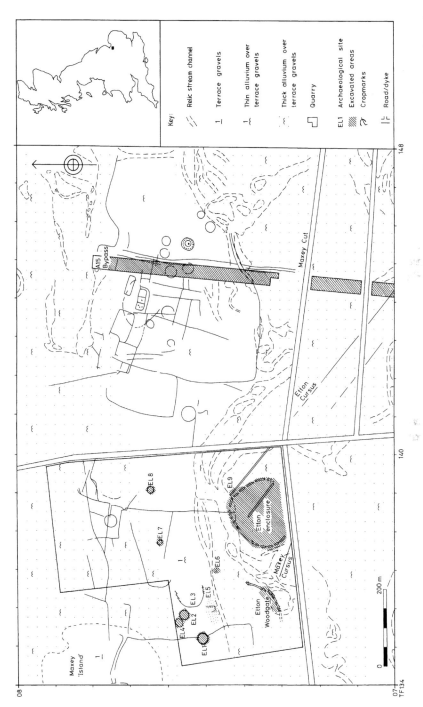

Figure 6.3 The Etton Landscape sites and the relict palaeochannel systems in the lower Welland valley (after French *et al.* 1992: fig. 16).

debris (Etton Landscape site 5; A15 Bypass). Several Iron Age and Romano-British dispersed farmstead sites with associated ditch systems occur on the highest parts of Maxey 'island' and the first terrace gravels (Pryor and French 1985; Simpson *et al.* 1993). In addition, the relict palaeochannel systems to the north, south and east of the Etton causewayed enclosure have been investigated by geomorphological survey and targeted sample excavation (French *et al.* 1992).

Buried soil evolution and prehistoric landscape change

Buried soils were sampled at all of these sites situated in different parts of the floodplain and the first terrace. Some forty soil profiles have been examined micromorphologically over a decade (French 1985a, 1985a, 1990, 1992a, 1995a, 1998a, forthcoming b), and their record examined in the light of the associated archaeological, plant macro-fossil (Green 1985; Nye and Scaife 1998), palynological (Scaife 1998), Coleopteran (Robinson 1998 and forthcoming), faunal remains data (Armour-Chelu 1992, 1998; Wallace 1995; Ainsley forthcoming) and relict palaeochannel system investigations (French *et al.* 1992). It should be noted that soil micromorphological analysis applied on such a landscape scale to buried soils as a 'new' technique had not been attempted before in Britain. The age of burial of the soils ranges from the mid-third to early first millennium BC, but the suite of information obtained from these palaeosols is remarkably consistent. What follows is a summary discussion of the analyses of the prehistoric palaeosols and their implications for land-use history in the lower Welland valley. This work is further augmented by the parallel studies of the lower Nene and Great Ouse valleys to the south (Figure 6.1) in Chapters 7 and 8.

The palaeosols preserved beneath the later Neolithic and Bronze Age monuments on the higher parts of the first terrace are always some form of argillic or brown forest earth. As one moves downslope towards the edge of influence of alluvial deposits, they become less well developed and tend to be a mixture of poorly developed argillic brown earths and brown earths, whereas those soils buried by Holocene river and overbank sediments are brown earths, often quite poorly developed and subject to considerable subsequent pedogenesis. Argillic brown earths (Figures 4.9 and 4.10) are created by the process of clay translocation under well-drained and stable forested conditions in which clay particles are moved down profile (leaving an eluvial or Eb horizon) and redeposited (illuviated) in what is termed a textural B (an argillic or Bt) horizon (Fedoroff 1968; Bullock and Murphy 1979; Avery 1980; Fisher 1982; McKeague 1983). This is considered to be a modal soil type under the earlier-mid-Holocene forests of southern England and many areas of northwestern Europe (Keeley 1982). Brown earths are essentially less well-developed argillic brown earths which consist of an A horizon overlying a cambic B (or Bw) horizon which exhibits some alteration of the parent material and some illuviation of fine material (Limbrey 1975; Avery 1980).

The formation of well-developed argillic horizons towards the base of brown earths testifies to extensive woodland development, probably by the Neolithic period, in the lower Welland valley, at least on the higher parts of the terrace just above the floodplain zone. This is corroborated to a great extent by the pollen and insect record at the Etton causewayed enclosure (Robinson 1998; Scaife 1998), the insect assemblages from A15 Bypass sites (Robinson forthcoming) and from pollen in peat deposits in earlier Holocene relict channels located just to the southeast (French *et al.* 1992; Scaife forthcoming). Moreover, the record of soil development suggests that this woodland began to be seriously disturbed by the latter part of the third millennium BC and into the second millennium BC, with a predominantly open environment existing by the latter period. This is especially well corroborated by the insect and pollen records from the middle Neolithic Etton causewayed enclosure ditch (Robinson 1998; Scaife 1998), and the insect record in later Neolithic to Bronze Age pits and ditches of the Etton Landscape/A15 Bypass (Robinson forthcoming).

When the proportion of wood- and tree-dependent Coleoptera from both the Etton and A15 Bypass sites are considered together (5–9 per cent of the terrestrial beetles), the assemblages indicate that there was extensive woodland remaining in this part of the valley, with possibly up to half or more of the catchment having tree and shrub cover at the end of the Neolithic or at the end of the third millennium BC (Robinson 1998 and forthcoming). It is suggested that there was alder in low-lying areas, grading into oak/hazel woodland on adjacent dried ground. Over the life of the Etton causewayed enclosure, there is not a great change in the insect assemblage, but the vegetation around the site may have become more thorn scrub dominated. Moreover, the groundwater table was relatively high and close to the ground surface in the floodplain zone as the insects assemblage within the Etton causewayed enclosure ditch formed under stagnant water conditions (Robinson 1998: 345), and there was a preponderance of aquatic and marginal aquatic plant taxa in the pollen record from the base of the enclosure ditch (Scaife 1998: 306–7). The pollen evidence also suggests that a component of this woodland was lime (ibid.), and this perhaps reflects the potential wider catchment for pollen as compared to insects.

Nonetheless during the life of the Etton causewayed enclosure, both the site and its immediate river floodplain-edge environs appear to have been relatively open, and more open than the general landscape. This landscape was set against a background which retained much alder woodland, partic-ularly along the floodplain of the contemporary stream which loops immediately around the site to the north, with oak, lime and hazel on higher areas of first terrace beyond, although even this woodland component had rapidly diminished by the time that the enclosure was constructed in the earlier to middle part of the fourth millennium BC. Some of this woodland was perhaps a vestige of the general former tree cover of the region as there were beetle species characteristic of over-mature trees and decaying wood in undisturbed woodland. The other major component of this landscape was grassland with a significant presence of grazing animals. Marsh environments appear to be only a background habitat to the co-dominant woodland and grassland. Notably, the insect evidence does not give much solid evidence for disturbed ground, let alone arable fields. But the pollen evidence obtained from a turf derived from the interior of the Etton enclosure did contain an assemblage with dominant herb taxa with ruderals, segetals and minor cereal-type pollen which indicates the possibility of some agricultural activity taking place, perhaps within the enclosure but more probably on the drier and higher land to the north (Scaife 1998: 308).

Towards the end of the second millennium BC or later in the Bronze Age, the insect assemblage tells a markedly different story (Robinson forthcoming). The wood- and tree-dependent Coleoptera have now fallen to below 2 per cent suggesting that there is very little woodland remaining in this landscape and what there is, is mainly willow and alder. The grassland is herb-rich and is supporting grazing animals. By way of comparison, Robinson (1992, 2001) suggests that the drier parts of the Flag Fen basin at the mouth of the adjacent Nene valley to the south (see Chapter 7 below) were probably more similar to the environment at Etton in the later Bronze Age. Again, there is no good evidence for arable or even much disturbed ground.

Associated with the deforestation process, several coincident and concomitant processes began to affect the lower parts of the terrace and the contemporary floodplain. By the third millennium BC it appears that both the ditch fills and the contemporary soil within the interior of the causewayed enclosure were receiving additions of silt and clay, probably derived from overbank freshwater flooding on a seasonal or episodic basis. At about the same time, the channel system skirting between the Etton Woodgate and Etton sites began to migrate southeastwards (Figure 6.3) and encroach upon the northwestern arc of the Etton causewayed enclosure ditch and infill it with colluvially derived silts and clays. The stream deposits were probably formed under almost year-round stagnant/standing water conditions as shown by its insect assemblage (Robinson 1998: 345). This same material also began to aggrade on the margins of the land surface occupied by the adjacent Etton Woodgate site under seasonal conditions of shallow standing water. This material was probably locally derived from immediately upstream and the higher ground of Maxey 'island'. This phase of soil movement and redeposition downstream was soon overtaken by the movement and deposition of alluvial silts and clays derived from overbank flooding both within the floodplain and on the lower margins of the first terrace gravels, for example the zone occupied by the later Neolithic and earlier Bronze Age sites of Etton Landscape and the A15 Bypass route.

The whole lower part of the Welland valley floodplain and first terrace was very active in terms of water movement and sediment transport and redeposition, at least on an episodic and/or seasonal basis. This occurred long before the major post-Roman phase of alluviation that was responsible for the deposition of silty clay alluvium which buried the prehistoric sites of the Etton Landscape and A15 Bypass. The Maxey-Etton floodplain was subject to channel migration, and widespread, low velocity freshwater flooding, ponding-back and the deposition of fine eroded soil and sediment in still water conditions over a wide area and a substantial period of time. Associated with these events was a seasonally higher but fluctuating groundwater table, much gleying of the lower part of soil profiles and the deposition of secondary calcium carbonate derived from the underlying base-rich terrace gravel subsoil. This increasing movement of water through the system is probably a consequent effect of increasing soil water and groundwater run-off associated with ongoing clearance activities in the catchment.

The most important processes in these floodplain and floodplain edge soils that were in operation at the onset of alluviation were frequent oxidation and gleying, and the inclusion or intercalation of fine material eroded from topsoils upstream and uphill in the valley system. The alternating rises and falls of the groundwater table led to accelerated leaching of the lower half of the soil profile, leaving a brown earth, for example, characteristically looking like a pale, greyish brown B horizon below an organic, but severely oxidized, A horizon, both in the field and in thin section. This was largely the result of the removal of the organic and much of the inherent fine components of the soil. Those pedofeatures that remained from the pre-alluvial soil, such as well-oriented clay coatings, tended to become impregnated with iron oxides and hydroxides, and turn a strong reddish brown to orangey brown colour. Indeed, the whole fine groundmass of the soil became generally oxidized and much affected by the impregnation of iron as well as calcium carbonate in a variety of forms.

Most importantly, how does the gradual deposition of alluvial material affect the soil that is being buried? As alluvial fine material (silt, clay and amorphous organic matter) began to accumulate on the soil's surface under temporary, shallow, standing water conditions in the late winter and spring, the topsoil or A horizon became increasingly dominated by the intercalation of dusty (or silty) clay, with or without the addition of finely comminuted, amorphous organic matter. This process also affected the B horizon below to a greater or lesser degree, leading to the formation of dusty/dirty or very impure silty clay coatings down profile. The combined effects of these processes caused the 'clogging-up' of the soil, much reducing pore space, gradually changing the soil's texture, that is from a sandy loam to a sandy clay loam, and eventually leading to the formation of blocky to columnar ped structures, especially in the upper half of the soil profile, as generally observed in field section today. In addition, this increase in soil density and change to a 'heavier' texture caused further impedence of water infiltration down profile, thus leading to two separate moisture regimes. The lower half of the profile remained more freely drained but subject to a seasonally fluctuating groundwater table, which was partially sealed from oxidation from above by a dense, silty clay soil now forming the upper half of the soil profile. Nonetheless, the soil profile continued to be affected by seasonal wetting and drying episodes, and the accretion of fine material under alluvial flood conditions. In addition, the deposition of fines and the blocky ped structure is often associated with shrink-swell clay types, meaning that the soil is periodically anaerobic and periodically aerobic, which occasionally allows the ingress of oxygen into the lower half of the soil profile. Thus, there is a gradually changing soil matrix and preservation status within the alluviated soil through time, which is at the same time both detrimental and advantageous to the preservation of organic remains and the *in situ* soil.

By implication this low-lying, flood-prone landscape was generally unsuitable either for settlement and/or arable agriculture, except perhaps for the occasional hay crop in the driest spring to summer months. This may go some way to explaining the lack of field systems in this area; perhaps it was treated as common land and used only for seasonal grazing, and therefore did not need defining by boundaries in the same way as on adjacent higher ground. Moreover, the active floodplain would have been a much more varied environment that we can envisage today, and this is aptly demonstrated in particular by the wood and insect evidence from the Etton and A15 Bypass sites (Taylor 1998; Robinson 1998, forthcoming). There would have been bare and shifting banks of sand and gravel, active channels, backwaters and stagnant ponds, eroding channel banks, scrubby willow and alder growing on banks and channel fringes, and the latter are often managed through coppicing or pollarding, patches of reed and sedge growth and areas of natural flood meadow. In the winter/early spring months much of the active floodplain would have been under shallow standing water and therefore less accessible to humans and domestic animals, and in summer/early autumn months large areas would have reverted to dry land and become much more accessible for exploitation by humans and animals throughout. In addition, there would have been seasonal variation in the wild resources available in the floodplain, for example for fish and fowl, or as a refuge for several wild species of animal like pine marten and bear (Armour-Chelu 1998; Wallace 1995).

Little reliable evidence for arable farming has been found at any of the sites examined. The soil micromorphological evidence is inconclusive at best (French 1985a, 1998a). Despite good evidence for soil disturbance, the absence of suites of convincing micromorphological features in the buried soils that are characteristic of ard agriculture (after Jongerius 1980, 1983; Gebhardt 1990; Carter and Davidson 1998, 2000; Lewis 1998a; Macphail 1998) precludes any definitive conclusion. Nonetheless, there were occasional agricutans (compound micro-laminated dusty clay coatings with included fine charcoal and organic matter) (Jongerius 1970, 1983) present in the pre-late Neolithic soil within the Maxey henge (French 1985a: 208). In addition, in the soil within the interior of the Etton causewayed enclosure, frequent mixing of fabrics occurred within the upper part of the buried soil and occasionally there were micro-laminated impure clay coatings present, both of which could have been caused by ploughing. Moreover, this rather ambiguous soil evidence does not mean that arable farming was not taking place in some parts of this valley floor landscape; it is just extremely difficult to recognize securely. Indeed, there are some hints in the pollen record at Etton of arable agriculture taking place on the adjacent drier and higher parts of the first terrace as indicated by a low presence of cereal pollen, but high values of ruderals and segetals (Scaife 1998: 306).

Conclusions

The combination of long-term field archaeological projects in the same area mainly undertaken by the same group of people combined with a variety of on- and off-site environmental sampling and analyses and geomorphological survey has enabled a detailed picture of the changing landscape to be built up over space and time. The result is not just a palaeoenvironmental sequence, but a series of landscape and land-use models through time and space in relation to the topography and archaeological record. Throughout there is a series of at least three major landscape zones available in the valley system – higher terrace, lower terrace and active floodplain – and it is likely that elements of each were exploited simultaneously, but for different needs and purposes as necessary in the past.

In the early Holocene, this valley was dominated by a wide anastomosing channel system situated to the south of the Maxey Cut and the location of the Etton causewayed enclosure (French *et al.* 1992: fig. 16.2). The herbaceous grassland with juniper and then birch/pine scrub woodland of the earlier Holocene soon gave way to a mixed deciduous forest dominated by lime and oak as the climate rapidly warmed and associated soil formation took place. When this landscape was entered in the earlier Neolithic period (early fourth millennium cal BC), the active floodplain had shifted some half a kilometre northwards and become a lazy, meandering stream, probably with marsh or sedge fen vegetation and alder carr woodland on either side. It would have provided the easiest avenue of movement as relatively impenetrable deciduous forest on well-drained forest brown earth soils would have dominated the higher and driest parts of the adjacent terraces. Indeed, much of the floodplain zone may well have been relatively quite open, say 50 per cent of it, and rapidly became more so during the mid to later fourth millennium BC. By the later third millennium BC, monument construction was taking place in all three landscape zones, implying a relatively fast and widespread opening-up of this landscape with it certainly becoming more scrubby. The presence of at least two lengthy cursus monuments (Maxey and Etton) crossing the valley diagonally from its highest to its lowest point across all three landscape zones corroborates this nicely. Despite the *in situ* absence of settlement evidence, except perhaps at Etton Woodgate on the edge of the active floodplain of the day, there is sufficient redeposited domestic debris found in pits and middens at the water's edge to suggest some occupation near the lower margins of the river valley. Undoubtedly further discoveries are here to be made, and, I suspect, will depend as much on recognition of something we do not know we are looking at, as much as anything else. Definite evidence of land-use is hard to come by except from the insect assemblages and to a lesser extent the palynological studies, despite the large areas of well-preserved buried soils present and already quite thoroughly investigated. Nonetheless, it does seem that the landscape was open and pasture dominated, and became more so throughout the third and second millennia BC.

By the end of the third millennium BC, there is the first encroachment of floodwaters on to the margins of the lower terrace with seasonal deposition of riverborne silts and clays. This previously stable and quite well-drained landscape becomes more and more affected by flooding in late winter and early spring months, with seasonally higher groundwater tables. The water-influenced margins would have become seasonally available rather than year-round pasture, but other resources such as fish, wild fowl, reeds, willow and alder for coppicing would have become more available and exploitable as a result. The gradual beginnings of erosion, transport and redeposition of sediment in the system are undoubtedly associated with the increasing opening-up of the higher parts of terrace to either side of the floodplain as well as hillslopes with clay-rich soil/geology inland. Nonetheless, it represents quite small amounts of material in terms of the scale of the disruption of the dryland, and may well only represent the erosion occuring concomitant with initial clearance activities. Despite the evidence for arable farming being rather rare and ambiguous, there certainly was some but it was limited and within a predominantly pastoral landscape.

The environment of the second millennium BC apparently was similar, but I suspect there were some major changes. The first change I cannot prove, but I suspect that later in the millennium, the main channel system shifted dramatically northwards, now going around Maxey 'island' to the north leaving the Maxey-Etton floodplain more as an overflow corridor. Although the former active floodplain remained seasonally damp and affected by flooding and sediment aggradation, the main channel around the former location of the Etton causewayed enclosure was now infilled and out of use, and there are no other evident sets of channels available in this southern part of the valley system. This former floodplain zone should have provided extremely lush grassland for all but the wettest months of the year. It would have been seasonally wet and receiving small incremental additions of silts and clay with each flood event.

The second change that was associated with this one was the establishment of extensive ditched field systems, as occurred in many other parts of England at this time such as the lower Nene (Pryor 1980), lower Ouse

(Evans and Knight 1997a and b) and upper Thames valleys (Lambrick 1992). This phenomenon became even more widespread on all parts of the terraces in the lower Welland valley within the later first millennium BC and Romano-British period. Unfortunately, there is little direct evidence for increased use of land for arable cultivation, and there is little secure evidence of the nature of the grassland or pasture, especially in the soil record.

It is not until the late and post-Roman period that further and rapid changes occurred within the valley system. This development was signalled by a marked change in the nature of sediment accumulation in ditch systems within and on the margins of the lower terrace/former floodplain area as well as by extensive alluvial aggradation across the valley (French *et al.* 1992; Passmore and Macklin 1993). First, Romano-British ditches became infilled with a dark greyish-green clay, which 'feathered' uphill along the ditches from their lowest points. New and greater amounts of material derived from new areas in the catchment were getting into the drainage system more quickly and on a much greater scale than previously (Passmore and Macklin 1993). It is suspected that not just eroded topsoils but eroded subsoil material as well was getting into the valley drainage system. Then, there is the beginning of a long period of substantial alluvial deposition occurring which was responsible for depositing up to 1.5 m of alluvial silty clay more or less across the whole floor of the lower Welland valley from Etton-Maxey downstream (some 28 sq km), essentially burying the whole former flood-plain zone and overlapping onto the lower parts of the terrace to as high as the 7.5 m OD contour. This was associated with late winter flooding when the main river system to the north of Maxey 'island' could no longer cope with the amount of water and sediment on the move. The whole process was undoubtedly caused by initial deforestation and taking into plough the clay-dominated uplands on either side of the Welland valley from about Ufford, Barnack and Uffington westwards. Possibly it began in the middle Saxon period and was associated with a major reorganization of settlement site location, land division and the creation of extensive systems of arable strip fields (Hall 1981). The disruption of these 'heavy' soils on slopes inland brought new sources of sediment into the system, quickly and in great quantities. In the Etton-Maxey area this situation continued to exist until 1953 when the Maxey Cut was enlarged to control it. It was not until quite recently (since the 1950s), with improved drainage and advances in tractor technology that this alluviated land could be taken into plough, and ceased to be used mainly as seasonal grazing land.

Essential reading

French, C. (1990) 'Neolithic soils, middens and alluvium in the lower Welland valley', *Oxford Journal of Archaeology* 9: 305–11.

French, C., Macklin. M. and Passmore, D. (1992) 'Archaeology and palaeochannels in the lower Welland and Nene valleys: alluvial archaeology at the fen-edge, eastern England', in S. Needham and M. Macklin (eds) *Archaeology under Alluvium*, pp. 169–76, Oxford: Oxbow.

Pryor, F. (1998). *Etton: Excavation at a Neolithic Causewayed Enclosure near Maxey, Cambridgeshire, 1982–7*, Archaeological Report 18, London: English Heritage.

Pryor, F. and French, C. (1985) *Archaeology and Environment in the Lower Welland Valley*, Cambridge: East Anglian Archaeology 27.

7   The Fengate shore, lower Nene valley and the Flag Fen basin, Cambridgeshire, England

Introduction

During the past thirty years, intensive and extensive archaeological excavations, environmental analyses and research have been carried out in the lower reaches of the Nene valley at Fengate, Peterborough, and in the adjacent fenland basin of Flag Fen (Figures 6.1 and 7.1), principally by Dr Francis Pryor and his teams. Few regions of lowland England have been the beneficiary of so much focused attention as this river terrace/fen-edge zone which contains such a wealth of associated archaeological and environmental data. This set of projects was dominated by two major projects – first Fengate and then Flag Fen, separated by a decade. These projects had the benefit of tending to have many of the same team members involved for the long term which enabled a high and detailed information return. Fortunately also, the numbers of sites and archaeological investigations in the area have allowed what is in effect a series of sample transects to be made across most parts of this fen and fen-edge landscape, with some of the most extensive and largest open area excavations ever seen completed at Fengate itself.

Not suprisingly, new sites continue to be discovered, assessed and excavated in this same area every year as a result of development-led archaeology. Rather ironically when Fengate was being excavated in the 1970s, we had little idea of what lay just to the east under the fen peats waiting to be discovered. It was not until the first project in the lower Welland valley at Maxey (Pryor and French 1985) had been completed, some experience had been gained by team members in Holland on the Assendelver Polders Project (Brandt *et al.* 1987) and the excavations at the Etton causewayed enclosure had begun (and see Chapter 6 above) (Pryor 1998a), that the real significance of the burial of landscapes by superficial deposits began to dawn on us. Only then did a return to the Fengate area and adjacent fen-edge become feasible in terms of our mind-set and the methodological techniques that we could bring to bear. Then the chance discovery of the Flag Fen site during systematic dyke survey (Pryor 1986, 2001; French and Pryor 1993) led to a focusing of attention on the Flag Fen basin itself. No one had any

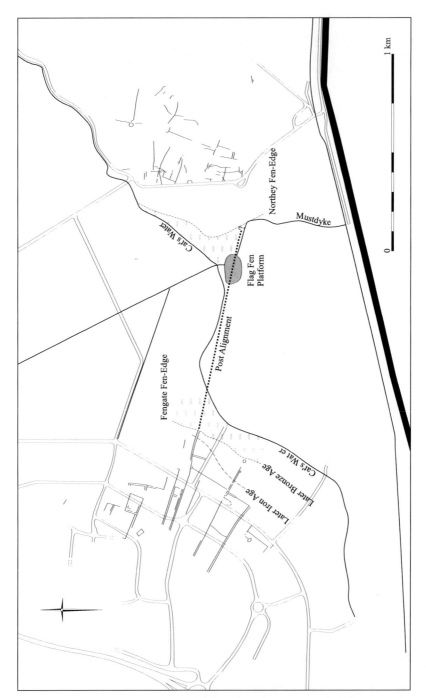

Figure 7.1 Location map of the Fengate and Northey 'shores', and Flag Fen (C. Begg after F. Pryor).

idea at the time that it would lead to so much research excavation over the long term. Then from 1990 with the advent of Policy Planning Guidance 16 (D.o.E. 1990), the continuing commercial development of the Fengate fen-edge meant that there were many new chances for prospection and discovery of buried archaeological landscapes which could be related to the previous Fengate sites and ongoing work in the adjacent Flag Fen basin.

What follows is a period-by-period attempt to draw together all of the available data that currently exists, presented as a landscape history of the Fengate/Flag Fen/Northey region (Figure 7.1) from the third millennium BC to the medieval period (Table 7.1). This case study is largely drawn from my own contributions to the Flag Fen volume (French 2001a and b), for which Francis Pryor is gratefully acknowledged for permission to repeat much information here. Throughout there are distinctive links and affinities in the story which are mirrored by similar events occurring in the lower Welland valley (see Chapter 6), lower Ouse valley (see Chapter 8) and the adjacent fen basins (see Chapter 9).

Fengate is located on the eastern outskirts of Peterborough (Figure 7.1). It contained an extensive archaeological record (Pryor 1976, 1978, 1980, 1984, each with references) discovered through the construction of a large modern industrial estate and road infrastructure, and more continues to be discovered every time a new development is undertaken in the area (e.g. Gibson 1997; Cuttler 1998). It is essentially the northern side of the River Nene system on First and Second Nene Terrace gravels (Horton *et al.* 1974) where it empties into the adjacent fen basin, or Flag Fen (Pryor 2001). This Fengate 'shore' sweeps northwards to conjoin with the Eye peninsula (Figure 10.3). Beyond this to the north are the fen basins of Newborough and Borough Fen into which the lower Welland river valley empties (French and Pryor 1993) (see Chapter 10).

Both the Fengate and Northey gravels witness later Neolithic and Bronze Age dispersed settlement associated with elaborately laid out field systems, known over at least 100 hectares and investigated over about half of this known area. This field system is one of the largest prehistoric field systems in Europe (Pryor 1980: fig. 4, 1996, 1998b), only recently rivalled by similar extents of field systems such as those discovered in the lower Great Ouse valley at Barleycroft Farm (Evans and Knight 1997a and b) (see Chapter 8). The next major phase of occupation at Fengate witnesses the building of small farming hamlets, first at Vicarage Farm Road in the Early Iron Age and then at the Cat's Water sub-site from about the fourth century BC to the mid-first century AD with a brief re-occupation in the later second century AD (Pryor 1984: 212–16, fig. 16). These small nucleated hamlets of up to ten structures in use at any one time are the only two to be more or less completely excavated in a fen-edge locale in England.

The Flag Fen basin is one of the most landward basins of the Cambridge-shire fens, and was bounded to the south by the former course of the River Nene, which looped to the south of the present embanked and canalized course

Table 7.1 Summary of the main landscape history events in the Fengate to Flag Fen to Northey region

Third M BC	Earlier second M BC	Later second/ earlier first M BC	Later first M BC	Roman/later

Fengate:

  mixed deciduous woodland → extensive and gradual deforestation and establishment of grassland

  argillic brown earths; well drained becoming seasonally wet; brown earths

  mixed land-use with extensive pasture; ditched field systems with droveways — abandonment of fields; ? hedgerow enclosed fields

  nucleation

  abandonment

Fen-edge:

  wide zone of natural flood meadow encroaching to 3m contour

  peat growth from 800 to 400 cal BC

  alluvial aggradation from 400 cal BC

  drier; then renewed alluvial aggradation

Flag Fen basin:

wide fringe of carr woodland – diminishes with time

  peat growth from 2030 to 1680 cal BC; reedswamp and zone of shallow open water which becomes more extensive

  Flag Fen platform and avenue

  peat surface drier

  renewed peat growth and alluviation

Northey 'island':

wooded, becoming more open with field systems   ? abandoned

  peat encroachment after 1090–840 cal BC

(Hall 1987: fig. 38). The eastern side of the basin is occupied by the Northey peninsula, composed of fen or March gravels, like an 'upturned foot-like extension' of the largest fen 'island,' Whittlesey (Figure 10.1). The Flag Fen basin coalesces with the open fen beyond through a narrow 'neck' oriented northeastwards. As such, this basin has its own sedimentary history, different from the main fen basin beyond but related to it in many aspects as well as to the river to the south. The site of the Late Bronze Age platform at Flag Fen is situated in the northeastern part of the basin, more or less centred just below the 'neck' of the fen basin. It is contemporary with (*c.* 1300–900 BC) and linked to the Fengate and Northey 'shores' by an avenue of multiple rows of posts (Pryor 2001: fig. 6.19). This site is again unique at a pan-European level, both in terms of size and extent of preservation, and in terms of the metalwork deposited at the landward edge of the associated avenue of timbers (Bradley 2000: 51–3; Pryor 2001). At the Fengate margin, large amounts of later Bronze Age and Early Iron Age metalwork are deposited in and around the timbers (Coombs 1992; Pryor 1992, 1993). This remarkable concurrence of monuments is still not satisfactorily explained (Pryor 1996, 2001), but it does mark out the area as extremely significant in later prehistory.

Third millennium BC

Although the earlier third millennium BC rectangular structure at the Padholme Road subsite, Fengate (Mahany 1969; Pryor 1974, 1993: figs 92 and 93), currently sits in isolation as the earliest archaeological evidence in the study area, by the end of this millennium considerably more human activity was evident. There are a series of relevant sites, all situated on First Terrace gravels on the northern side of the lower Nene valley at Fengate. These include the Grooved Ware settlement and associated field system north of Storey's Bar Road sub-site at the 5 m OD contour (Pryor 1978), the small hengiform monument discovered in 1990 (Pryor 2001) at the Co-op site just to the south of the Cat's Water Iron Age complex at the 3 m OD contour (Pryor 1984), and the post-built rectilinear structure of the later Neolithic discovered just to the southwest of this 'hengiform' site in 1997 (Gibson 1997).

In addition, a length of later Neolithic ditch was discovered immediately to the east of what was to become the easternmost extent of the subsequent second millennium BC field system at the Power Station site (Pryor 1992: fig. 8). This zone, at the break of the 3 m OD contour, had always previously been considered to be the fen-edge, but it may well have remained dry land at this stage. This picture of a much wider zone of delimited dry land fringing the Flag Fen basin was further corroborated by the watching brief at the Peterborough sewage treatment works in the southwestern or most landward corner of the Flag Fen basin. It revealed a *c.* 150 m wide swathe of thinly alluviated terrace gravel soils, which supported well-drained brown earth soils which remained unburied to at least post-Bronze Age times (French 2001a and b).

Palynological (Scaife 1992, 2001) and micromorphological (French 1991a and b, 1992a–d, 1995a, 2001a and b) studies would suggest that this Fengate fen-edge had been a wooded environment developed on argillic brown earth soils in the earlier to mid-Holocene. A mixed deciduous woodland dominated by lime with oak, ash and hazel to a lesser extent was developed on a stable and well-drained argillic brown earth soil. Obviously by the time that the later Neolithic enclosures and field systems were constructed, some substantial clearance inroads had been made into this environment, and the elm decline had already occurred. What is noticeable in the soil evidence is that there has been little truncation, and no apparent degradation in terms of soil developmental changes and/or the advent of poorer conditions of drainage. These soils were well structured, freely draining and of loamy texture, all of which would have contributed to their ease of use and ready fertility. Unfortunately, there is no absolute evidence of the nature of the land-use on the fen-edge itself in the soil micromorphological evidence (twenty-nine profiles analysed from across the basin, plus another six evaluated) (French 1991a and b, 1992c and d, 1995a, 1997a–c, 1998, 2001a and b; French and Pryor 1993: 94–100; French and Lewis 2001). For example, there are no definitive plough marks evident underneath any of the many upstanding banks investigated, except at the Second/Third Drove site excavated in 1992, and these are rather enigmatic and probably of much later date (French and Lewis 2001). There are only hints of limited arable use in the pollen record, but much stronger evidence of a pastoral environment on these Fengate shores in the pollen (Scaife 1992, 2001), insect (Robinson 1992, 2001) and macro-botanical assemblages (Wilson 1984; Scaife 2001).

The pollen record contained in the old land surface from beneath the Flag Fen platform in the adjacent fen basin, Scaife (1992, 2001) suggests that the surroundings were dominated by a combination of woodland and mixed agricultural land by the beginning of the second millennium BC. In addition, there was strong evidence for nearby wetland, especially alder and willow comprising carr woodland in a marginal or 'skirtland' zone around the basin, with patches of open water and reed/sedge fen in the basin itself. Radiocarbon assay of organic mud deposits representing the onset of waterlogging in the deepest part of the Flag Fen basin suggests that this process began at about 2030–1680 cal BC (3500±60 BP; GU-5618), most probably in response to the marine inundation phase responsible for the deposition of the 'fen clay' in the main fen basin to the northeast (French and Pryor 1993; Waller 1994) which undoubtedly interrupted the easy outfall of freshwater rivers such as the Nene.

Given these fragments of evidence from the fen basin and Fengate terrace areas, it is possible to suggest the following scenario :

There was a gradual opening-up of the deciduous woodland on the first terrace (above the 3 m OD contour) throughout the third millennium BC, with only very minor and demonstrable evidence of arable cultivation. The lower gravel terraces were characterized by open scrubby pasture, probably grazed mainly by cattle. The contemporary fen-edge was anything up to 150–200 m further to the east of the perceived fen-edge as defined by the Cat's Water Drain (Pryor 2001: fig. 2.10), thus substantially extending the flood-free zone of dryland on the fen-edge, that is effectively adding all the available land between the 1.5 m and 3 m OD contours. The eastern and southern limit of this zone (around the 1.5 m OD contour) was fringed by a wide zone (perhaps 200 m across) of carr woodland dominated by alder and willow, with a shallow reed swamp occupying most, if not all, of the remainder of the then very small Flag Fen basin beyond (at <1 m OD). There probably was a small area of shallow standing water in the northeastern part of the basin, more or less in the position where the Flag Fen platform came to be built, perhaps *c.* 150–250 m across, which shrank and swelled depending on the season and the influence of the open fen beyond.

Earlier second millennium BC

This period witnessed major changes. The most extensive development was the large scale division of the landscape by the establishment of the rectilinear, ditched field systems and east–west aligned droveways of the Padholme Road, Newark Road, Cat's Water and Fourth Drove subsites of Fengate between the 3 m and 6 m OD contours (Pryor 1980, 1984). A similar and contemporary field system was discovered on the fen 'island' of Northey on the eastern side of the Flag Fen basin (Gurney 1980), and is now known to extend over a much greater area to the north on the Fengate shore and just east of Flag Fen to either side of where the timber avenue reaches the western edge of Northey (Upex, Palmer and Pryor pers. comm.; Pryor 2001).

Until the excavations took place at the Power Station site in 1989 and Co-op site in 1990, the eastern limit and nature of these field systems on the Fengate terrace were unknown. At the Power Station site, ditches 8 and 9 of the Newark Road system (Pryor 1980: fig. 5) returned at right angles to themselves and parallel to the contour/fen-edge of the day. Perhaps significantly, these enclosures ended just upslope from a seasonal stream channel which was situated along the break of slope (French 1992a and b; French *et al.* 1992).

At the Co-op site, some 100 m further upstream to the south, the southeastern fen-edge aspect of the fields were completely different. The ditched enclosures (associated with the Newark Road ditches 3 and 4) which lay beneath the adjacent and later Cat's Water site (Pryor 1984: fig. 16) appear to have changed to open-ended fields defined only by fencelines. It is possible that this was a 'tacked-on' extension to the enclosure system as originally laid out, or perhaps even an earlier system. Nonetheless, it appears that these fields opened into the formerly unenclosed fen-edge zone, which effectively acted as common grazing areas of flood meadow available on a seasonal basis depending upon the level and prevalence of localized flooding.

Micromorphological analysis of eight palaeosol profiles from the Co-op and Power Station sites suggests that stable, well-drained, brown earth soils developed on this lower half of the First Terrace gravels (French 1991a and b, 1992a and b, 2001b). These soils had once supported a woodland cover and allowed the development of argillic brown earths. Subsequent to clearance and the establishment of the field enclosure system, these soils exhibited no indication of disturbance caused by cultivation and remained flood-free. The sedimentary and molluscan analyses of the Newark Road second millennium BC ditch system (French 1980a and b) suggested that these enclosure ditches became infilled by natural weathering processes under ostensibly open conditions, with no evidence of the influence of freshwater flooding, except at the extreme eastern edge of the system (i.e. at the Fourth Drove, Fengate subsite (French 1980b: 210–12).

The palaeobotanical evidence from the Newark Road enclosure system ditches just to the northwest indicated similar open conditions, dominated by species indicative of pasture, with some evidence of the presence of hedge-row species and wet ground (Pryor 1980; Wilson 1984). There was only a minor presence of cereals, and it has been suggested that corn supplies may have been brought in from elsewhere, ready threshed.

Peat growth began at about 1500–1320 cal BC (3130 ± 60 BP; GU-5617) in the Flag Fen basin consequent upon a regionally rising groundwater table (Scaife 2001). The pollen record from the lowermost peat beneath the Flag Fen platform recorded a further expansion of wet fen. It was a diverse assemblage containing many aquatic species, which suggested that the water depth was increasing in the lowest part of the basin (and by implication spreading out over a much greater area of previously marginal land). It suggests that the small lake in the northern part of the basin began to deepen and widen in extent, slowly but surely. There was sedge fen in and around the lake and probably over the greater part of the basin, which was effectively surrounded by a belt of alder carr woodland on the fringe of this gradually enlarging and encroaching fen. At the same time, there are indications of a decline in lime (*Tilia*) probably caused by a combination of factors such as woodland clearance and fen encroachment leading to waterlogging of former dryland soils. There was also the continuous presence of cereal pollen, Poaceae and dryland herbs which are indicative of clearance and mixed agriculture on the dry areas of the terraces around the Flag Fen basin.

Combining all of these strands of evidence, the following picture of landscape change is suggested:

The earlier second millennium BC witnessed an extensive and long-lived opening-up and management of large tracts of the lower part of the First Terrace gravels. Although there is evidence of clearance and co-existing arable and pastoral land-use, there was continued evidence of woodland in the immediate hinterland, in which oak was now more dominant than lime. The ditched enclosure system, with droveways aligned at right angles to the adjacent fen basin to the east, suggests that this system was intended as an integral part of a wider landscape. The various presence of water, fen carr and marsh probably acted as the real boundaries that existed previously – physically, ritually and symbolically. Pryor's (1980) original suggestion of the Newark Road field system being an area for over-wintering livestock (whether cattle or sheep) (Pryor 1996, 1998b) in enclosed pasture has been reinforced. In the absence of good evidence that arable farming was practised, a pastoral landscape was probably much more predominant. Indeed the zone of lowermost terrace (*c.* 1.5–3 m OD) fringing the fen-edge, more or less corresponding to the 50–100 m area just upslope from the Cat's Water Drain and perhaps 100–200 m downslope into the fen basin beyond the Cat's Water Drain, was available for unenclosed pasture and seasonal grazing. This zone would have been most ideal for late spring and summer grazing as the winter floodwaters receded, and the area acted as natural flood meadow. Over the millennium, this resource would have diminished very gradually, almost imperceptibly in terms of a human life-time. A belt of alder carr fringed this flood meadow to the southeast, with sedge fen and shallow, open water beyond that in the lowest part of the Flag Fen basin. Again, over the millennium, the zone of open water would have begun to deepen and widen, ultimately beginning to 'drown' the fringing carr vegetation, independently of human exploitation and denudation of this woodland resource.

The later second millennium BC

This is a period of marked change in organizational terms for the environment and landscape of the Fengate and Flag Fen area.

Over the last few centuries of the first millennium BC, the easternmost set of fields (i.e. in the Fourth Drove and Cat's Water subsite areas) would have succumbed to seasonal flooding, as witnessed by the infilling of these ditches with silts containing a rich freshwater molluscan assemblage (French 1980) and the formation of thin peat deposits overlying the hengiform site and eastern field at the Co-op site (French 1991b). At the same time, the eastern part of the Fourth Drove subsite area of natural flood meadow, characterized by thin alternating laminae of peat and minerogenic deposits (Figure 7.2) (French 1991a, 1992a and b; French *et al.* 1992), became dominated by the avenue of timbers (from 1363–967 BC) (Neve 1992: 473) which led to and crossed the Flag Fen platform in the adjacent basin. The timbers of the avenue were set in place on a similar alignment to the earlier second millennium BC droveway ditches 8 and 9, overlying them and crossing a small stream channel at the break of 3m OD contour. Furthermore, the remainder of the field system on the higher terrace to the north began to fall into disuse by the end of the second millennium BC (Pryor 1980).

The surrounding dry land vegetation that existed at the time of the construction of the Flag Fen platform and avenue consisted of a mixture of open ground for pasture and arable activities as well as some areas of mixed

Figure 7.2 Section of alternating minerogenic and peat deposits capped by alluvium
at the Fengate fen-edge.

deciduous woodland, possibly with some lime remaining (Scaife 2001). It is suggested that the recorded decline in oak may reflect the diminution of timber as a result of felling for the avenue and platform in the locale. There may also have been some woodland management of hazel for coppicing. After this clearance and/or management of the existing woodland, there is some evidence for woodland regeneration, perhaps indicating a slight recovery, albeit localized, after the felling of at least some of the timber for the platform and avenue.

During this period, the argillic brown earths to brown earth soils in the lower first terrace zone became affected by the incorporation of considerable quantities of fines (or silt and clay), as well as minor amounts of eroded soil material derived from forest soils, presumably immediately upstream and inland (French 1992b). These features suggest that this part of the terrace was subject to seasonal flooding carrying fine alluvial sediment. This evidence corroborates Scaife's (1992) pollen evidence for the development of a natural flood meadow environment fringing established pasture at the Power Station site. Furthermore, this environment was subject to a fluctuating water table and probably variable human exploitation.

Evaluation work on this same lower terrace zone further upstream between the modern Second and Third Drove roads by the Cambridge Archaeological Unit (Evans 1992; Gdaniec 1997) and off Third Drove by the Birmingham University Field Archaeology Unit (Cuttler 1998) has provided further corroboration. This contract rescue work has revealed an extensive area of Iron Age fields with upstanding banks. The buried soils (twelve profiles) sealed beneath these banks consistently show a rather poorly developed argillic brown earth soil that is receiving alluvial fine material prior to burial, and exhibiting isolated signs of disturbance, which in one case has been caused by a narrow 'ridge and furrow' type of cultivation which is believed to be pre-Iron Age in date (French 1998b; French and Lewis 2001).

To the east on Northey 'island', with its steeper and more abrupt fen-edge, the 'island' remained relatively drier and less affected by the encroachment of freshwater deposits than the Fengate 'shore' (French and Pryor 1993: 94–100). Nonetheless, there were indications that the brown earth soils were occasionally subjected to periods of peat encroachment, then drying and perhaps occasional episodes of cultivation. Also, major peat growth on the fringe of Northey began to occur at sometime after 1090–840 cal BC (2800±100 BP; HAR-8511) (French and Pryor 1993: 96), possibly somewhat earlier than observed on the opposite Fengate shore.

At the same time, the area of open water in which the Flag Fen platform was now under construction was deepening and enlarging, but nonetheless still fringed by sedge fen, with the avenue of timbers crossing this whole landscape complex. In particular, the analysis of the insect assemblages associated with the Flag Fen platform has provided evidence which corroborates that indicated by the palynological and micromorphological studies (French 1992b, 2001a and b; Robinson 1992, 2001; Scaife 1992,

2001). It gives a uniform picture of well-vegetated, shallow, stagnant water or reedswamp, with permanent to near-permanent water and pools of water present around the platform. In addition, there is a background element to the assemblage which indicates the presence of a few trees, such as alder and willow, in a peat fen landscape with grassland on drier ground and minerogenic soil surrounding the fen.

In summary, the end of the second millennium BC witnessed a substantial increase in the extent and influence of the Flag Fen basin. The area of open water immediately around the platform had increased in extent and depth, to a lesser amount, and the fringing sedge fen with associated peat development had encroached up to about the 3 m OD contour on the Fengate shore to the northwest, and begun to affect the edges of Northey 'island' to the east. The alder carr fringing the fen remained despite the gradual progression to more aquatic conditions and undoubted exploitation by humans, but was probably diminishing in lateral extent. In this context, as originally postulated in Pryor (1992), the timber avenue linking dry land to dry land across a narrow 'neck' of open fen of about a kilometre in length takes on much greater significance. Perhaps it acted as much as a symbolic and human-made boundary against the rising water table of the encroaching deep fen to the east as a physical and spiritual access between the dryland and the platform itself. In contrast, the hinterland or terrace landscape to the west continued to support a diverse assemblage of woodland and dry land herb taxa, with some evidence for a reduction in oak and an increase in alder which may have been associated with the construction of the Flag Fen platform and avenue (Scaife 2001).

The first millennium BC

A similar progression of the events to those already set out for the later second millennium BC may be envisaged for the remainder of the later Bronze Age and throughout the Iron Age.

The first half of the first millennium BC spanning the later Bronze Age/ early Iron Age transition sees groundwater base levels rising significantly in the Flag Fen basin (Waller 1994), the disuse of the platform and the timber avenue by the seventh century BC at the latest, and their submergence by water and peat growth (Pryor 2001). All of the known field systems on the adjacent first terrace and Northey 'island' are now substantially infilled and apparently out of use. Despite this 'abandonment', the pollen evidence suggests continuing mixed agricultural land-use in the immediate region (Scaife 2001). In particular, there are cereal pollen percentages of 5 per cent plus a variety of other weed taxa present (Brassicaceae, Polygonaceae and Chenopodiaceae) plus typical indicator species such as *Plantago lanceolata*, *Ranunculus* type and *Rumex* spp., and consistency of pastoral type herbs with Poaceae which suggest that a mixed arable/pastoral agriculture was being practised. Perhaps associated with this are indications in the palaeobotanical record that hedgerow species reached a relative peak in the later Bronze Age (Wilson 1984). This suggests that there may well have continued to be land division in this period, but it just did not necessarily comprise ditches and banks.

Throughout this period it appears that there were frequent, alternating conditions of peat formation and minerogenic soil accumulation associated with alluvial deposition episodes over the fen-edge fringe zone between the 1.5 m and 4 m OD contours (Figure 7.2) (French 1992a; French *et al.* 1992). These stratigraphic features were best observed at the Power Station and Co-op sites. Radiocarbon assay at the Power Station site suggests that the first major growth of peat (as opposed to earlier intermittent growth) on the Fengate fen-edge occurred at about 800–400 cal BC (2840±50 BP; GU-5620). Slightly further upstream at the Fengate Second/Third Drove site, the fen-edge landscape was solely dominated by the seasonal deposition of silty clay alluvium (Figure 3.3) (French 1998b; Scaife 1998; French and Lewis 2001), with substantial periods of drying out inbetween.

This first half of the first millennium BC apparently witnessed a largely open, pastoral landscape on the fen margins and first gravel terrace which was perhaps divided by a system of hedgerowed boundaries. As no associated later Bronze Age settlements have been found on the Fengate/Northey gravels, this may imply a shift in settlement somewhere, possibly to higher ground above the 6 m OD contour which has yet to be discovered. On the other hand, it may simply imply a very dispersed, small farmstead type of settlement pattern, with large areas of common land between which did not necessitate enclosure, on sites that have yet to be located. The gradually encroaching peat fen of the Flag Fen basin would have begun to limit the available and permanent dry land, but on the other hand would have created more extensive zones of natural flood meadow on its margins which would have been available on a seasonal basis for pastoral exploitation. Unfortunately, the distinct absence of relevant archaeological discoveries for this period in both the fen and terrace landscape zones makes these suggestions no more than surmises.

As early as the fifth century BC, there are the first archaeological signs of nucleation at the Vicarage Farm Road, Fengate, subsite (Pryor 1976) and by the third century BC with the development of the substantial 'hamlet' at the Cat's Water subsite, occupied throughout the middle and later Iron Age (Pryor 1984: 210–27). Most of the archaeological features, namely pits and enclosure ditches, have semi-waterlogged primary fills which suggest that there was a reasonably constant and high groundwater table over most of the first terrace gravel zone between the 3 m and 5 m OD contours. Palaeobotanical evidence for weed species associated with arable land and cultivation reached a peak in the Iron Age, a feature which continued into the earlier Roman period, as do species of cultivated plants (Wilson 1984). This is corroborated by the relative increase in the number and diversity of herb pollen (Scaife 2001). Nonetheless, evidence for cereal cultivation remains minor, as does evidence for hedgerow and woodland species. But there is a distinct increase in the species of water and marsh plants with a wide range of species represented which inhabit wet mud, shallow water and wet ditches. The faunal remains indicate that cattle predominated slightly over sheep as the mainstay of the livestock component of the economy (Biddick 1984). In addition, there were fish remains of pike, tench, bream and carp, as well as evidence for a variety of birds, such as duck, swan, goose, heron, stork, cormorant, sea eagle and goosander. Incidentally, this is the best evidence recovered from the fenland for the exploitation of fish and fowl resources other than that from the Iron Age site at Haddenham in the Cambridgeshire fens to the south (Evans and Serjeantson 1988) (see Chapter 8).

It would appear that by the later part of the first millennium BC the Fengate fen-edge was being much more extensively settled and exploited. It was very much a mixed economy, utilizing the best of the adjacent fenland resources as well as the fen margins and drier terrace hinterland. There was an evident increase in the enclosure and division of the landscape by ditch systems on the terrace gravels, with the fen-edge well defined at the southern edge of the Cat's Water settlement site at about the 3 m OD contour. The adjacent Flag Fen basin was now ostensibly open and dominated by peat growth and a large area of open water in the centre/deepest part of the basin, with many semi-aquatic and marginal aquatic plants present suggesting numerous shallow pools between hummocks of peat. The remaining alder/willow carr fringing the higher ground around the basin became progressively inundated, giving rise to a shallow, muddy water fen community (Scaife 2001). Finally, as suggested by the diatom analysis (see Juggins in Pryor *et al.* 1986), there may have been very brief periods of the influence of brackish water within the basin in the later first millennium BC which probably derived from the backing-up of freshwater against high spring tide conditions further to the east.

At the very end of the first millennium BC, there began the widespread deposition of alluvial silty clays in the basin. Radiocarbon assay from the Fengate and Northey 'shores' suggests that this occurred shortly after 400–90 cal BC (2290±50 BP; GU-5619; 2180±60 BP; GU-5616) (Pryor 2001). This suggests that clearance and soil disturbance on a greater scale than hitherto and of different parts of the landscape had begun in the hinterland to the west. Associated with this were increases in the number of herb taxa and their relative percentages (Scaife 2001). Increases in arable and pastoral indicators may suggest a local intensification and extensification of agricultural land-use on the dry terrace areas.

The Roman and later periods

The landscape and environmental setting of the Fengate/Flag Fen basin areas during the first two centuries AD probably witnessed a continuation of the earlier conditions. Nonetheless, there may have been a period of drying-out of the surface of the peat fen as the Roman gravel road or Fen Causeway was constructed across the peat surface of the Flag Fen basin in the later first century AD (Pryor 1984, 2001).

By the third century AD, most of the remaining open ditches at the Cat's Water site were affected by the deposition of silty clays. These clastic sediments were undoubtedly derived from a renewal of freshwater flooding and the deposition of alluvially derived fines over a much larger and higher area of terrace for the first time – that is above the 3 m OD contour. Similar feature infills have been observed in similar situations in the lower Welland valley at Etton (French *et al.* 1992; French 1998a) and at Barnack (Passmore and Macklin 1993) (see Chapter 6). It suggests that exploitation, or clearance and arable cultivation, of the 'heavier' soils on the limestone higher ground to the west of present day Peterborough and Stamford had begun by this period. This new uptake of land led to increased hillwash erosion and alluvial transport of these silt/clay-rich sediments in floodwaters and their deposition downstream. The main difference at Fengate is the distance from the river of the day. Here the main River Nene channel was at least 1.5 km further to the south, and the silt and clay-rich floodwaters must have spread out over the whole of the Flag Fen basin in order to have affected the northern fringe of this basin in this way.

The remainder of the surviving stratigraphic sequence on the Fengate fen-edge continues to be dominated by the deposition of silty clay alluvium deposits. This process has been observed more or less continuously along the Second to Fourth Drove area on the terrace gravels, across the whole Flag Fen basin and up to about the 4 m OD contour. There are also several major levels of alluvial deposition evident in the Flag Fen basin sections, with at least one phase visible below and one phase above the Fen Causeway Roman road section (Pryor *et al.* 1986: fig. 3) and two phases evident above the timber avenue at the Power Station site (French 1992b: fig. 7). Indeed the micromorphological analyses of these alluvial silty clay deposits (French 2001b) confirms that they are composed of eroded topsoils and fine material derived from elsewhere, presumably from upstream and inland in the Nene valley catchment. Similar and extensive post-Roman alluvial deposits have also been observed in the Nene floodplain overlying the Orton Longueville barrow group on the western side of Peterborough (French 1983; O'Neill 1981), and overlying the post-Roman landscape of the lower Welland valley to Borough Fen area to the north of Peterborough (see Chapter 6) (French 1990, 1998a; French and Pryor 1993: 68–79, 105–7).

The late Roman and medieval landscape of the Fengate fen-edge was therefore dominated by freshwater flooding and the gradual accretion of fine sediments carried in these floodwaters. It would have provided natural meadows for grazing on an extensive scale but which were prone to seasonal inundation. Their lateral extent would have varied considerably on an annual basis, very much controlled by land-use upstream and the drainage pattern of the day, as well as by peat growth and the influence of high tides acting as physical barriers further to the east in the fens. The naming of the present day roads across this Fengate fen-edge as First, Second, Third and Fourth Droves must refer to this long-term land-use, as well as hinting at the movement of stock from enclosed fields to unenclosed meadow on the fen-edge and perhaps sometimes in the basin itself. Mustdyke and the medieval toll house on the site of Flag Fen itself (T. Halliday pers. comm.) suggest that the site as a place continued as a functioning and important nodal point in the watery landscape.

The Flag Fen basin continued to be subject to shallow, muddy water, sedge fen and peat growth conditions, with additions of alluvially derived sediments often captured from time to time in this basin throughout the medieval and post-medieval periods. Very little of this peat has survived the impact of post-seventeenth century AD drainage, and today it is very much confined to the central part of the basin. This peat may have been up to 2 m or more in thickness above the present day ground surface (R. Evans pers. comm.).

Conclusions

The influence of gradually rising base water levels in the fens as well as seasonal, lateral and vertical variation peat formation and alluvial deposition were all intrinsically linked to the development of the landscape in the Flag Fen basin and the adjacent terrace gravel and 'island' margins. Although seasonal episodes of flooding, aggradation and erosion may have been disruptive of this organized landscape, the layout of this landscape as recovered in the archaeological record throughout the second and first millennia BC took good advantage of and was adapted to the dry, seasonally and permanently wet zones of this evolving landscape. Moreover, the Fengate gravel terrace, the Flag Fen peat and alluvium-infilled fen basin and Northey 'island' landscapes must now be viewed as integrally associated and part of a much more extensive system in terms of human use and exploitation. Throughout, shrinkage of the usable land base would have been a serious long-term restriction in terms of human activities.

Essential reading

French, C.A.I. (1992) 'Alluviated fen-edge prehistoric landscapes in Cambridgeshire, England', in M. Bernardi (ed.) *Archeologia del Paesaggio*, pp. 709–30, Firenze.

Pryor, F.M.M. (1980) *Excavation at Fengate, Peterborough, England: The Third Report*, Northampton/Toronto: Royal Ontario Museum Monograph 6/Northamptonshire Archaeological Society Monograph 1.

Pryor, F.M.M. (1984) *Excavation at Fengate, Peterborough, England: The Fourth Report*, Northampton/Toronto: Royal Ontario Museum Monograph 7/Northamptonshire Archaeological Society Monograph 2.

Pryor, F. (1992) 'Current research at Flag Fen', *Antiquity* 66: 439–531.

Pryor, F. (2001) *The Flag Fen Basin: Archaeology and Environment of a Fenland Landscape*, Archaeological Reports, London: English Heritage.

8   The lower Great Ouse valley, Cambridgeshire, England

Introduction

The chapter that follows is an expanded version of a paper that was prepared for the 2000 Leeds Alluvial Archaeology in Northwestern Europe conference (French and Heathcote in press), much of which is repeated here with the kind permission of the volume editors. Combined archaeological and palaeoenvironmental investigations by the Cambridge Archaeolological Unit in advance of large-scale, commercial sand and gravel extraction and by the English Heritage sponsored Fenland Project has enabled a number of prehistoric sites to be analysed between St Ives and Haddenham in the lower Great Ouse valley and adjacent fen-edge of Cambridgeshire (Figures 6.1 and 8.1). In particular, the recent work has centred on the lower Great Ouse valley between the villages of Over and Willingham to the south and Bluntisham and Earith to the north, at St Ives (Pollard 1996) and the Haddenham complex of sites, building on the work of many archaeologists (e.g. Evans and Hodder 1984, 1985, in press a and b; French and Wait 1988; French and Pryor 1992; Hall and Coles 1994: 51–5; Waller 1994; Hall 1996).

As for previous work in the lower Welland valley (see Chapter 6), the lower Nene valley (see Chapter 7) and the adjacent fen-edge in northwestern Cambridgeshire (French 1988 a and b; French and Pryor 1993) (see Chapter 9), there is an extensive alluviated floodplain which has witnessed considerable archaeological intervention with associated environmental analyses and terrain modelling (French and Wait 1988; Waller 1994; Evans and Pollard 1995; Wiltshire 1996, 1997a and b; Burton 1997; Evans and Knight 1997a and b; French et al. 1999). In this case, the alluviated terrace zone as it widens to merge with the fenland basin contains earlier peat deposits as well as at least two substantial palaeochannel systems which are traceable upstream, with gravel levee banks occasionally emerging at the surface on either side (Figure 8.2). This zone meets the calcareous marl deposits of a relict lake, Willingham Mere, located just to the south of the Old West River, and beyond that the fenland marine and freshwater deposits of the Haddenham, Lower Delphs and Foulmire Fen area (Figure 8.1) (Waller 1994: fig. 8.1).

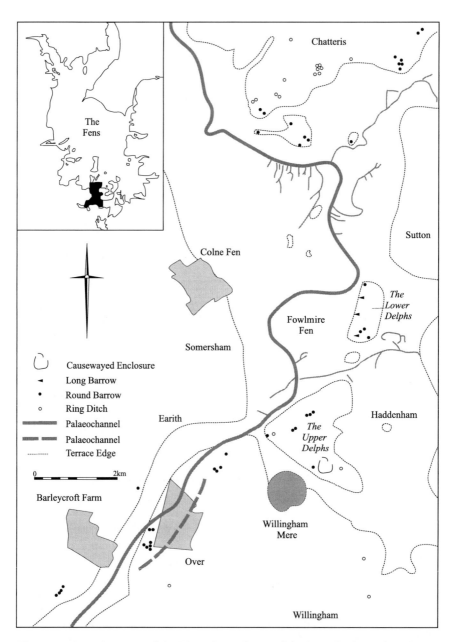

Figure 8.1 Location map of the River Great Ouse valley, Over, Barleycroft Farm
and Haddenham sites, and the position of the relict palaeochannels and
Willingham Mere (C. Begg).

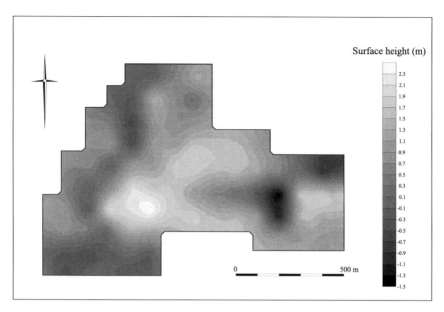

Figure 8.2 Terrain model of the buried topography and channel systems in the southwestern corner of the Over quarry site with the paler areas indicating
gravel levees and the darker zones representing former channels and pools
in the floodplain (C. Begg after C. French/HLE Ltd).

With the exception of the Haddenham sites, the archaeological work has
largely been made possible through recent pre-planning and development
work in which extensive areas of the alluviated and unalluviated landscapes
have been exposed through large-scale gravel extraction. This allows the
bigger, valley-scape picture to be visualized. Moreover, the same personnel
have largely been involved with these investigations, thus permitting a great
familiarity with the subtleties of these landscapes. Nonetheless, one major
problem remains and that is easily linking the three main foci areas together
in terms of their soil and geomorphological histories. In the Haddenham to
Over area, this will be possible over the next couple of decades as the Over
'super-quarry' expands methodically northeastwards, whereas it will be more
difficult on the inland stretch from Over to St Ives because of urban
development and extensive areas of former gravel extraction in between.

The major sites that have been and/or are currently still under investigation include the Haddenham complex, Over, Barleycroft Farm, Needingworth,
and Meadow Lane, St Ives (Figure 8.1). The Haddenham complex of sites is
situated on terrace gravels where the Great Ouse river valley meets the fen
basin (Figure 8.3). It is comprised of Neolithic and Bronze Age barrows, a
Neolithic causewayed enclosure, Iron Age settlement and a Romano-British
temple complex (Evans and Hodder 1984, 1985, in press a and b; French in
press b). Further inland at Barleycroft Farm (Gdaniec 1995; Evans and

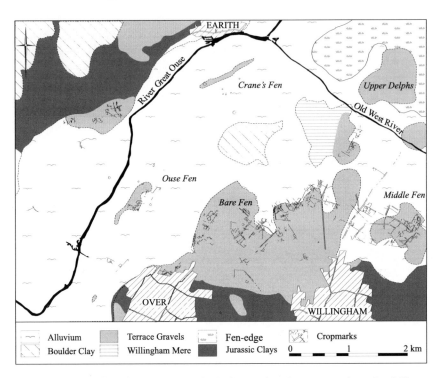

Figure 8.3 Map of the known archaeological record at Over set against the drift
         geology (C. Begg after C. French).

Knight 1997a) on the northern side of the alluviated terraces of the modern
lower Great Ouse River near Needingworth, there are Bronze Age barrows.
Also later Bronze Age post-alignments and structures have been discovered
along with an Iron Age settlement. In the floodplain to the south of the
modern Great Ouse River and to the north of Over village, there are
dispersed later Neolithic occupation sites, Bronze Age barrows, and middle-
later Bronze Age field systems and occupation which comprise the other half
of the Barleycroft Farm archaeological landscape (Evans and Knight 1997b).
At Meadow Lane, St Ives, some 8–10 km upstream from the other sites,
there was an extensive zone of later prehistoric and Roman pit alignments
and boundaries parallel to the river system (Pollard 1996: fig. 3). There is a
gradient from west to east in terms of heights above sea level from about
+10m to −0.5 metres Ordnance Datum, alluvial overburden thickening
downstream and broadening out as the valley widens to *c.* 4 km across at
Needingworth/Earith to Over/Willingham, with fenland peat deposits
present from the centre of the Over quarry site northeastwards (Figure 8.1).
Ironically, most of the Haddenham sites were very shallowly buried by
alluvial overburden on terrace deposits where the river valley meets the fen-
edge, with the upper peat cover of the medieval period long since wasted

away through a combination of drainage and desiccation, arable farming and wind-blow. Crucially, most of the new sites in the Over area, for example, are buried by 1 m or more of alluvial overburden (and/or basin peat deposits), making physical preservation better but detection more difficult without conducting major earthmoving exercises.

This essay sets out to summarize what is known of the palaeoenvironmental sequences along this 10 km stretch of river valley during the early-mid Holocene at the three main study areas (Figure 8.4). The emphasis is on the micromorphological investigations of buried soils and land surfaces, topographical relationships and several sets of good palynological information, although these have a fen-edge and fen basin bias. The story suggests some models and interactions over time to explain the relationships of archaeological sites and human activities. This study may be viewed as an attempt at assembling this information, building on the work of Waller (1994), Evans and Knight (1997b) and Evans and Hodder (in press a and b), and at the same time acknowledging that there are some significant gaps in our resolution and knowledge, both spatially and in terms of most classes of data (i.e. field survey, geo-prospection, excavation, soils, faunal, palaeobotanical and insect evidence). It has also great comparative value to the other Cambridgeshire fen edge valleys of the Nene and Welland (see Chapters 6 and 7).

The lower Great Ouse and Haddenham fen-edge in the fifth millennium BC to early first millennium AD

The only good and available environmental evidence for the fifth to fourth millennium BC comes from the pollen studies of Waller *et al.* (1994: 164–83) in the Haddenham area. In the Mesolithic and earlier Neolithic periods, the terraces between Haddenham and the Over area (or the Upper Delphs) appear to have been dry and well wooded, except along the rivers and tributary streams of the day. Woodland was predominant (averaging 70 per cent of total land pollen or TLP), and dominated by lime, with hazel, ash and oak to a lesser extent. At Haddenham, this dense woodland existed prior to 4370–4165 cal BC (Q-2814; 5420±100 BP). Associated with this was the development of an argillic brown earth soil, well drained, well structured,

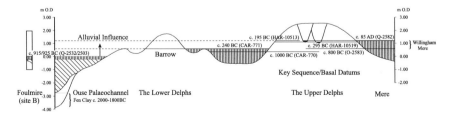

Figure 8.4 Schematic, cross-sectional model of fenland and lower Ouse valley alluvial peat and fen clay deposits (C. Begg; with the permission of Chris Evans).

clay-enriched and nutrient-rich (French 1985b, in press b). Fen-type environments appear to have been restricted to either side of the river channels with alder carr in a belt a few hundred metres wide.

To digress briefly, there is some debate as to where the Ouse channel was at this time upstream from Haddenham (see Waller 1994: 180). Nonetheless, the recent work in the Over quarry suggests that there were two previous major systems, situated predominantly to the east of the present day Great Ouse embanked channel (Figure 8.1). The earlier of the two palaeo-channels is situated on the southeastern edge of the floodplain, about 1 km east of the modern channel. It survives as a series of disconnected but wide meanders and is infilled with organic mud and silty clay with flint gravel deposits. This disjointed effect suggests that subsequent gravel deposition has reworked this part of the terrace, and that the channel is of much greater antiquity, probably of Devensian or last glacial times. But it is probable that parts of this system remained as either an occasional channel and/or as open pools with reed swamp vegetation until at least the later Bronze Age when peat began to blanket the whole area. The second main palaeo-channel is both wide (*c.* 100 m) and deep (up to 5 m) and is situated just to the southeast of the modern river and immediately northwest of the southern and northern barrow groups. Although there is as yet no absolute dating evidence for this relict channel, the fact that numerous later Neolithic and Bronze Age sites are situated along its banks implies that there was some kind of contemporary relationship. For example, both groups of Bronze Age barrows at Over are situated on its southeastern banks, along with the Grooved Ware settlements and later Bronze Age field systems, and the whole of the Barleycroft Farm complex is on its northwestern side. The Old West River channel flowing east from the current junction of the main Great Ouse channel and Forty Foot Drain does not appear to have been cut until post-Roman times (Waller 1994), and probably represented a major reorientation of the valley in the Haddenham area from northeast to east due to accumulations of marine sediment and peat growth in the south-central fens blocking its outfall route.

Clearance of the forest upstream from Haddenham appears to have begun later in the fifth millennium BC, or within the earliest Neolithic period. At Haddenham at 4370–4265 cal BC (Q-2814) there was a distinct but very slight fall in elm coincident with the first appearance of grass grains with a large annulus diameter (Evans and Hodder in press a; Peglar in press). The presence of other herbs indicative of open and/or disturbed ground such as *Plantago lanceolata*, Liguliflorae and *Solidago* type, suggests the beginnings of disturbance caused by clearance and cultivation of this dry land wooded environment. Tree pollen values diminish rapidly to only 24 per cent TLP, and lime and oak in particular, whilst herbaceous vegetation becomes predominant. It is in this gradually opening-up environment that the Haddenham causewayed enclosure was constructed from about 4700 BP or the mid-fourth millennium cal BC. A similar picture is available for the Etton causewayed enclosure in the lower Welland valley when it was constructed in the earlier fourth millennium cal BC (Pryor 1998a; Scaife 1998). As at Etton, waterlogged deposits were found in the bases of both the Haddenham causewayed enclosure and long barrow ditches, suggesting that the goundwater table was never far below the ground surface, even in the earlier Neolithic. Moreover, these ditches often held standing water for much of the year.

Plant macro-fossil evidence from the ditch of the Haddenham causewayed enclosure and in the buried soil of its interior provides the most definite evidence that there was some cereal cultivation in the vicinity (G. Jones in press a and b). The charred plant remains consisted mainly of barley of the six-row species *Hordeum vulgare*, with wheat (*Triticum dicoccum*) in small amounts, as well as hazelnut shell fragments, a possible apple pip and one seed of cultivated flax. Unfortunately, there is no positive evidence for crop processing on site, and it is impossible to discern whether the grain was brought into the enclosure in a fully cleaned state or whether it was processed on site. Given that the enclosure was probably used only inter-mittently and over a lengthy period (Evans and Hodder in press a), and like many other causewayed enclosures was probably peripheral to the main area of contemporary settlement (Edmonds 1999: 104–5), this evidence is probably skewed in some fashion and does not have much wider relevance.

The palaeosol evidence from beneath the Neolithic long barrow at Haddenham did not provide unequivocal evidence of cultivation despite extensive micromorphological investigation (French in press b). The pre-mound soil was a well-developed argillic brown earth (Avery 1980), which exhibited micro-laminated illuvial clay features indicative of former forest development and clearance (Figure 4.10). Similar soil material was found incorporated within the turf and soil make-up of both the east and west long mounds. This soil had suffered considerable disturbance, some possibly due to initial clearance activities and the coincident soil truncation and the construction of the mortuary structure and the subsequent mounds. The occurrence of relatively large amounts of finely comminuted organic matter and charcoal in the groundmass and in dusty (or impure) clay coatings (named 'agricutans' after Jongerius 1970) (Figure 4.5) is also indicative of biological mixing and soil disturbance. In addition, there are very rare fragments of micro-laminated clay present which were originally interpreted as fragments of eroded palaeo-argillic horizons, but these could be fragments of surface crusts formed by ard ploughing (Jongerius 1970; Macphail *et al.* 1990; Lewis 1998a) which have subsequently become broken-up and mixed with the soil by later disturbance and bioturbation. Nevertheless, the soil fabrics are not sufficiently heterogeneous to suggest prolonged tillage, nor were the suite of characteristic features present in thin section that are often produced by ard ploughing (Gebhardt 1990; Lewis 1998a). Also the pollen record provides only slight indications of cultivation in the vicinity of the site (Waller *et al.* 1994). Unfortunately, most of the specific micro-features that are considered to be indicative of ard agriculture (Lewis 1998a) may have been largely destroyed by subsequent bioturbation, hydromorphism and the disruption caused by mound-building itself, so there is no way of being absolutely sure on the question of tillage.

Why is there so little evidence for earlier Neolithic activity in this landscape other than in the decline in tree pollen, minor amounts of charred cereal grain and enigmatic indications in the buried soils? The short answer is that either it is not there or it is impermanent and/or we are unable to locate and recognize it. One suspects that the evidence is slight and generally buried and therefore not easily detectable by current methodologies, and that there is very little to be found because it is dispersed and scanty. That people are there from at least the late Mesolithic is indicated in the lithics record – for example a considerable number of late Mesolithic and early Neolithic flints were found within the mound make-up of the Haddenham long barrow and the buried soil beneath (Middleton in press). Moreover, there may be a scenario operating similar to what has been observed in meticulous and detailed pollen and sedimentological work examining the nature of woodland clearance in southeastern Europe. It is often observed that there is a considerable time lag between the first evidence of clearance seen in the pollen record and the appearance of the first archaeological remains to testify to this (Willis *et al.* 1997; Gardner 1999). The first clearances are extremely subtle and amount to just very slight and short-lived variations in the relative abundance of different tree species. Unless the pollen sampling is done at very close intervals and immediately adjacent of the archaeological site creating the clearance (i.e. within *c.* 200 m), the first very minor clearances, which are really just slight changes in forest composition, are unlikely to show up in the pollen record at all. Thus in the Haddenham area, the indications of clearance and monument building that are evident by the late fifth-early fourth millennium BC suggest that inroads into the forest were already quite advanced, and that the clearance process had begun sometime previously and that the cumulative effect of these first inroads only appear on a rather coarse scale.

In the later Neolithic or in the third millennium BC, there is quite good evidence for some regeneration of woodland coincident with a diminution of cleared areas and a decline in herbaceous pollen (Peglar and Waller 1994: 179; Peglar in press). In particular, oak dominated the woodland areas, with ash and lime to a lesser extent, and hazel and yew, possibly as understorey and woodland fringing trees. It has been suggested that this could have coincided with the first rises in groundwater table that affected the dry terraces, causing a shift in human activity and therefore clearance activities to higher ground (Evans and Hodder in press a). If it was the first real effect of a rising groundwater table, increases in fen-edge and fen carr communities would most probably have occurred and been reflected more strongly in the pollen record. Instead, it is perhaps better to see it as the product of a shift in the focus of human exploitation upstream to the floodplain and lower terraces upstream, for example at the Over and Barleycroft Farm sites.

The terraces above about Ordnance Datum do not really appear to have been affected by waterlogging, marine inundation and peat formation until about 4000 BP onwards. But the deposition of the 'fen clay' under marine and tidal influence did gradually begin to encroach up the Ouse channel and into the fen and fen-edge in the Haddenham area from about the middle of the third millennium BC (2590–2305 cal BC (Q-2813; 3950±95 BP) to 2470–2150 cal BC (Q-2585; 3855±80 BP)), reaching its maximum extent several hundred years later (Peglar and Waller 1994). In Foulmire Fen to the northeast, fen clay deposition appears to have occurred somewhat later between *c.* 3600 and 3200 BP, or within the earlier Bronze Age (Waller *et al.* 1994: 182).

During this period, three main zones would have been identifiable in the landscape. The channels themselves would have been meandering and dendritic in pattern, tidal occasionally and gradually becoming infilled with fine sand, silt and clay-size mud and with an associated reed swamp, represented by *Phragmites* reeds and standing water. The channels would have been fringed with a linear zone composed of some combination of reed swamp, sedge fen and/or alder/willow carr woodland which was suffering through having its roots drowned by brackish water from time to time. Beyond this was dry terrace land, with woodland that was becoming gradually more open and less dominated by lime and hazel, and with an increasingly greater diversity of shrubs and herbs, and some fairly consistent indications of disturbed ground and limited cereal cultivation. Although the argillic brown earths exhibit signs of disturbance, it is not yet possible to ascribe these particular signs to arable farming *per se*. Somewhat unusually, after the cessation of 'fen clay' deposition, there seems to have been a slight recovery in tree pollen, except for lime and hazel, which occurred at each of the main pollen profiles investigated, presumably because of a lessening influence of brackish water and higher local water tables.

The second and first millennia BC witnessed a gradually rising groundwater table and an increasingly open environment (Waller *et al.* 1994: 182). This was indicated by renewed peat formation in the whole area, except where the terrace surface was above *c.* 1 m OD, and distinctive changes in the vegetation assemblage. The crown of the Lower Delphs at just under 1 m OD may have just survived as a fen 'island' in the summer months and even the fringes of the higher (at 1.5–2.5 m OD) Upper Delphs were becoming affected by the encroachment of peat from about 800 cal BC (Evans and Hodder in press b). The pollen analyses indicate that on the drier terraces just inland there was a decline in tree pollen, and lime in particular, accompanied by an increase in grasses, some probably cereals because of their large annulus diameters, considerable increases in *Plantago lanceolata* (ribwort plantain) and other weeds of disturbed ground often associated with arable cultivation such as mugwort (*Artemisia*) and the goosefoot family (Chenopodiaceae). This began to occur from about 2800–2600 BP or within the late Bronze Age–early Iron Age. At the same time at the fen-edge or within seasonally waterlogged zones around 0–2 m OD, there was fen carr woodland dominated by alder and willow, grading in places into sedge fen and/or reed fen with areas of open water beyond. For example, there is peat growth dated to 845–660 cal BC (Q-2583; 2595 ± 50 BP) beneath Willingham Mere, which suggests that peat growth was beginning to encroach inland up into the lower Great Ouse valley at that time. It appears that from about this time, groundwater levels began to rise significantly and faster than previously. Nonetheless, the bulk of the Upper Delphs terrace surface at 1.5–2.5 m OD remained sufficiently dry for a whole series of farmsteads with enclosures and field systems to be built and used for most of the second half of the first millennium BC. But high groundwater tables would have been the norm and most ditches at least partially filled with standing water for most of the year. It would have been a truly damp, misty and chilly place much of this time. It was not until the last century BC that freshwater flooding finally gained the upper hand and made the continued use of these Iron Age sites as farmsteads untenable. This is nicely attested by the tertiary fill of the Haddenham site V enclosure ditch with its alternating lenses of peat development and alluvial clay deposition (Simms in press), and the complete lack of Iron Age material on the levees upstream in the Over area.

Towards the end of the first millennium BC, Willingham Mere began to form in a small northward draining valley where the River Great Ouse had emptied into the fens just south of the Haddenham complex of sites in the Upper Delphs (Figure 8.1). The pollen record from the mere itself suggests that a tripartite environment similar to that previously discussed existed well into the Roman period and beyond (Waller *et al.* 1994: 158–64). The groundwater table was continuing to rise with open water in the mere, there was a reduction in sedges around the margins of the mere, an open woodland of oak and hazel on the drier and higher terraces to the north and inland to the west, with indications that the cultivation of arable crops was an important component of this landscape. It is suggested that the first century BC witnessed some alluvial aggradation in the mere, followed by a relative drying out phase in the second century AD, and then renewed alluvial deposition from the third to fourth century AD. This process of alluvial deposition which was responsible for the aggradation of silts and clays both in the mere and within the floodplain of the day was probably associated with an increase in arable farming on the drier terraces some 5–20 km upstream to the west, as well as late winter/spring floodwaters that did not easily drain away northeastwards due to poor river outfall and the upwards growth of peat in the fens beyond.

The best non-organic evidence for arable agriculture in the study is comprised of at least seven sets of superimposed ard marks that were found beneath the enclosure bank and the floor of Building 7 at the middle Iron Age Haddenham site V (Evans and Hodder in press b). It is postulated that this evidence for arable agriculture coincides with the laying-out of a linked series of field enclosures in the middle Iron Age on the Upper Delphs (ibid.). Unfortunately, these ard marks were not sampled for micromorphological analysis at the time, nor was the sampling of the buried soil as intensive as it should have been, knowing what we know now about the importance of prehistoric ploughsoils and ard marks (cf. Lewis 1998a).

The micromorphological investigation of the buried soil beneath the same bank unfortunately produced rather equivocal evidence for past arable activities (French 1985, in press). There are two fabrics present in an heterogeneous mixture. The predominant fabric is a depleted very fine quartz sand which is suggestive of a leached lower A or Eb horizon fabric, and the subordinate fabric is a silty clay loam which includes minor, micro-laminated and non-laminated pure and dusty (or impure) clay coatings in its ground-mass that are indicative of B horizon, brown earth material. On one hand, the incomplete mixing is suggestive of mechanical disturbance such as is created by ploughing (Jongerius 1970, 1983; Macphail *et al.* 1987, 1990; Gebhardt 1990; Lewis 1998a). But the various clay coatings present are just as likely to be associated with disturbance such as caused by clearance and the construction of the bank as ploughing itself, as well as the occasional influence of introduced fine material through overbank flooding. Unfortunately no other definitive microfeatures were present which would make a micromorphological identification of ploughing possible in its own right. In this case, without the ard marks themselves and the pollen and abundant plant macro-fossil evidence, there would be insufficient data to make a reliable judgement (cf. Carter and Davidson 1998).

The plant remains, charred and uncharred, from the same Haddenham site V, are indicative of there being a mixture of arable land and damp pasture present in the immediate vicinity (G. Jones in press b; Hunt in press). Barley and the glume wheats emmer and spelt occurred regularly along with a range of wild species, most of which could have been weeds of crops or grown on waste or damp ground. In particular, the small-seeded *Eleocharis palustris/uniglumis* predominated amongst the wild species, and the preference this genus has for damp ground also suggests the cultivation of damp ground. The regular contamination of the grain with weeds suggests that the grain had not yet been cleaned and was unprocessed, and the type of weed assemblage suggests that the grain was cultivated locally. Jones (in press b) and Hunt (in press) have concluded that the evidence at this site in its earliest phase combined with the ard mark evidence and limited pollen evidence from the enclosure ditch (Simms in press) 'constitutes an unusually good case for local cereal cultivation.'

Moreover the faunal remains from the Haddenham site V Iron Age settlement site produced a unique (to southern Britian) assemblage of domesticated and wild species (Serjeantson in press). Along with the plant macro-fossil and pollen evidence, it illustrated that the inhabitants were exploiting both the drier hinterland for grain crops and sheep and cattle husbandry, and that the fen-edge carr woodland, reed marsh and open water adjacent for wild animals for pelts, birds for plumage and fish were used to a lesser extent.

What is the model for soil erosion and alluvial aggradation in this type of terrace/fen-edge system that is slowly but surely succumbing to the effects of a rising groundwater table? The brown forest soils of the dry, relatively flat terraces of this part of the lower Great Ouse valley would have been relatively stable despite deforestation and associated soil disturbance as long as they were well managed and flood-free. This would require putting organic material back into the soil on a regular basis to provide some structure and stability whilst fallow, and/or the establishment of grass sward for pasture. Recognition of manuring through geo-chemical 'finger-prints' in the soil is possible (Bull *et al.* 1999; Simpson *et al.* 1999), but it is difficult, expensive and a relatively new technique. But perhaps the best indication of this practice is indicated by the common occurrence of a general background scatter of artefacts in soils discovered during the archaeological fieldwalking survey. Long fallow periods, deep ploughing and episodes of prolonged rainfall when soils were exposed would be detrimental and would encourage instability and soil movement especially on slopes, but in this quite flat river valley environment these types of event would most probably have been relatively few and far between. The soils on the lower terraces of the valley were probably not therefore adding much if any eroded sediment to the contemporary drainage system. Instead, it is the gradually rising water table associated with the regional rise in the groundwater table and the encroachment of peat growth throughout later prehistory which largely initiated both soil change and transformation, and possibly the movement of saturated soils over short distances downstream and into cut features such as field system ditches. This is reflected in the ubiquitous gleying/oxidation mottling of the soils on the fen-edge (at *c*. 0–2 m OD), the calcitic component and the relatively high proportion of the fine illuvial material found within both the A and B horizons of the brown earths on the fen-edge.

The channel fills themselves at this earlier Holocene/earlier prehistoric phase result mainly from slow infilling processes with fine organic material associated with channel avulsion in the floodplain. The slow meandering system with little outfall gradient would have been prone to gradual, natural silting-up. Thus, it is suggested that the two large meandering relict systems in the Ouse valley between Over and Needingworth/Earith and into Fowlmire Fen (Figure 8.1) indicate long periods of relative stability in this landscape. The major channel shift northwestwards over a distance of about 0.5–1 km observed at Over quarry (Figure 8.1) may well have resulted from a combination of extreme flood events associated with high spring tides and disruption of the outfall route to the east in the fens through upward peat bog growth, as much as from any direct human influence, forcing the river to find a new and easier outfall route. This same circumstance may have also been responsible for the major change in the river course in the fens to the northeast from the Neolithic-Bronze Age channel along the northwestern side of the Upper Delphs terrace into Fowlmire Fen to the easterly course occupied by the Old West River from at least post-Roman times (Figure 8.1).

It is only with much increased run-off and soil erosion occurring some way inland and upslope beginning in the later prehistoric period that one can envisage drastic channel avulsion, bank and channel scour and overbank flooding occurring in the lower Great Ouse valley. This had to be associated with more intensive and extensive clearance and cultivation, aggravated by the slight slopes and gravity, on the higher terraces to the northwest and some distance inland. With increased run-off and more bare and disrupted soils on slopes, soil erosion began in earnest. This was responsible for the major phase of alluviation with silty clay material that is seen all the way upstream from the Haddenham sites to at least St Ives. It seems to have begun to intensify from the later first millennium BC onwards, possibly reaching a peak in the earlier medieval period when the English midlands generally witnessed the establishment of extensive ridge and furrow systems on clay-rich subsoils on hillsides (after Hall 1982). This had the long-term associated effect of seasonal waterlogging and gleying over a wide area of the floodplain and lower part of the first terrace, probably up to about 3–5 m OD. Associated overbank flooding containing fine organic matter, silt and clay then became added to the *in situ* soil over the long term, thus changing its soil structure and texture over time. This alluvial overbank flooding undoubtedly affected many river's-edge soils and made them no longer suitable for arable agriculture, that is making them 'heavier' (or finer in texture) and consequently more poorly drained, until the advent of modern machinery. In fact, these alluviated silt and clay-rich soils remained only useable for seasonal pasture in the drier months of the year. These soils are called gleyed calcareous brown earths.

In more detail, what happens in these former brown earths when they become seasonally waterlogged on a regular basis? The alternating rise and fall of the groundwater table leads to accelerated leaching of the lower half of the soil profile. This results in a brown earth characteristically looking like a pale, greyish brown B horizon below an organic, but severely oxidized, A horizon (both in the field and in thin section). This is largely the result of the removal of the organic and much of the inherent fine component of the soil. Those pedofeatures that do remain from the pre-alluvial soil, such as clay coatings, tend to become impregnated with iron oxides and hydroxides, and turn a strong red, reddish brown or orangey brown colour. Indeed, the whole fine groundmass of the soil becomes generally oxidized and much affected by the impregnation of iron oxides and hydroxides. In addition, if the groundwater is very calcareous, there are often numerous types of secondary calcium carbonate formed when the soil begins to dry out.

As a result of overbank flooding and associated seasonal waterlogging, the upper half of the brown earth soil profile becomes transformed from a well-drained and friable loamy soil to a dense, poorly drained soil dominated by silt and clay. As alluvial fine material (silt, clay and very fine organic matter) begins to accumulate on the soil's surface under temporary, shallow, standing water conditions in the late winter/spring, the A horizon becomes increasingly dominated by the intercalation of dusty (silty or impure) clay, with or without the addition of finely comminuted, amorphous organic matter. This process also affects the B horizon below to a greater or lesser degree, leading to the formation of dusty/dirty silty clay coatings down profile. The combined effect of this process is to 'clog up' the soil, much reducing pore space, changing the soil texture, and eventually leading to the formation of blocky ped structures, especially in the upper half of the soil profile. In addition, this increase in soil density and change to a 'heavier' texture causes further impedence of water infiltration down profile, thus leading to two separate moisture regimes. The lower half of the profile becomes more freely draining and subject to a fluctuating groundwater table. This is all partially sealed from oxidation from above by a dense silty clay soil (the upper half of the profile), which is affected by seasonal wetting and drying and the gradual accretion of fine material. In addition, the deposition of fines and blocky ped structure is often associated with shrink-swell clay types, meaning that the soil is both periodically anaerobic and aerobic, and oxygen can get into the lower half of the soil profile. Thus, there is a gradually changing matrix and preservation status within the alluviated soil through time, which is at the same time both detrimental and advantageous to the preservation of organic remains and the original features of the *in situ* soil.

Over to St Ives

The archaeological, palaeobotanical and palaeosol records for this area upstream of the fen-edge are not nearly so extensive as downstream, but there is good site-specific evidence from Barleycroft Farm and Meadow Lane, St Ives, further upstream.

The southwestern corner of Over quarry and Barleycroft Farm quarry to the northwest provide a typical sequence of brown earth soil on gravel terrace deposits buried by thin, silty clay alluvial deposits (<1 m thick). The buried soils appear to be best preserved in terms of development and thickness adjacent to relict palaeochannel systems.

At Barleycroft Farm, the palaeosols exhibited well-oriented, pure or limpid clay throughout the groundmass and as linings of voids (Table 8.1). These are indicative of the development of a forest brown earth or argillic brown earth (Avery 1980). This soil type is associated with clay illuviation occurring beneath stable woodland cover on a well-drained calcareous subsoil (Bullock and Murphy 1979; Fisher 1982). The absence of evident horizonation in the field suggests the subsequent influence of fluctuating groundwater tables and seasonal flooding episodes, associated with alluvial deposition, leaching, eluviation/illuviation and alternating oxidation/reducing conditions as well as soil faunal mixing. This has resulted in the established dryland soil becoming progressively leached with considerable secondary deposition of silty clays, formation of secondary iron and calcium carbonate, and organic depletion. The final result is the homogeneous silty/sandy loam palaeosols now visible beneath silty clay alluvial sediments.

Table 8.1 Summary micromorphological descriptions and interpretations, Barleycroft Farm

Sample	Major characteristics	Interpretation
BCF/92: Pr 1/1	poorly sorted silty sand loam; 2–5% porosity; vughy	glacial/fluvial origin of quartz, felspars and rock; root penetration; pedogenesis; groundwater fluctuations, saturation, reduction/oxidation, translocation/eluviation of fines, illuviation/clay coatings; organic matter degradation; iron oxide formation; former brown forest earth, now a leached, homogeneous brown earth buried by silty clay alluvial sediments
BCF/92: Pr 1/2	as above; quartz rich; various rock fragments; degraded organics; granostriated/undifferentiated/ weakly developed speckled b-fabric; clay coatings	as above; extensive removal of clay and fine silt by groundwater (eluviation) and limited translocation (illuviation)
BCF/94: Pr 2/1	poorly sorted silty sand loam; 5-10% porosity; planar and polyconcave voids; quartz rich; various rock fragments; mixed fabric as above; iron oxides and organics; clay coatings; possible fragments of burnt clay	as above
BCF/94: Pr2/2	as above	as above; water movement concentrated in areas of root channels
BCF/94: Pr 3/1	as above; but with calcium carbonate as calcite crystals & sparite nodules; shell fragments; clay coatings; *in situ* and detrital organics; rounded daub fragments	glacial/fluvial source of mineral and rock components; turbation, rootlet penetration; formation of calcium carbonate; groundwater fluctuations; limited compaction; limited eluviation/illuviation; reduction/oxidation; former brown forest earth, now a leached, calcareous brown earth buried by silty clay alluvial sediments

At Over, the terrestrial sequence exhibited a fine-grained minerogenic alluvium, a complex sequence of laterally variable peats and alluvium (minerogenic and of variable organic content) overlying a sandy loam to sandy clay loam buried soil developed on the surface of terrace sands, sandy clays and gravels. In all profiles, the unit directly overlying the buried soil is highly organic and characterised by relatively high porosity, moderate impregnation with amorphous iron compounds, strong cracking and fine, angular peds. It is well humified and desiccated. In particular, the organic component is fragmentary and exhibits poor internal preservation and much comminution by the soil mixing fauna.

The buried soil at Over, although apedal, does display some pedogenesis in terms of two major episodes of translocation of fine material, first a pure clay and second dusty/dirty clay, as well as considerable impregnation with amorphous iron, often replacing organic matter. Nonetheless, it is not as well preserved here as at Barleycroft and the Haddenham sites. The sequence reflects what has been observed to occur elsewhere in the valley, namely soil development under stable dryland conditions followed by disturbance and the addition of fines derived from overbank flooding. This argillic to brown earth to gleyed brown earth sequence suggests a well-drained and wooded landscape becoming disturbed by two major influences, first, human activities such as clearance and a mixed agriculture, and then increasingly, the aggradation of alluvial soil material associated with seasonal flooding and waterlogging. The main evident archaeological use of the area is in the later Bronze Age on all parts of the first terrace gravels and in Romano-British periods on the upper parts of the first terrace in the form of field systems and dispersed settlement (Evans and Knight 1997a and b). This is typical of similar geographical locales in the lower Nene and Welland valleys to the north (French 1992a) (see Chapters 6 and 7).

Palaeobotanical study (both pollen and plant macro-fossils) of later Bronze Age pits and ditches at Barleycroft Farm has indicated the general presence of open, rather damp, weedy grassland, with periodic standing water in cut features (Stevens 1997; Wiltshire 1997a). The faunal record suggests that cattle and relatively much fewer sheep are grazing in this landscape (Yannouli 1997). Scrubby birch, hawthorn, sloe and bramble are present, as well as some damp alder woodland in the vicinity. Water's-edge or fen-edge environments also exist nearby. There are possibly areas of disturbed, open soil that is nutrient-rich and supporting arable crops. Weeds of arable fields, barley, emmer and spelt wheat are present, as well as broad bean. Unfortunately, the botanical assemblages are small, not the best preserved and insufficient to tell whether the wheat crops are being grown in the fields on site or represent crop-processing sites nearby. The Romano-British period ditches contain clay-rich fills suggestive of a high groundwater table and eroded soil material carried in overbank floodwaters from upstream. As indicated previously, this is a widespread occurrence in the fen-edge region at this time.

About 4 km upstream at Meadow Lane, St Ives, area excavation in advance of extraction revealed a sequence of Neolithic, Iron Age and early Romano-British boundary features adjacent to an active floodplain now buried by silty clay alluvium (Pollard 1996). There are two large relict palaeochannel meanders to the southeast of the site and a relict lake beneath the southern channel. The lake and the overlying, southernmost palaeochannel have their origins in the early Holocene (C. Goa pers. comm.). The main channel, adjacent to the site and *c.* 100–150 m northwest of the earlier channel, was active from at least the Neolithic period, but was becoming infilled during the first millennium BC and was out of use by the first century AD. It is tempting to compare these earlier and later prehistoric channel systems to the pattern observed downstream at Over quarry which appears to be quite similar in terms of form, position and relative dating.

During the latter part of the infilling process of the northern channel, there was some overbank aggradation of silty clay at least on the western bank. The excavator suggests that there was a slight (relative) drying out and hiatus in alluvial deposition in the Roman period, with renewed flooding and sediment accumulation beginning in the fourth century AD (Pollard 1996). Subsequently, up to 1.3 m of alluviation has occurred in post-Roman to modern times over the whole floodplain and adjacent terrace edge.

The palaeoenvironmental evidence recovered from the mid-first millennium BC pit alignment at Meadow Lane is quite similar to that obtained from the later Bronze Age features at Barleycroft Farm downstream. The plant macro-fossils suggest an open and herbaceous landscape with wet fen-type environment adjacent (Fryer and Murphy 1996). Unusually, the wood remains were strongly indicative of an adjacent hedge with sloe and occasionally field maple and oak present (Taylor 1996: 105–8). Pollen was poorly preserved and is suggestive of intermittent wetting and drying conditions occurring within the pits (Wiltshire 1996), as one would expect in a seasonal floodplain edge position. Preservation of buried soils was also poor given the amount of disturbance created by the construction of the various boundary alignments. Nonetheless, the truncated remnants are indicative of a brown earth soil subject to alternate wetting and drying episodes and the intercalation (or addition) of fine material as a result of overbank flooding (French 1994a).

Here it appears that the channel system and active floodplain was much more restricted in its wider effect on the valley floor. There were two major periods of channel avulsion prior to the creation of the modern river channel, and each system was apparently long-lived. Finally the area was extensively affected by later alluvial aggradation, in places up to 2 km away from the present river position to about the 5 m contour.

Conclusions

The major environmental events recognizable in the lower Great Ouse valley bear remarkable similarities to a combination of the evidence available from the lower Welland and Nene valleys to the north, but exhibit differences of scale, extent and timing. Deforestation seems to have begun a little earlier in the lower Great Ouse as opposed to the valleys to the north, that is in the late fifth millennium BC rather than in the earlier fourth millennium BC. At about this period, there is a major period of river channel avulsion north-westwards in the lower Great Ouse valley, and somewhat later downstream within the Upper Delphs/fen basin itself. Even though the floodplain area may have been more open naturally in the Mesolithic/early Neolithic than previously envisaged, earlier inroads may well have been made into these woodlands than are readily apparent in the existing pollen diagrams because of problems of sample locale and resolution. Forest composition is very similar in all three study areas, but fen-edge or fen carr woodland may have lingered a little longer in the lower Nene/Flag Fen and the lower Welland/Borough Fen basins to the north. The recognition of arable agriculture remains problematic in this period, but there are hints that it was occurring on a limited scale from the fourth millennium BC. Unfortunately, the surest examples do not occur until the Iron Age, for example at Haddenham site V. Relatively open pasture appears to predominate within a landscape that is gradually becoming cleared, with a groundwater table, at least seasonally, close to the contemporary ground surface.

Well-preserved argillic brown earths and brown earths have been observed in this valley, developed on gravel terrace deposits just above the active floodplain level of the day. Such soils have been found repeatedly in the Welland and Nene valleys and on much of the fen-edge between these valleys (see Chapters 6, 7 and 9). On the higher parts of the terrace they occur regularly either associated with or beneath Neolithic and Bronze Age monuments, and in the lower parts of the first terrace are found extensively beneath thin alluvial silty clay cover. As the subsoil terrain dips across the slope margin either into the floodplain or into the fen basin, more poorly developed argillic brown earths and brown earths tend to occur. On these margins, the palaeosol preservation and extent is seen in terms of many, many hectares, even if the colours and upper parts of the profile have often been transformed by various burial processes. Thus these lower river valley/fen-edge locations contain one of the greatest areas of relict forest soils in England.

The gravel terraces of the floodplain edge witness much organized human activity throughout the second millennium BC or Bronze Age, but by the end of this period are becoming increasingly susceptible to seasonal freshwater flooding and the gradual deposition of flood-derived, eroded soil material from upstream. Nonetheless, relatively small quantities of soil/sediment are involved at this stage (as compared to the post-Roman period), more or less in the order of less than 50 cm of deposition in the floodplain up to about the 1.5 m OD mark. This has a combined effect of widespread clearance and cultivation upstream leading to increased run-off and soil erosion, as well as the rising groundwater table of the fen-edge associated with the development of the later Neolithic salt marsh and subsequent Bronze Age and Iron Age peat formation in the fen basin to the east.

Where would the eroded soil/sediment found in the lower Great Ouse floodplain have been derived from? For example, there is evidence of extensive later prehistoric activity (Bronze and Iron Age) at Broom on the western slopes of the River Ivel valley in Bedfordshire, a tributary of the Great Ouse (Mortimer 1997), and Iron Age and Romano-British activity beneath river alluvium at Warren Villas, Bedfordshire, in the middle reach of the Great Ouse valley. The site of Broom is about 50 km to the southwest at about 30 m OD on glacial sand and gravels overlying Oxford Clay, and there are indications of thin, rather poorly developed brown earth soils being present there in the Bronze Age (French 1996a). At Warren Villas, some 5 km downstream from Broom, both the Iron Age and Roman periods witnessed arable ploughing in the floodplain zone of the Great Ouse (Macphail 1995). Although quite a distance inland and upstream, both of these would be the type and location of activity that would have generated small amounts of soil material which could have found its way into the drainage system. Surface run-off from bare soils between crops in the autumn and winter months would have been the most likely source, finding its way into the small streams as colluvium and on into the main river channel. It would have stayed in suspension with sufficient flow rate and water volume until the lower valley/fen-edge zone was reached some 40–50 km downstream, whereupon it spread out in overbank flooding episodes, and gradually settled out of suspension in quiet, standing, shallow water conditions. The seasonally aggrading increments would have been small, mostly imperceptible to the eye and over a lifetime. But over several centuries the repeated alluvial events began to change the nature of the soil, making it more silt- and clay-dominated and more poorly drained. As this was coincident with generally rising groundwater levels in the fens and valley floor, the lower floodplain zones that were affected by this alluvial aggradation would have become less and less usable for anything other than seasonal, summer-time grazing. A similar scenario would have taken place in late Roman and post-Roman times, but on a greater scale of soil disturbance and at a faster rate of accumulation downstream with more extensive flooding in late winter/early spring.

The earlier Roman period or first two centuries AD may have seen a slight fall in the groundwater table along the fen-edge, but there is soon renewed freshwater flooding and overbank accretion of silty clay sediments in the later Roman period. This may have been initiated as another major clearance inroad into areas of higher ground and heavier clay soils in the midlands to the west (now Bedfordshire, Leicestershire and Northamptonshire). Initially, only the immediate floodplains were affected by silty clay alluvial aggradation, but throughout the next millennium, a very wide area was affected, often over a width of 1–4 km of the valley floor, up to the 5 m OD contour and up to 1.3 m in thickness. This undoubtedly reflects the massive uptake and utilization of land for arable crop production in the English Midlands during the medieval period. Such drastic landscape change was exacerbated by peat growth upwards and laterally in the adjacent fens, which seriously affected river and drainage outfall to the east. The last major drainage and rationalization of the river channel system was coincident with the drainage of the fenlands from the seventeenth century onwards.

Essential reading

French, C. and Pryor, F. (1992) 'Floodplain gravels: buried Neolithic and Bronze Age landscapes along the fen margins', in M. Fulford and E. Nichols (eds) *Developing Landscapes in Lowland Britain: The Archaeology of the British Gravels: A Review*, pp. 63–77, London: Society of Antiquaries Occasional Paper 14.

French, C., Davis, M. and Heathcote, J. (1999) 'Hydrological monitoring of an alluviated landscape in the lower Great Ouse valley, Cambridgeshire: interim results of the first three years', *Environmental Archaeology* 4: 41–56.

Evans, C. and Hodder, I. (in press a) *The Emergence of a Fen Landscape, The Haddenham Project: Volume I*, Cambridge: McDonald Institute Monograph.

Evans, C. and Hodder, I. (in press b) *Marshland Communities and Cultural Landscape: The Haddenham Project: Volume II*, Cambridge: McDonald Institute Monograph.

Pollard, J. (1996) 'Iron Age riverside pit alignments at St Ives, Cambridgeshire', *Proceedings of the Prehistoric Society* 62: 93–116.

Waller, M. (1994) *The Fenland Project, Number 9: Flandrian Environmental Change in Fenland*, Cambridge: East Anglian Archaeology 70.

9 The development of the Cambridgeshire fenlands of eastern England

Introduction

Before looking at some of the detail provided by the dyke survey project specifically for the northwestern part of Cambridgeshire in Chapter 10, it is worth attempting to summarize the known stratigraphic and environmental sequence for the whole of the Cambridgeshire fenlands. The palaeoenvironmental history of this area is important to understand given the effect it has on the river and valley systems entering into it throughout the Holocene.

There is now a considerable body of stratigraphic and palynological evidence available from the Cambridgeshire fens with which to reconstruct the development of this part of the East Anglian fenland in the Holocene (Figure 9.1). This data derived from English Heritage-funded, extensive field survey and mapping programme with associated palynological studies. Although not every topographical basin has been examined in the same degree of detail, and there is a considerable degree of non-synchronicity between the various basins that comprise the fens, there is now sufficient consistency and breadth in the stratigraphic and palynological data to offer a broad synthesis of the environmental events of this region from the Mesolithic through to the medieval period.

The study area is effectively defined by the River Welland to the north, Peterborough to the northwest, the A1 to the west, the Isle of Ely to the east, the southern Cambridgeshire fen-edge between Waterbeach, the Swaffhams and Burwell villages to the south, and the chalk/gravel uplands of the Suffolk/Norfolk borders skirting northeastwards from Cambridge towards Mildenhall and Lakenheath (Figure 6.1).

Waller (1994) has already summarized much of the previous environmental work (i.e. based on Clark 1933, 1936; Clark *et al.* 1935; Godwin *et al.* 1935; Clark and Godwin 1940, 1962; Godwin 1940; Churchill 1970; Gallois 1988). In addition, Waller (1994) has contributed with various other authors such as Cloutman, Alderton and Peglar (in Waller 1994) and Scaife (1993) numerous well-dated palynological studies of the region. Also, Smith *et al.* (1989) have re-examined the Shippea Hill complex first investigated by

Clark *et al.* (1935, 1960). Shippea Hill was a Mesolithic flint scatter and occupation site on a sand ridge dated to between 8500 and 6800 BP (uncalibrated) which may have seen repeated short-term use over as long as 700–1,500 years, and remains a unique site in the East Anglian fens. It was also one of the earliest and first sites in lowland England to indicate damage to the landscape or limited reduction of the tree cover through human activities at about 8500 BP and again more intensively at *c.* 8250 BP (Smith *et al.* 1989). There were several benefits of this, such as attracting game through the replacement of trees by herbs and shrubs and therefore improving hunting success as well as greater predictability of resource scheduling (Mellars 1976). Finally there was a small, repeated but short-lived Neolithic use of the same sand ridge at Peacock's Farm and nearby at Letter F Farm (Clark *et al.* 1935), as at other fen-edge sites such as Hurst Fen (Clark *et al.* 1960) and more recently at sites such as Crowtree and Oakhurst Farms in Newborough Fen (see Chapter 10).

The following account attempts to summarize briefly this previous and more current palaeoenvironmental work, based on an already published summary (French 2000c).

The Flandrian sequence

Essentially, there is a six-part sequence of Flandrian sedimentary events in this fenland region – channel peat, limited marine incursion, basal peat, 'fen clay' marine incursion, upper peat and an 'upper silt' marine incursion (Figures 9.1 and 9.2). Although each event is not represented everywhere and/or uniformly across the county, there is a relative synchronicity of the occurrence of major events. The dating of these episodes of deposition is no longer based solely on the Shippea Hill site sequence as first set out by Clark *et al.* (1935), as the sedimentary sequence there has been demonstrated to be atypical in date range in that it represents the infill of a large, partially eroded channel (Smith *et al.* 1989). Also, Godwin's pollen diagrams of the 1930s and 1940s (see Godwin 1940) only show arboreal or tree/shrub types of vegetation, therefore making it very difficult to draw inferences concerning any human impact on the vegetation.

As the post-glacial period (post-10000 BC) began, the fen basin was dryland dissected by river valley systems with narrow floodplains (Perrin and Hodge 1965). The surface geology and soils differed little from the adjacent river terrace areas and uplands (French 1988a and b; French and Pryor 1993) (see Chapters 6–8), although there were a number of low knolls or 'islands' that have remained relatively dry throughout the development of the fens. During the post-glacial amelioration, deciduous forest established itself across the fen basin, with lime as the predominant species in this woodland (Scaife 1993; Waller 1994). Throughout the first half of the post-glacial era, the sea level continued to rise, more or less reaching its present height during the first millennium BC (Jelgersma 1979; Shennan 1982). Conse-

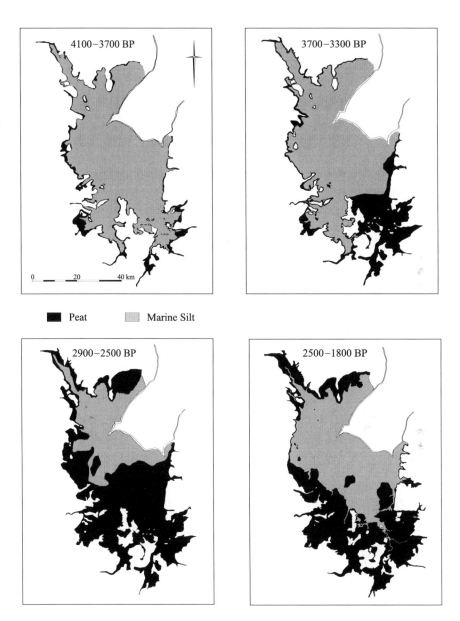

Figure 9.1 Development of the Cambridgeshire fenlands showing the late
Neolithic marine zone, the growth of the peat in the Early Bronze Age,
the later Bronze Age salt marsh and the post-Bronze Age upper peat
development (C. Begg after Waller 1994).

Figure 9.2 Typical fenland profile of palaeosol, basal peat, fen clay and
wasted/desiccated upper peat in Newborough Fen.

quently the drainage of the fenland basin became increasingly impeded, resulting in increasing overbank freshwater flooding and the formation of a marsh.

In the deepest parts of the fenland basin, at *c.* 7–9 m below Ordnance Datum, a eutrophic wood/reed peat first began to form as early as the sixth to fifth millennia BC as a regional response to rising base water levels. Examples occur at Tydd St Giles in the northeastern corner of the county at −9.1 m OD with a date of 7690±400 BP (SRR-1757), Adventurer's Land east of Thorney at *c.* 6575 BP (Hv-10011) (Shennan 1986a), and Welney Washes at −7.04 to −7.23 m OD dated to pre-6170±110 BP (Q-2824) (Waller 1994: 143–52). Nonetheless, for most of the Mesolithic, fen vegetation must have been relatively unimportant and confined to channels and the lowest parts of the basin, with marine influence absent and dryland vegetation predominant.

In addition, there is now evidence to suggest some minor marine influence resulting in shallow incursions and the deposition of marine silts during the later Mesolithic or within the fifth millennium BC. Examples are known from Adventurer's Land after 6415 BP and again at *c.* 6200–5600 BP (Shennan 1986b) and at Welney between 6170 and 5850 BP (Q-2823; 4970–4485 cal BC) (Waller 1994: 143–52), but their limits/extent are unknown and not mapped.

The long-lived Mesolithic use of the seminal site of Shippea Hill at Peacock's Farm was over by this period of first peat deposition at Welney and elsewhere. Smith *et al.*'s (1989) re-investigation of this site has indicated that there was Mesolithic occupation on the sand ridge at Peacock's Farm between about 8500 and 6800 BC. The whole area was a very well wooded landscape which witnessed its first, minor openings at *c.* 8500 BP and again at *c.* 8250 BP, marked by a decline in pine, hazel and oak and an associated slight increase in alder and grasses, but nevertheless indicative of a pronounced human impact on the local environment. These relatively open conditions persisted for some 700 to 1,500 years before forest cover was re-established by about 6100 BP, coincident with the first peat development in the most low-lying part of the fens such as at Welney to the northwest.

The minor marine influences in the fifth millennium BC were overtaken by the onset of the main period of basal peat formation from the later fourth millennium BC, continuing until the end of the third millennium, coincident with rising base water levels (Figure 9.1) (French and Pryor 1993: 6; Waller 1994: 153). For example the pollen analyses in the southeastern part of the county at Wicken Fen, Peacock's Farm and Adventurer's Fen indicate peat formation from about 4500 BP (or *c.* 3365–3000 cal BC). At Wicken Fen, a lime-dominated woodland became subject to rising water levels and the development of an alder-dominated fen carr with abundant marsh ferns and a hazel-dominated fen-edge woodland (Peglar and Waller 1994). This then gave way to sedge fen, with evidence of more extensive clearance. It is marked by decreases in oak, lime, elm, ash and hazel, increases in *Plantago lanceolata* (ribwort plantain) and *Pteridium* (bracken) with charcoal, and a rise in Poaceae (grasses) with large annulus diameters of >8um which is suggestive of cereal-type grasses. This evidence all points to some anthropogenic influence in the few hundred years prior to the subsequent 'fen clay' inundation in the later Neolithic. In contrast, pollen analyses in the north of the county and on the fen-edge in Newborough Fen suggest basal peat growth was continuing into the Early Bronze Age, as late as 3660±60 BP (2270–1890 cal BC) (Har-8513) and 3740±100 BP (2460–1890 cal BC) (Har-8510) (French and Pryor 1993: 36) (Figure 9.2).

At Shippea Hill, the earlier Neolithic use of Peacock's Farm would appear to have been minimal, whereas at Letter F Farm it was mainly an earlier Neolithic occupation in the first half of the fourth millennium cal BC (Smith *et al.* 1989). But at both of these sites, there was very little evidence of damaging and sustained effects to the local environment observable in the pollen record. It is suggested that this is indicative of short duration use, perhaps brief visits by hunting/foraging parties as part of a more differentiated settlement pattern (ibid.), and unlike more permanent sites on the fen-edge such as Hurst Fen to the east (Clark *et al.* 1960). Nonetheless, in the most recent pollen analyses, there is evidence for a major elm decline at about 5600 BP (or *c.* 4715–4270 cal BC) and a more minor one at about 5300 BP (or *c.* 4370–3850 cal BC), which equates with other dates for the elm decline in the region and beyond (Clark and Godwin 1962; Godwin 1975). At most, the pollen evidence suggests very limited local clearance. More sites of this period in this region need identification and analysis. Certainly, all activity at Shippea Hill had ceased by the onset of the 'fen clay' deposition, and perhaps its abandonment may have been ultimately associated with this event itself.

Prior to recent research, the 'fen clay' marine incursion (or the Barroway Drove Beds) was dated to a period of about 600 years during the later Neolithic within the third millennium BC. But it is now recognized that this incursion comprised a number of episodes which were not necessarily synchronous across the whole of fenland and which occurred over a much longer time-frame.

The maximum extent of the 'fen clay' is well established, rarely occurring above −1.0 m OD (Figure 9.1) (Waller 1994: fig. 5.18, map 6, 71). The earliest date for 'fen clay' influence is found again at Welney Washes, of 4865–4355 cal BC (Q-2822), where it continued to 2465–2075 cal BC (Q-2821). This latter date is similar to its end date at other locations on the fen-edge, such as at Redmere (3095–2720 to 2485–2130 cal BC; Q-2596, Q-2595), Wood Fen (2925–2495 to 2465–2040 cal BC; Q-2581, Q-2580) and Feltwell Common (2910–2495 to 2470–2050 cal BC; Q-2548, Q-2551) (Waller 1994: 152). Outside of the lowermost parts of the fen and channels, the 'fen clay' transgression occurred throughout the third millennium BC across the region (ibid.: 153) and into the earlier second millennium BC in the north of the county (French and Pryor 1993: 7).

The 'fen clay' represents a brackish/salt marsh or coastal reedswamp environment, dissected and drained by tidal creeks or roddons in a dendritic pattern. It was probably not lagoonal as there is no solid evidence for coastal barriers, nor areas of deep water present. The 'fen clay' as a deposit tended to accumulate in the creeks/channels, and then spread out over a much wider area under high tide conditions. Perhaps initially, it would have provided a new set of perimarine resources, before becoming a more inhospitable landscape, made especially difficult to get across because of the deep, shifting, wet silt mud in the channels bounded by dense reedbeds. The closest modern analogue environments to this can be found today on the coasts of Essex and south Lincolnshire.

On the landward, fen-edge fringes of the influence of the 'fen clay', freshwater peats continued to form. At present, there is insufficient data with which to accurately map this fringing peat zone. For example at the Isleham Snail valley sites (Gdaniec 1995; Hall 1996) and West Row, Mildenhall (Martin and Murphy 1988), there would have been peat growth on the immediate dryland/fen-edge interface, with the 'fen clay', tidal creek, perimarine zone several hundred metres to 1–2 km beyond to the northwest and west, respectively (Waller 1994: fig. 5.18, map 6, 71). A similar situation has been observed in the north of the county in Newborough Fen where peat growth fringed still-active tidal creeks (French and Pryor 1993). This type of transitional environment would have given the late Neolithic/Early Bronze Age people use of a number of different environmental zones – a partly wooded upland, fringed by a fen-edge zone of willow/alder carr to sedge fen type of environment, with peat growth and pools of open water and a tidal, perimarine zone beyond.

From about the second half of the third millennium BC or in the late Neolithic/Early Bronze Age transition period, a seaward extension of freshwater conditions began, overlapping the period of 'fen clay' marine incursion on its landward side (Figure 9.1) (Waller 1994: figs. 5.19 and 5.20, maps 7 and 8, 73–4). The existing radiocarbon determinations are quite consistent and indicate that this change occurred over a relatively short time over a wide area. Waller (1994: 154) suggests that this upper peat formation and coincident rising base-water levels occurred over the whole region. In many instances, it may have led to the abandonment of sites and/or made them difficult to continue using, particularly for sites located below about 1 m OD. Certainly this has been the case in the northern Cambridgeshire fenland region where detailed archaeological and environmental studies have been done, for example at several sites in Borough Fen and Flag Fen (Pryor 1992, 2001; French and Pryor 1993).

The development of the upper peat was initially associated with willow and to a lesser extent alder carr. In many cases, coincident with rising base-water levels, this gave way to sedge fen and more open water conditions. In several pollen diagrams (e.g. Wicken Fen, Redmere, Welney Washes, Crowtree Farm and Oakhurst Farm in Newborough Fen, Fengate/Flag Fen), this change is accompanied by the virtual disappearance of lime trees, with oak relatively increasing as lime and alder fall (Scaife 1992, 1993; Waller 1994). Also, *Plantago lanceolata* and Poaceae occur more regularly, and may indicate more widespread clearance in the region (Waller 1994: 154). This is occurring throughout the first half of the second millennium cal BC.

A second marine transgression (or Upper Barroway Drove Beds) occurred in the fen to the north and northwest of Thorney in the north of the county during the later Bronze Age or late second/early first millennium BC (Hall 1987; French and Pryor 1993; Waller 1994). This phase of marine flooding deposited a grey silty clay, similar to the 'fen clay' but less sticky and plastic in consistency and containing a greater proportion of silt. It has been mapped by Hall (1987: fig. 32) and by the British Geological Survey (Zalaciewicz 1986; Zalaciewicz and Wilmot 1986), and is associated with remnants of the former tidal dendritic drainage system of the former 'fen clay' episode.

A further phase of marine influence affected the extreme northeastern part of the county beyond Thorney to Wisbech but mainly in south Lincolnshire during the late Iron Age or during the late first millennium BC/early first millennium AD (Hall 1987; Waller 1994). It is possible that the development and upward growth of the upper peat meant that most of the remainder of the southern fens was not significantly affected by this marine incursion.

In one instance at about the same time in the south of the county, another marine or 'upper silt' phase has been observed in the Washes at Welney. Here, between about 425–140 cal BC (Q-2819) and 10–605 cal AD (Q-2818), marine influence interrupted freshwater peat growth in the northern part of the region (Waller 1994: fig. 5.20, map 8, 74). It is coarser than the silty clay of the 'fen clay' and was therefore deposited in a higher energy environment. The maps of Waller (ibid.), Seale (1975) and Gallois (1988) indicate its limited extent; effectively it is found in a confined zone around Welney and does not extend landward to the fen-edges such as around Isleham. There has been insufficient mapping and analysis to be sure of how extensive and synchronous this event was, but as it does not occur in channels, it probably occurred in a wide range of overbank environments.

At about this same time, several freshwater meres began to develop within the southern fens. For example, the mere at Redmere, immediately to the east of Shippea Hill, had begun to form after 15–280 cal AD (Q-2593). Both Jennings (1950) and Waller (1994: 124–33) suggest that it may have formed during and in response to the 'upper silt' marine transgression, with the 'upper silt' effectively blocking drainage of freshwater out to the sea and leading to ponding-back of freshwater. Specific work at the other meres in the region is needed to establish any synchronicity in their formation patterns. But with nearby Willingham Mere beginning to form by 40 cal BC to 220 cal AD (Q-2582) (ibid.: 158–63), there may be a greater regional cause/effect relationship at work which is as yet not understood.

Beyond this marine interruption and mere formation formation phase, upper peat formation continued over the whole southern fenland region until the advent of seventeenth century AD drainage (Figure 9.1) (Waller 1994: figs 5.21 and 5.22, maps 9 and 10, 76–7). In extent, the upper peat influenced most areas up to the 2 m OD contour which defines the present day fen-edge in southeastern Cambridgeshire. The development of the upper peat was coincident with a continued and gradual opening-up of the landscape and a greater intensification of land use, and often associated with overbank flood deposits of alluvial silty clays, particularly where the main river systems entered the peat fen (French and Pryor 1993). Since the drainage of the fens began in the mid-seventeenth century AD, it is estimated that the surface level of peat in many places in the Cambridgeshire fens has fallen by as much as 4–5 m (Hutchinson 1980; Purseglove 1988: 83).

Conclusions

The considerable amount of recent work by Waller (1994) and a variety of colleagues associated with the Fenland Project (funded by English Heritage) has enabled the development of a much more detailed and accurate account of the formation of the southern fens of Cambridgeshire. This has both complemented and enhanced the picture revealed by the seminal investigations of Clark and Godwin in the 1930s to 1960s. But the best way to think of the development of the fens is as a series of individual histories of basins or embayments which can either share aspects of developmental history or exhibit their own particular variations on the 'theme sediments' of marine silts, freshwater peats and floodwater alluvial silts and clays.

The fen-edge embayments would have been best placed to take advantage of various resources presented in the changing fen landscapes from the Mesolithic through to the medieval period. Gradually rising water tables by the later Neolithic/Early Bronze Age were probably detrimental in some aspects, but at the same time useful to life for a variety of processing activities and the procurement of various natural resources. Potentially, the fen-edge sites would have been able to take full advantage of the landscape in all directions. Inland and on higher ground there was woodland which was gradually being cleared throughout the last three millennia BC, with well-drained, calcareous and fertile, former woodland soils, as well as solid geology for stone and flint resource procurement. The river valley and fen-edge fringes provided natural spring meadow grassland, reeds, willow and alder for building materials, gravel riverbeds and banks for flint pebble raw materials, and water for a variety of preparation activities, that is for working stone, bone, hides and bark as well as various cooking activities. Fish, fowl and bird life would have abounded in the fens beyond, all accessible by numerous avenues of transport by water. In short, a varied and resource-full landscape would have been available year round, rather than the monotonous, 'agri-business' flatlands of the Cambridgeshire fens today.

Essential reading

French, C.A.I. and Pryor, F.M.M. (1993) *The South-west Fen Dyke Survey, 1982–6*, Cambridge: East Anglian Archaeology 59.

Smith, A.G., Whittle, A., Cloutman, E.W. and Morgan, L. (1989) 'Mesolithic and Neolithic activity and environmental impact on the south-east fen-edge in Cambridgeshire', *Proceedings of the Prehistoric Society* 55: 207–49.

Waller, M. (1994) *The Fenland Project, Number 9: Flandrian Environmental Change in Fenland*, Cambridge: East Anglian Archaeology 70.

10 The dyke survey in the northwestern Cambridgeshire fenlands

Introduction

The dyke survey project (French and Pryor 1993) arose from the extensive excavations on the fen-edge/lower river valley at Fengate in the lower Nene valley (Pryor 1980, 1984) (see Chapter 6), Maxey (Pryor and French 1985) and Etton (Pryor 1998) in the lower Welland valley (see Chapter 7) and the survey work of David Hall for the Fenland Project (Hall 1987). In particular, Hall's work (ibid.) revealed that many prehistoric sites and landscapes were emerging from beneath later peat cover as a result of drainage and desiccation (see Chapter 11). At the same time, the whole Welland valley team had worked briefly on the Assendelver Polders Project in the Netherlands (Brandt *et al.* 1987) and had been exposed to a very successful form of dyke survey and extensive augering survey techniques used to prospect for sites in the peatlands of Holland.

It was immediately obvious that there was a huge buried landscape present northeast and east of Peterborough where the Rivers Welland and Nene debouched into the fens. This landscape was largely unexplored archaeologically and this potential resource would provide new data, free from the worst of the post-depositional distortions that normally affect the interpretation of surface field survey data (Crowther *et al.* 1985). Significant buried and waterlogged deposits both on- and off-site were to be expected, and there would be special emphasis on the monitoring of post-drainage effects on the fenland landscape and the archaeolological record.

Nonetheless, there was the major archaeological problem of how to gain access to this vast buried landscape. The answer was there all along, but hitherto unappreciated. Each spring and autumn the various drainage boards in the fenland district carry out cleaning, deepening and widening works on the dykes on a regular basis, approximately every five to seven years. These drainage works exposed very long sections through the buried stratigraphic record of the fens, and would allow topographical and archaeological survey, plus sampling of significant deposits. Obviously the selection of the dykes was done for engineering and drainage reasons, not on archaeological criteria. But the drainage authorities were addressing problems in the wetter parts of the fens, and that therefore would behove archaeologists to examine those areas closely before they become dewatered. The approach had a haphazard, random element because the dykes are of differing orientations, but on the other hand gave access to kilometres of buried landscapes that had never before been investigated. The dyke survey approach was flexible, relatively quick and cheap, allowing anything from simple recording to augering to sampling (for example for pollen, micromorphology, phosphates), or even small-scale, problem-oriented excavation (French and Pryor 1993: 3–5).

The end result was the discovery of new sites and new landscapes of the major prehistoric and Romano-British periods. Schematic maps were drawn of different fen embayments through time relating surficial deposits and the archaeological records in the days before the use of Geographical Information Systems. Also, detailed palaeoenvironmental sequencing data, mainly from pollen and soil micromorphological evidence, was obtained from a number of locations which augmented the work of the Fenland Project palaeo-environmental survey and analyses (Waller 1994).

The main survey area (or the North Level) that is discussed here is bounded by the River Welland, Lincolnshire border, Crowland and the Old South Eau to the north, an imaginary line drawn between the villages of Parson Drove, Guyhirn and March to the east, the Twenty Foot River and King's Dyke to the south, and Peterborough, the Car Dyke and Peakirk to the west (Figure 10.1). It is based on the already published work of French and Pryor (1993), and should be read in tandem with Chapters 6, 7 and 9. This case study gives a very different view of the long-term sequence detailed for Shippea Hill and the southern Cambridgeshire fens.

Archaeology and environment by major period

The late Mesolithic and Neolithic (fifth to third millennia BC)

Few earlier prehistoric sites have been discovered in the North Level area, but on the other hand extensive areas of buried landscapes of that period have been. These areas hold tremendous potential for the future if our powers of detection of buried archaeology improve in methodology and reliability.

During this period one must envisage two meandering river systems bounding the north and southern parts of the survey area. The River Welland to the north was probably more or less flowing along its present course where it enters the fen today between Peakirk and Deeping St James, whereas the River Nene was flowing much more southeastwards along the line of what became the King's Dyke and to the south of Whittlesey island, before turning abruptly northwards towards Guyhirn and then eastwards again towards Wisbech (Hall 1987: figs 21 and 38; French and Pryor 1993: fig. 2). Deep peat deposits of the later fifth millennium BC are found only in a former channel of the River Nene near Guyhirn (Shennan 1986a and b; Waller 1994).

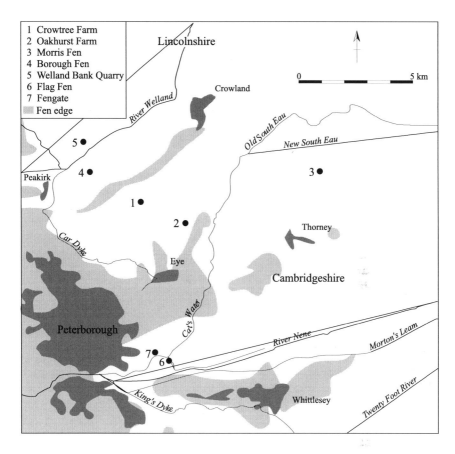

Figure 10.1 Location map of the northwestern Cambridgeshire fens and sites
discovered (C. Begg after French and Pryor 1993: fig. 2).

The remainder of this area was ostensibly dryland until the third millennium BC with peat formation previously only really occurring in deep,
relict channels in the base of the valley systems. Even then, it was only the
eastern half of the study area that was being particularly affected by rising
base groundwater levels and freshwater peat growth. The area affected
includes the fen northeast of Newborough towards Crowland, fen to the east
of Northey 'island', the fen south, east and north of Thorney 'island', the fens
east of Whittlesey, and land between Thorney/Crowland and Newborough
(Figure 10.2) (Hall 1987: figs 9, 29 and 38; French and Pryor 1993: fig. 70).
As far as one can tell from the sections examined in Newborough Fen, the
northeastern edge of Newborough is as far westward as the basal peat deposits
ever extended in this part of northern Cambridgeshire. This basal peat growth
is drowning the Mesolithic/earlier Neolithic woodland, up to at most about
the 0.3 m OD level (not taking into account any peat compression factor).

Nonetheless, this large area of dryland may have been affected by seasonal freshwater flooding influences from the two main rivers attempting to find new drainage routes through the growing peat fen to the east. The zone of influence is probably relatively small and confined to the lowest parts of the active floodplain of the day (i.e. less than 1 m OD), just as is seen upstream in the Etton/Maxey and Fengate areas (see Chapters 6 and 7).

Two of the sites found in the eastern part of Newborough/Borough Fen suggest that early prehistoric groups of people were utilizing small 'islands' of dry land within the encroaching peat fen. The Crowtree and Oakhurst Farm sites (Figure 10.2: 1 and 2) lie on small areas of higher ground (up to 0.4 m OD and just below −0.2 m OD, respectively). Two other 'island' sites have been found in Morris Fen to the east, but only one of them had indications of human presence in the form of Neolithic flints within the buried soil (at −0.7m OD) (Figure 10.2: 3). The nature of these sites' use is not well understood and probably never will be, but it is possible that they were frequented briefly or intermittently, perhaps on hunting and/or foraging routes for raw materials.

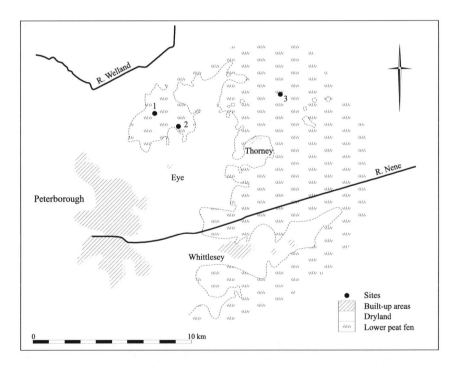

Figure 10.2 The development of the northern Cambridgeshire fens: the extent of the basal peat versus dryland in the Mesolithic to earlier Neolithic periods (site 1: Crowtree Farm; site 2: Oakhurst Farm; site 3: Morris Fen) (C. Begg after French and Pryor 1993: fig. 70).

The soil micromorphological and palynological evidence from the palaeosols present on these 'islands' indicates the existence of well-developed forest soils associated with a mixed deciduous tree assemblage dominated by lime of fourth to third millennia BC date (French 1988 a and b; French and Pryor 1993: 33–60 and 79–88; Scaife 1993). As inland in the lower Welland valley in the Etton-Maxey area, there are well-developed developed argillic brown earths of about 25 cm in thickness surviving on the fen 'islands' and skirtland area westwards. These soils exhibit characteristic well-oriented, pure clay structures in their lower halves or argillic (or Bt) horizons (Figures 4.9 and 4.10), suggesting that they formed under stable, well-drained woodland cover (Fedoroff 1968; Bullock and Murphy 1979; Fisher 1982). On the fringes of these 'islands' where the basin dips beneath about 0.5 to −0.5m OD, there are thin, immature and poorly developed soils which have been waterlogged for much of their lives. This scenario is very much mirrored in the lower Nene and Great Ouse valleys to the south (see Chapters 7 and 8).

The pollen sequences at Crowtree and Oakhurst Farm sites (Scaife 1993) indicate that the vegetation was dominated by lime woodland, with oak and hazel already present. At Crowtree Farm in particular, there is some evidence in the pollen record for human disturbance. This is suggested by woodland depletion with a decline in lime trees and the presence of ruderal herbs indicative of more open ground. The herbs present, especially *Chenopodium* type (goosefoot) and ribwort plantain (*Plantago lanceolata*), are weeds which can indicate both human occupation and animal husbandry, and these are increasing in diversity up-profile. Grasses and sedges were also present. These palaeosols and these 'islands' do not appear to have become waterlogged until the subsequent deposition of the 'fen clay' in the early second millennium BC, although their margins had been previously affected by basal peat growth.

One problem of note is the possible truncation of many of the buried soil profiles investigated, and the obvious knock-on effect on the interpretation of the palynological profiles. In only two cases, within the Borough Fen ringwork and on the western edge of Northey 'island', the buried soil profile is apparently complete. In the former case this is because of burial by an upcast gravel bank in the Iron Age, and in the latter case it is due to the slow peat encroachment on to the margin of the 'island'. Elsewhere the soils are preserved in a very open system, usually buried under some combination of either marine silt and/or alluvial silty clay deposits. In many cases, their deposition has apparently had the effect of eroding and/or transforming the upper part of the *in situ* soil profile. Originally, this was believed to have been caused mainly by the physical erosion of the upper mull horizon and lower A horizons of the soil (French and Pryor 1993: 107). Whilst there may have been some post-clearance surface erosion caused by clearance and exposure leading to a certain amount of instability of these soils, the depositionary environments associated with flooding are not envisaged as being so violent that they could strip off the upper layers of a soil so efficiently and over such wide tracts of land. Rather, it is much more probable that one is seeing a longer-term, depositional and post-depositional transformation of the upper soil horizons out of all recognition through textural change caused by the addition of eroded fine sediments carried in water, combined with the effects of waterlogging and bioturbation. This process of the effect of alluvial deposition has been described in the Welland valley (see Chapter 6).

Where might be the main focus of Mesolithic and Neolithic occupation in this area? The wide area of 'skirtland', between the Etton area and Newborough to either side of Peakirk in the lower Welland valley, the fringes of the Eye peninsula, and most of the Flag Fen basin at the interface with the lower Nene valley, are possible candidates. In this extensive area, the main problem is the blanketing effect of later alluviation which is preventing detection, although the sites may be both very infrequent and of enigmatic nature. Ironically, it is the extensive impact of extraction for gravel in the lower river valleys and fen-edge zone that will lead to new discoveries in time.

The Bronze Age (second to earlier first millennia BC)

The earlier second millennium BC witnessed the major marine incursion responsible for the deposition of the 'fen clay' (Barroway Drove Beds) (Figure

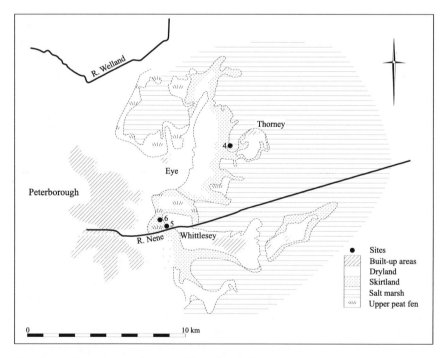

Figure 10.3 The extent of marine silt and peat fens in the later Neolithic and earlier Bronze Age (site 4: Eye; sites 5 and 6: Fengate) (C. Begg after C. French 1993: fig. 71).

10.3). The tidally influenced salt marsh drained by creeks (or rodhams/ roddons) that was created was quite a hostile environment for people and would have had a definite impact on land that had previously been available for at least seasonal exploitation. The tidal creeks are generally oriented southwest to northeast, and exhibit a dendritic pattern much like the branches of an upturned oak tree. For example, there are large rodham systems visible from the air and on the ground east of Whittlesey and Thorney (Hall 1987: figs 30, 38 and 43).

Pollen was recovered from the basal part of the 'fen clay' at both the Crowtree and Oakhurst Farm sites (Scaife 1993). The onset of marine conditions is indicated by the dominance of *Chenopodium*-type pollen, particularly glassworts and oraches, which are characteristic of saline environments. In addition, the regional vegetation is represented. Areas of dry land, presumably inland to the southwest from less than half a kilometre away, were dominated by oak and hazel with alder growing on the fen margins.

The commonest monument of the second millennium present is the round barrow and ring-ditch. There are least forty-nine barrows known on Thorney 'island' (Hall 1987: fig. 30), the Eye peninsula (Hall 1987: fig. 15) and the western part of Newborough Fen (Hall 1987: fig. 10), and at least double that number of barrows and ring-ditches has been found in a similar fen-edge or 'skirtland' position between Deeping St James and Bourne in south Lincolnshire to the north (Palmer 1994: fig. 2). These sites exhibit a distinctive linear aspect, just inland of the furthest extent of peat encroachment at this period along the fen-edge. Excavations at Borough Fen barrow 10d suggest the ditch and barrow became overwhelmed by peat from the Roman period onwards (French and Pryor 1993: 61–7, pl.VII), and at Deeping St Nicholas barrow 28 from the late second millennium BC or 1260–1000 cal BC (2850 ± 50 BP; GU-5346) (French 1994: 44 and 87). To use a conventional archaeological argument, these barrows are sited on more marginal land in terms of drainage and its ability to grow crops or allow occupation for any length of time. Perhaps also, the barrows are sited at an important conceptual interface between wet and dry worlds (after Downes 1993: 29).

The silting up of the network of tidal creeks was well underway by the middle of the second millennium BC, and would have caused considerable disruption to the outfalls of the fen rivers. A consequence of this was the initiation of peat growth on the landward side of the influence of the 'fen clay', as freshwater began to pond-back behind the salt marsh. For example, this was occurring at Deeping St Nicholas (ibid.), the western edge of Borough Fen (French and Pryor 1993: 61–5 and 68–77), on the southwestern edge of Northey island (ibid.: 92–100) and in the Flag Fen basin immediately to the north (French 1992a and b).

The importance of the palaeoenvironmental studies at the later Bronze Age Flag Fen complex (see Chapter 7) is considerable. They indicate that throughout the later second and earlier first millennia BC zones of open water were increasing steadily in extent and depth in the central, deeper parts of fenland basins, with reed beds surrounding these pools, and alder fen carr woodland fringing the margins between wet fen and dry land. The fen carr woodland appears to have mainly disappeared by the end of the Bronze Age, perhaps due to a combination of a rising water table and ever increasing exploitation without the lengthy time periods necessary for rejuvenation.

Along the fen-edge of the clay marked by the barrow cemeteries over the latter part of the Bronze Age (and continuing throughout the Iron Age), seasonal pasture would have gradually diminished as an available resource. This is hard to quantify, but must have intensified pressure on good land on the First Terrace gravels inland and westwards up the lower parts of the Welland and Nene river valleys over at least a millennium. Human adaptation to this must have been extremely gradual rather than calamitous, but may well have strengthened the desire and necessity to physically enclose parcels of land in ditched and embanked fields on drier ground inland, at least in this region. This is aptly demonstrated by the later Bronze Age field systems at Maxey (Pryor and French 1985) and Welland Bank in the lower Welland valley (Pryor 1998), Fengate in the lower Nene valley (Pryor 1980), and Barleycroft Farm (Evans and Knight 1997a) and Over (Evans and Knight 1997b) in the lower Great Ouse valley. Only the highest parts of the fen 'islands', that is above about 2.5 m OD, would have remained sufficiently dry for settlement within the fen basins themselves. There is one such possible site on the Eye peninsula (Hall 1987: fig. 15, site 2) that was found by field survey, and there are excavated sites at Welland Bank (A. P. S. 1996; Pryor 1998), Whittlesey (M. Knight pers. comm.) and Barleycroft Farm (Evans and Knight 1997a), but these are few and far between.

Whilst the upper peat was growing over most of the North Level area and encroaching onto the fen margins westwards, the fens around Thorney 'island' were subject to another major episode of marine incursion. This deposited the 'younger' or Upper Barroway Drove Beds, which were formed under salt marsh conditions, probably during the earlier half of the first millennium BC (Hall 1987: 50, fig. 30). Effectively over the eastern half of the North Level area, the landscape became extremely inhospitable and essentially unusable except for forays for fishing, fowling and possibly reed harvesting.

The Iron Age (later first millennium BC)

During the latter half of the first millennium BC, the influence of marine salt marsh conditions dwindled in the northeastern parts of the North Level, with peat growth continuing over all but the extreme western third of Borough Fen (Hall 1987: fig. 10) and the main 'islands' of Thorney and Whittlesey/Northey (Figure 10.4). The last marine incursions of this part of Cambridgeshire occurred just to the north of Thorney 'island' and just to the south of Crowland 'island' during the late Iron Age (Hall 1987: fig. 32). These marine silt deposits are called the Terrington Beds and are mainly

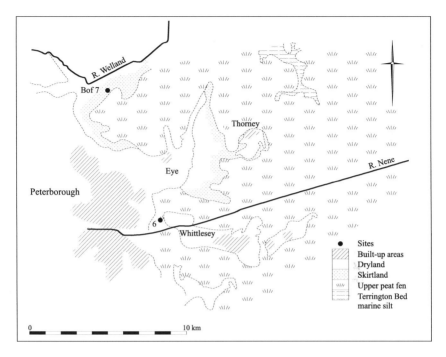

Figure 10.4 The extent of the peat fen in Iron Age times (site 6 : Fengate; BoF 7:
Iron Age ringwork) (C. Begg after French and Pryor 1993: fig. 72).

located in the fens of south Lincolnshire. Peat growth had continued to
advance both westwards and upwards, again shrinking the dryland area
available for human use.

Iron Age occupation appears to have been confined to the larger fen
'islands' and the western fen margins, at sites such as Welland Bank (Pryor
1998b), Borough Fen ringwork (site 7) (French and Pryor 1993: 68–76),
Thorney (Hall 1987: sites 31–3), Eye (Hall 1987: site 4), Cat's Water,
Fengate (Pryor 1984), Northey (French and Pryor 1993: 92–100) and
Whittlesey (M. Knight pers. comm.) (Figures 10.4 and 10.6). Most importantly at Fengate, there is now evidence for the nucleation of settlement from
the fourth to the third centuries BC (Pryor 1984). Although these sites may
have been relatively dry to begin with, they soon appear to have become
plagued by rising groundwater tables, undoubtedly aggravated by the
continuing upwards growth of peat to the east and the difficulties of the main
rivers in finding satisfactory outfalls through the fen basin. For example, a
common feature of the settlement sites is the repeated digging of the same
ditch on slightly different alignments or frequent recutting of the same
feature. This is seen particularly well, for example, at Cat's Water, Fengate
(Pryor 1984: fig. 36, M77). In addition, the first relatively thick and extensive
deposits of alluvial silty clays were being deposited as a result of seasonal

overbank flooding, for example at Welland Bank, Borough Fen ringwork and Fengate. There is insufficient data on the dating of these deposits, but the process appears to have begun in the later Iron Age and then resumed in earnest from late/post-Roman times (Figure 10.5). But it does appear that the extent of influence of these Iron Age alluvial deposits was relatively limited to the active floodplains and fen-edge of the day, up to about 3 m OD.

One site on the northwestern edge of Borough Fen and just over the Cambridgeshire/Lincolnshire border, Welland Bank, has produced excellent evidence for arable agriculture in the region based on soil micromorphological evidence alone (Figures 4.4–4.8, 10.1, 10.6 and 10.7) (French and Marsh 1999). It is important to describe this agricultural soil in some detail given the nature of recent debates on the subject of the recognition of arable farming using micromorphological techniques (Carter and Davidson 1998; Macphail 1998; Lewis 1998a; Usai 2001) (see Chapter 4). In 1997 archaeological investigations were carried out in advance of mineral extraction at the Sly Mason Field, Welland Bank Quarry, Deeping St James, Lincolnshire. Later Bronze Age/earlier Iron Age settlement activity was revealed which was associated with an extensive area of 'dark earth' (*c.* 100 m by 150 m) containing abundant charcoal and artefacts, sealed beneath the alluvial

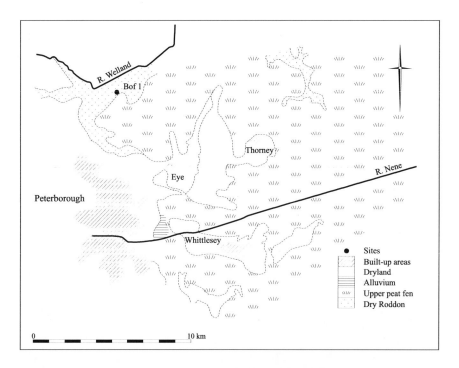

Figure 10.5 The extent of the peat fens in Roman times (BoF1: Roman farmstead) (C. Begg after French and Pryor 1993: fig. 73).

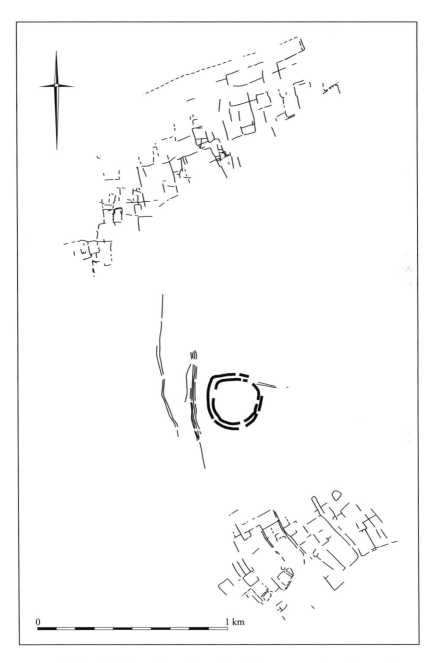

0   1 km

Figure 10.6 Plan of the later Bronze/Iron Age field systems and settlement sites at
Welland Bank, south Lincolnshire, and Borough Fen, north
Cambridgeshire (C. Begg after R. Palmer, Air Photo Services and
A.P.S., 1996 and F. Pryor 1999: fig. 55).

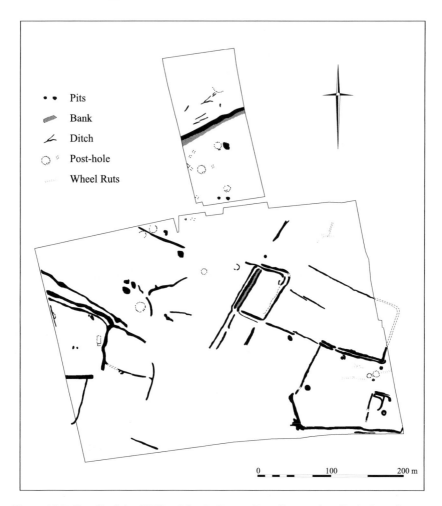

Pits

Bank

Ditch

Post-hole

Wheel Ruts

0   100   200 m

Figure 10.7 Detail of the Welland Bank Quarry Late Bronze Age/Early Iron Age
enclosures (C. Begg after A.P.S. and F. Pryor 1999: fig. 58).

overburden and developed on a well-preserved palaeosol (Figure 10.8) (A.P.S.
1996). The 'field' was defined on its northern side by a large internal bank
and external ditch. Thirteen soil profiles were taken through the pre-alluvial
soil profile for micromorphological analysis, with the aim of investigating
the archaeological integrity and importance of this rural 'dark earth'.

It should be pointed out that 'dark earth' material was found both beneath
the bank and overlapping its southern side, which suggests that it may have
undergone a lengthy period of accumulation and development from the later
Bronze Age into the earlier Iron Age. The 'dark earth' is generally characterized by one fabric with a reasonably well-developed structure, although in a
few instances there are admixtures of two or three different but more minor

Figure 10.8 Typical profile at Welland Bank showing the alluvial overburden, 'dark earth' and palaeosol developed on river terrace sand and gravel deposits.

soil fabrics present. The 'dark earth' is a sandy to sandy clay loam character-ized by large amounts of finely comminuted, humified and mainly carbon-ized organic material throughout (Figure 10.9). Despite much bioturbation, there is a rather weakly developed, small to sub-angular blocky ped structure. The soil fabric exhibits evident but irregular depletion zones of silty clay and amorphous iron, and occasionally small intrusive aggregates of reddish brown silty clay derived from the overlying alluvium. These features suggest partial mixing by some form of physical disturbance, and variable leaching and illuviation. It also contained small amounts of midden-like inclusions, namely bone fragments as well as calcitic ash. This horizon is the upper, organic A horizon of the buried soil profile.

The buried soil, both inside and outside the 'dark earth' field, is a brown earth developed on terrace/fen-edge gravels, with argillic brown earth horizon material present in places at the very base of the soil profile (Figure 4.9). This brown earth contains moderately to well oriented, intercalated fine material, exhibits a blocky ped structure and is generally decalcified, at least inside the 'dark earth' field. The subsoil here has a high silt and clay content at its upper surface, leading to localised poor permeability, which may account for some of the oriented silty clay component of the fine groundmass of the soil. A certain amount may be derived as well from subsequent alluvial aggradation and intercalation of fines down profile. This palaeosol type is characteristic of many soils in the lower Welland valley and fen-edge

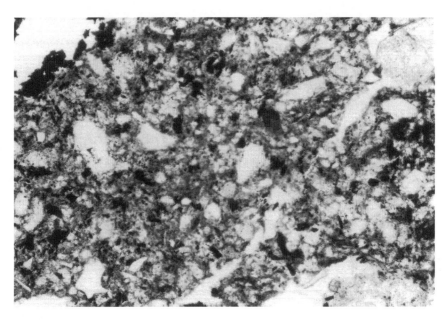

Figure 10.9 Photomicrograph of the fine groundmass of the 'dark earth' horizon at
Welland Bank illustrating the fine humified and carbonized organic
component (in plane polarized light; frame width=2 mm).

of Cambridgeshire and Lincolnshire (French 1990, 1994b; French and Pryor
1993), although it is not as well developed here as at some of the other sites
in the near vicinity (see Chapters 6–8).

In several instances, there were particular sets of microscopic features within
the 'dark earth' which suggest that some other form of disturbance of this soil
took place in the past. These occurred either in the groundmass, or in small
peds within or in a linear zone at the base of the 'dark earth' horizon. For
example, there are well-developed dusty clay coatings present as linear bands
arranged at 45 degrees within the fine groundmass. These clay bandings often
alternate with thin lenses of very fine to fine quartz sand (Figures 4.6 and 4.7),
and in one example exhibit thin crusts of strong impregnation with
amorphous iron. In two examples, these alternating clay/sand bandings occur
within sub-rounded aggregates of less than 2 cm in size. In addition, in two
profiles there are distinct concave feature cuts, less than 5 cm across and less
than 2 cm deep, infilled with 'dark earth' material (Figures 4.4 and 4.5), and
in another a near-horizontal set of laminae in a band some 15–18 mm thick
may suggest either the base of a wider ard furrow or cut of a small feature. It is
suggested that these are plough or ard marks. There is also occasionally iron
impregnated silty clay defining the edge or surface of a ped. Despite the rather
pessimistic statements by Carter and Davidson (1998) regarding the
recognition of plough agriculture from micromorphological features, the

combination of characteristics present in the dark earth at Welland Bank, all of which were observed in experimental ard ploughing exercises by Lewis (1998a), suggest that this 'dark earth' was once an ard-cultivated ploughsoil. Moreover, these diagnostic features have survived despite the usually detrimental combination of bioturbation and alluvial aggradation.

There are several other sets of microfeatures present which also indicate plough disturbance of this 'dark earth'. The common feature of inter- and intra-ped impure clay coatings within the 'dark earth' horizon (Figures 4.5 and 4.8) suggests some within-soil mass movement of fines caused by the slaking of fine material from exposed ped surfaces, probably associated with ploughing (Jongerius 1970, 1983; Kooistra 1987; Gebhardt 1990; Lewis 1998a). There are also micro-aggregates of oriented clay and fine silt called 'agricutans' (Figure 4.5) (after Jongerius 1970). The term 'agricutan' refers to the downward movement of silt, clay and very fine organic matter that occurs as coatings or infills down profile as a result of trapped water within a zone causing internal or sub-surface slaking. Finally, there is probably a minor component of the unoriented dusty clay incorporated within the groundmass which may derive from introduced fines through seasonal flooding and subsequent alluvial deposition, slaking and intercalation.

Certainly from the fieldwalking evidence, there are vast amounts of charcoal of all sizes present in the 'dark earth', which if nothing else suggests an intense concentration of fires and the deliberate collection and deposition of the carbonized material. The more minor anthropogenic-derived constituents present in the 'dark earth' are pottery, daub, bone, wood charcoal, plant remains, phytoliths, ash and rarely coprolitic material. These inclusions probably derived both from the nearby, contemporary occupation sites within the field and to the south, as well as from salt production as attested by the saltern debris (M. Dymond and T. Lane pers. comm.). Here it appears that the pre-later Iron Age organic A soil horizon has been transformed by the introduction of midden and saltern production material, and has in effect become a 'plaggen' or man-made soil. The result was the creation of an organic-rich, friable tilth on a rather poorly draining subsoil, suitable for either grain and/or vegetable crops in a fen-edge area increasingly prone to high groundwater tables and the 'clogging-up' of topsoils with fine sediment derived from overbank flood episodes.

The Roman period

As in the preceding period, archaeological evidence for settlements and field systems of the Roman period is similarly confined largely to the main 'islands' of Thorney and Whittlesey, the Eye peninsula and at Fengate (Figures 10.1 and 10.5). About ten new sites have been discovered by Hall (1987) by surface survey alone in the North Level area. It has been suggested that to enable the construction of the Fen Causeway or later first century AD Roman road from Fengate across to Whittlesey, March and eventually to

Denver in Norfolk (Potter 1981; Pryor 1984), the surface of the peat fen must have undergone a period of relative drying out. This is given further credence by the lack of subsidence of the sand and gravel dump construction road not sinking into the peat fen across Flag Fen (Pryor *et al.* 1986). Additional corroboration is also given by the presence of a Roman site situated on the Terrington Beds in the northern part of Thorney parish (Hall 1987: 51). Although this relative drying out of the surface of the peat may have enabled a degree of pastoral expansion and exploitation of the peat fens, it is unlikely that there was any settlement on these peat areas themselves.

As mentioned in Chapters 6–8 on the lower Welland, Nene and Great Ouse valleys, there does appear to be a renewal of sediment aggradation occurring from the later Roman period. This was also commonly occurring elsewhere in England such as in the upper Thames valley (Lambrick and Robinson 1979; Robinson 1992). In many areas, such as at Etton (French *et al.* 1992; French 1998a), Fengate (French in Pryor 1984), Hockwold-cum-Wilton (Salway 1967, 1970), Earith (Churchill 1970) and Stonea Grange (French 1996b) there is good soil, molluscan and/or palynological evidence for the onset of increasingly wet conditions on the fen-edge, more open conditions everywhere, and new clearance and exploitation of heavier subsoils inland and upstream. This led to fine silt and clay sediments being eroded downstream in the stream/river systems and deposited through seasonal overbank flooding where the lower river valleys met the peat fen-edge. As a result, vast tracts of land became at least seasonally flooded and subject to alluvial aggradation. For example, the area between Etton and Peakirk/Borough Fen, Deeping St James to Werrington where this was occurring in the lower Welland valley encompasses an area of about 10 sq km. The whole of the Flag Fen basin and the Fengate 'shore' to the south would have been similarly affected (see Chapter 7). Undoubtedly, this would have caused changes in the physical use of the landscape, that is constriction of land available in the winter/early spring months, and expansion of usable land in the summer/early autumn months. This probably explains the apparent absence of late Roman and later sites over vast tracts of the fen-edge and lower river valleys, and perhaps may have led to different forms of land ownership and husbandry which we have yet to decipher.

Essential reading

French, C.A.I. (1994) *Excavation of the Deeping St Nicholas Barrow Complex, South Lincolnshire*, Heckington: Lincolnshire Archaeology and Heritage Report Series No. 1.

French, C.A.I. and Pryor, F.M.M. (1993) *The South-west Fen Dyke Survey, 1982–86*, Cambridge: East Anglian Archaeology 59.

Pryor, F. (1998) *Farmers in Prehistoric Britain*, Chapter 8, pp. 109–23, Stroud: Tempus.

11 Monitoring desiccation, erosion and preservation of sites and landscapes in the East Anglian wetlands and elsewhere

Introduction

Any archaeologist who has worked in the East Anglian fens of eastern England has witnessed the generally low level of the groundwater in drainage ditch systems and the paucity of waterlogged archaeological remains discovered and reported on. Although the historical reasons for this in terms of drainage history are relatively well known (Darby 1940), there is little in the way of concrete data to chart the processes and timescales involved in the dewatering and the actual destruction of the archaeological resources. There are only a few experiments currently in operation which have tried to halt and reverse the processes of dewatering, desiccation and erosion in the fenland region, namely the establishment of reserves at Wicken and Holme Fens and Fowlmere in Cambridgeshire (Figure 5.6). More particularly, there are only a few monitoring projects attempting to find out the parameters of destruction (French and Taylor 1985; Caple 1993; Corfield 1993, 1996; Caple et al. 1997; French et al. 1999; Van de Noort et al. in press). What follows is an attempt to set out the known processes at work and to chronicle the current state of research into the hydrology of the East Anglian fenland region and elsewhere in Britain, and the implications for the survival of the archaeological record, as a series of case study examples directly relevant to Chapter 2. Much of this essay has already been published (French 2000d) and is reproduced here with the permission of the Heritage Trust of Lincolnshire and the Fenland Management Project, but it also includes up-to-date details from various current hydrological monitoring projects.

Drainage, erosion and peat wastage in the East Anglian fens

Although the drainage of the fens began some 350 years ago (Darby 1940) with concomitant soil/sediment erosion and peat wastage, the pace of destruction has increased dramatically since the 'Dig for Victory' campaign of the Second World War.

Peat wastage occurs as a result of desiccation and coincident oxidation, in combination with much increased micro-biological action. The whole process is hastened by wind erosion (R. Evans 1981; Evans and Cook 1986), especially when peat and sandy peats are exposed in the spring and early summer (Davies *et al.* 1972; Hodge and Arden-Clarke 1986; R. Evans 1992). For example, a recent survey of wind-blows in the Cambridgeshire fenland and Nottinghamshire between 1968 and 1977 indicated that moderately and severely damaged crops occurred about one year in every two for each month from March to May (M.A.F.F. no date). In another survey of farms on erodible sands and peats in Lincolnshire and Nottinghamshire, 36 per cent of the total area surveyed was liable to erosion, although it only affected small parts of the fields (Wilkinson *et al.* 1969). The type of crop also influences the susceptibility to erosion, with the smooth seed-beds and slow germination for crops such as sugar beet, carrots or onions being more prone to wind-blow than land sown to cereal crops (R. Evans 1992).

Drainage and peat wastage combine in a deleterious cycle of aeration, deflation and erosion. The digging of ditches for drainage initiates dewatering and deflation of the peat making it susceptible to wind-blow, the ditches run dry and silt up, thus necessitating their regular deepening and widening. This in turn leads to further wastage and the start of another cycle of degradation. Up until the mid-1980s, many of the internal drainage boards of the East Anglian fenland region were re-cutting drainage dykes throughout the region on a five to seven-year continuous cycle. In many cases, the setting of levels in the cuts, dykes and ditches was controlled by individual judgement and existing land-use, rather than according to any overall monitored scheme. If drainage on this kind of scale continues, organic archaeological remains whose continued preservation depends on the maintenance of anaerobic environments will degrade and eventually disappear from the record.

Rates of peat wastage have been well recorded (see Seale 1975; Richardson and Smith 1977; Hutchinson 1980). For example, peat wastage following a new drainage scheme in the fens is very rapid and can be up to 220 mm per year, although this slows to a longer term average of *c.* 10–18 mm per year. It has been calculated that the ground level of peat in the Cambridgeshire fens has fallen by up to 4.6 m in places since 1652 (Purseglove 1988: 83). Indeed at the Holme Fen post, 3.9 m of peat has wasted away between 1848 and 1950 (Figure 2.2) (Hutchinson 1980).

Now, a decade on from this, personal observation would indicate that this process has begun to slow and stabilize to a considerable degree, at least in some areas of the fens. Often only the minerogenic material now remains in place of peat, the organic fraction largely having disappeared through defla-tion and microbial decay. Indeed, in many places for example, the underlying fen clay or marine-derived clastic material is being ploughed up onto the surface. Here the peat resource is effectively gone. A similar state of affairs was observed repeatedly by the writer on site visits in all three fenland counties during the Fenland Management Project (1981–5). Today, the upper peat is now rarely more than the ploughsoil, *c.* 20–30 cm thick. Often, where peat does just survive, the farmers are actively encouraging its destruction by subsoiling to increase its fresh mineral content.

The inherent, humic qualities of peat which give it great agricultural value also cause its susceptibility to erosion once it becomes dry. Similarly, the humic component of soil has an advantageous effect on its structure, stability and fertility (see Chapter 4), and any reduction in organic matter content is a primary factor in a soil's increased susceptibility to erosion (Hodge and Arden-Clarke 1986: 13). The almost total dominance of arable farming practices in the fenland today has led to accelerated losses of organic matter caused by the increased oxidation consequent upon the improved drainage and aeration of ploughed soils. For example, the organic matter content of arable soils may be as low as 1–2 per cent, as opposed to 5–10 per cent for pasture soils (Johnston 1973). In addition, soil structural stability may be reduced by about a factor of five between pasture and arable fields (Low 1972), and soil ped structural cohesion by a factor of 12 (Dettman and Emerson 1959). In both these cases, the organic matter content is well below the critical level of 3.4 per cent, below which soils may become liable to structural instability (Greenland *et al.* 1975). Thus the intensively drained and deflated former peaty organic soils of much of the southern fenland region are extremely fragile and in many areas largely past conservation, if not non-existant. The 'sponge' cannot just be rewetted nor the peat become rejuvenated!

Groundwater and soil moisture

Given this pessimistic assessment of the status of the surviving upper peats of the fenland region of eastern England, what of the preservation conditions in the underlying fenland sediments, soils and subsoils? In large measure, this is dependent on the level and quality of the groundwater in the system, as well as the variable composition of the underlying drift geology.

The ability of a soil to absorb and retain moisture is crucial to the hydrology of an area (Ward and Robinson 1990: 129). The groundwater or the subsurface water in soils and rocks that are fully saturated acts as a vast regulator in the hydrological cycle and sustains streamflow during periods of dry weather (ibid.: 174). Rainfall enters the soil at ground surface and moves downwards to the water table, which marks the upper surface of the zone of saturation. Just above the water table is the capillary fringe in which most of the soil pores are full of water. Between this zone and the soil above is an intermediate zone where the movement of water is mainly downwards. For example, in the floodplain of a typical river valley situation, the capillary fringe often extends into the soil zone or even to the ground surface itself, whereas on the valley sides water drains into the intermediate zone and the saturated groundwater zone beneath.

In the fenland region, this model becomes much more complex, but the principles remain the same. There are extant and relict river systems draining into and through the fens, different types of palaeosol and subsoil, and overlying sediments in varying thicknesses (see Chapters 6–10) (French 1992a; French *et al.* 1992; French and Pryor 1993; Waller 1994). The maintenance of a consistently high groundwater table and sufficient soil water in the capillary fringe, intermediate zone and soil is essential both for the well-being of the organic component in agricultural soils as well as the organic archaeological and environmental components of the stratigraphic complexes in the fenland basin.

As the East Anglian fenland is a former wetland, there are obviously numerous regional and more global threats to the maintenance of the soil- and groundwater system. Although Coles (1995: 9–20) has already set out these threats of terrestrialization, changing climate and sea level, acid rain, water pollution and drainage, it is worth reiterating some of the points made about water abstraction in particular. Groundwater abstraction for domestic, agricultural and industrial uses continues to increase. If forty rivers in England are suffering from excessive abstraction (N.R.A. 1993), ground-water levels in the lower reaches of the river valleys entering the fenland system and the associated fenland basins will all be similarly affected. By implication, the groundwater levels in the fenland basin will also be falling, and with a knock-on but little known or understood effect on the archaeo-logical record. Specific instances of deterioration have now been observed, for example of wetland sites of special scientific interest (SSSI) such as at East Runton Fen SSSI in Norfolk where up to about one-third of the protected area has been adversely affected by water abstraction from boreholes in the surrounding vicinity (N.R.A. 1993). Personal observations during the dyke survey in Cambridgeshire (French and Pryor 1993) and whilst subsequently examining buried soil profiles at the forty-two sites examined in the Fenland Management Project indicated that well-preserved, waterlogged sediments and archaeological contexts were the exception rather than the rule. Unlike the Netherlands, where groundwater tables are generally maintained at 0.5–0.75 m below the ground surface, water levels in the fenland are kept at substantial depths (i.e. 2–4 m) below the ground surface. Only where there was a combination of features cut deep into relatively impermeable subsoils, or in deeply incised palaeochannels or the deepest parts of drainage basins, was waterlogging encountered,.

Hydrological monitoring projects of archaeological sites and landscapes in England

Although there is a long-standing interest on the part of most archaeologists in the effects of groundwater table fluctuations and water abstraction on the preservation of the archaeological record (e.g. Raikes 1984; Biddle 1994), very little long-term investigative research has been conducted. Fortunately, this problem is now beginning to be addressed through a variety of research projects.

Pioneering, small-scale hydrological survey work in relation to the perceived threat to the preservation of organic remains posed by gravel extraction was carried out at the Neolithic causewayed enclosure at Etton, in the lower Welland valley, Cambridgeshire (French and Taylor 1985; Pryor 1998a). There, groundwater level monitoring before and during extraction was carried out for fifteen months in 1982–3 using dipwells set out at 20 m intervals across the site. The results were compared with the maintained water levels in the adjacent drainage channel (Maxey Cut) and the local rainfall records. Within four months of the quarry pumps being turned on, the groundwater table within 200 m of the quarry fell by over 1 m and never recovered. Most importantly this maintained level was now below the level of the deepest archaeological feature in the same area. Moreover, the lower surface of the wood found in the ditches of the causewayed enclosure began to exhibit serious surface degradation within the same period. This project dramatically demonstrated how fast the groundwater table could fall as a result of continuous pumping of the adjacent gravel quarry, and how rapidly this dewatering from below could lead to the deterioration in organic preservation of the wooden remains in primary archaeological contexts.

This type of baseline research work has been extended in recent years to several new monitoring sites in England, namely the waterlogged Iron Age/Romano-British site at Market Deeping on the margins of the south Lincolnshire fens (Corfield 1996), the quarry site of Willingham/Over in the southern Cambridgeshire fenland/Ouse river valley (French *et al.* 1999), the Iron Age sites at Sutton Common in south Yorkshire (Van de Noort *et al.* in press) and in urban medieval York (Kenward and Hall 2000). Most of these research projects been funded and monitored by English Heritage, and there are relevant results available from all of them.

At Market Deeping, the soil water content has been recorded using a neutron probe, the groundwater table has been measured using dipwells and at the same time changes in the chemical state of the soil/water complex and the preservation of a variety of buried wood types are being measured (H.T.S. 1997). Although the groundwater table generally correlates with the rainfall pattern, the level of soil moisture below about 0.4 m from the ground surface appears to be being maintained regardless of external events. Unless the external conditions change, for example through an approaching gravel extraction programme, reasonably good waterlogged conditions can be expected to be maintained below a depth of about 1.5 m below the modern ground surface. Nonetheless, the dissolved oxygen content of the soil water drops in the summer months, and the conductivity figures fluctuate in no apparent pattern. These observed changes could be detrimental to continued good organic preservation, especially in the capillary and intermediate zones of the subsoil and palaeosol.

At Willingham/Over there is a new quarry development affecting about 450 hectares of alluviated river gravels, fen-edge and the area of the former Willingham Mere (Figures 8.1, 8.4 and 11.1). Here, a hydrological monitor-

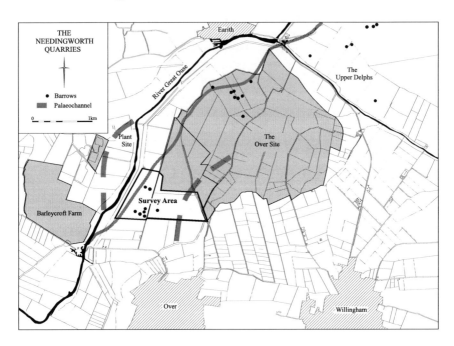

Figure 11.1 Location map of the Willingham/Over extraction area, hydrological monitoring programme study area, palaeochannels, and northern and southern barrow groups (C. Begg).

ing project has been instigated to examine long-term changes in the soil and groundwater systems associated with buried Neolithic-Bronze Age landscapes before, during and after commercial gravel extraction with associated water abstraction, and archaeological intervention (French and Davis 1994; French *et al.* 1999). Three years of monitoring (1994–7) prior to gravel extraction (French *et al.* 1999), and two years of monitoring since extraction began have now passed. The results are summarized here.

No soils or sediments have been found to be completely saturated at any time of the year except within the relict channel systems (Figure 11.2). Nonetheless, there is a trend towards reducing conditions in the ground-water over the three-year monitoring period (Figure 11.3). In particular, the fine-textured and higher organic content of the peat and alluvial overburden deposits leads to better moisture retention than in the more open and coarser textured buried soils beneath. It is suggested that the crucial level below which preservation is favoured is below about 1 m OD, which is equivalent to the marginal fringes of the higher ground of the gravel levees in the floodplain and the lower edges of the first terrace. As peat formation (with associated waterlogging) did not reach this kind of height until the later Bronze Age, this suggests that it was still substantially dry land in earlier prehistory, thus explaining the general lack of earlier prehistoric waterlogged

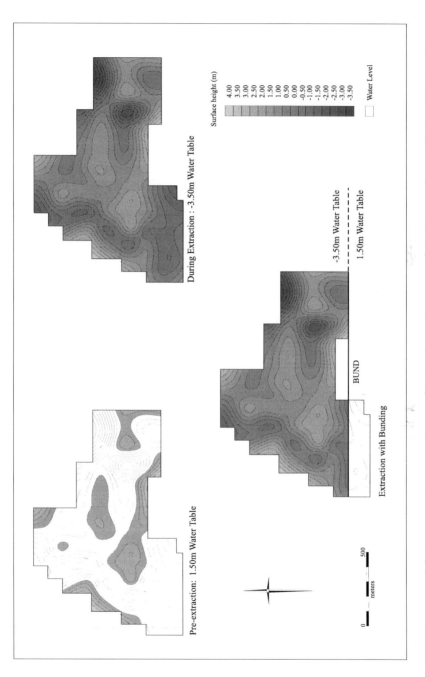

Figure 11.2 The pre- and during extraction groundwater tables in the southern part of the Over study area (C. Begg/C. French).

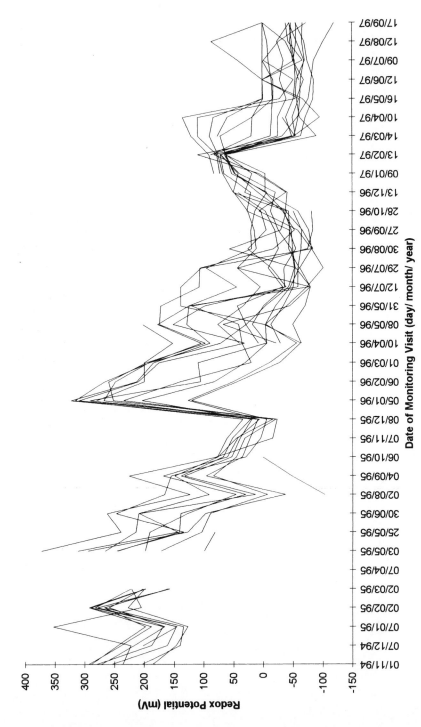

Figure 11.3 The redox changes in the groundwater over three years of pre-extraction monitoring (after HLE Ltd. in French *et al.* 1998: fig. 6).

sites and evidence found in the area. It is not really until the Iron Age when groundwater tables are sufficiently high and encroaching on the land above 1 m OD that waterlogged archaeology is found, such as at Haddenham site V to the east (see Chapter 8).

The electrical conductivity levels appear to act as a guide to whether a soil/sediment horizon is drying out and subject to physical/chemical change. The well-preserved buried palaeosols on the higher areas of the valley floor (i.e. above 1.5 m OD) exhibit high conductivity levels (French *et al.* 1999: fig. 6), and tend to coincide with those deposits which are drying out. Desiccation leads to change in the chemical state of the soil/sediment, the outcome of which often has detrimental results, such as the frequent formation of secondary minerals (e.g. micritic calcium carbonate, gypsum), iron oxides and hydroxides acting to change base status, soil texture and organization.

Soil moisture levels in the alluvial ploughsoil are considerably influenced by periods of increased rainfall, the stage in the arable cycle and periods of irrigation, as well as the ability of the fine, silty clay texture of the alluvial overburden to retain moisture (French *et al.* 1999: fig. 9). In contrast, soil moisture levels in the top of the sand/gravel terrace subsoil are mainly influenced by the influx of groundwater either through seasonally higher levels and/or deliberate irrigation. The various soil, peat and alluvial deposits situated between the groundwater table and the alluvial ploughsoil show much more variation in soil moisture content depending on their organic content, texture, relative proximity to the groundwater table and alluvial ploughsoil, and the absolute height above sea level.

The data from the southern barrow group at Over indicate lower and more variable moisture contents than those recorded in the northern barrow group (French *et al.* 1999: fig. 10) (Figure 11.1). In the latter, the mineral soils are located at a lower height OD, closer to the groundwater table and contain more silt and organic matter, and therefore have a higher moisture-holding capacity.

The specific data from the ring-ditch fills of one barrow of the southern barrow group suggest that the silt- and clay-dominated tertiary infill of the barrow ditch is acting as an anaerobic seal (Figure 11.4). Conversely, the moisture content drops off dramatically in the coarser matrices of the secondary and primary fills below. It is only the primary fills that are affected by the seasonal rise and fall of the surrounding groundwater table, but their coarser texture prevents the efficient retention of bound water. Thus, it is probable that the ditch is acting as a 'sump', both in terms of groundwater levels and atmospheric moisture percolating partially down profile. Nonetheless, the seasonal rise and fall of the groundwater table may pull water out from below. Whether or not air then invades this vacant pore space probably has more to do with the effectiveness of the alluvial 'cap'. Whether the evident waterlogging in the lower half of the barrow ditch is contemporary or not with the monument, the barrow ditch will certainly be susceptible to the general effects of dewatering, such as would be caused by future

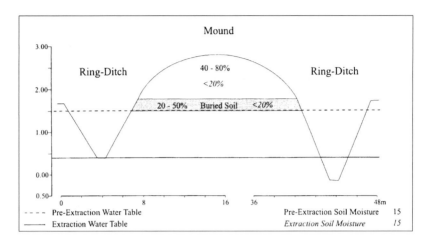

Figure 11.4 Schematic representation of the pre- and during extraction soil
moisture content of the southern barrow (C. Begg after C. French).

quarrying operations. In time, this would negate any of the beneficial effects
of the alluvial overburden and the fine-grained infilling of the tertiary ditch
fill.

Gravel extraction with associated water abstraction has now been underway for two years. Three 6-inch water pumps are in continual use to drain
the working extraction area, removing about 1,800 gallons per minute.
This has maintained a lowered groundwater table in this area at a depth of
some 5 m below the present ground surface or at about −3.5 m OD (Figure
11.2).

Results from the monitoring since extraction began suggest that several
rapid changes are occurring in the system. Although the conductivity values
of the groundwater have remained as before, the pH values have become
more calcareous and the groundwater table for the whole southwestern area
of the quarry has dropped by about 5 m (Figure 11.2). The sphere of influence
of the pumping operation in the active quarry has an effective radius of at
least 600 m from the active quarry face. In addition, large amounts of iron
oxides have found their way into the modern ditch systems of the study area
from the subsoil and groundwater, the redox values are generally low negative values and the dissolved oxygen component of the groundwater is now
higher than pre-extraction values. Moreover, now that the southern face of
the quarry has been bunded with impermeable clay (after 1.5 years of extraction), the groundwater table has recovered outside the extraction area to the
south, upstream and inland, but continues to fall within the extraction area
beyond the working face. This set of results suggests that anoxic preservation
conditions are no longer being maintained and that all organic deposits
within the extraction area are now under the threat of destruction during the
life of the quarry (in this case 25 + years).

The most striking data are the soil moisture values for the one barrow mound and ring-ditch remaining within the extraction area (Figure 11.4). Here the ploughsoil has effectively dried out, topped up occasionally by ambient rainfall, and the buried soil/gravel terrace transition has less than 20 per cent moisture content. The barrow mound has really begun to dry out with values rarely above 25 per cent soil moisture content. The only zone of real moisture retention remains the alluvial overburden acting as the tertiary fill of the ring-ditch (at *c.* 40–60 per cent), at depths of about 0.7–1.3 m below the ground surface. Moreover, these results have remained consistent since extraction and pumping began. But, once beyond the influence of the water abstraction by pumping, that is more than 1 km away, the soil moisture results appear to be very similar to the pre-extraction phase results.

This monitoring work suggests that several indicators are very important. It is probably the combination of the proximity to the groundwater table as well as the speed of burial that controls the extent of waterlogging. If the soil/deposit was not quickly sealed by the alluvial deposits, thereby preventing the ingress of oxygen, there will be a well-oxidized soil/deposit with a low potential for organic preservation regardless of its proximity to the groundwater table.

Other monitoring research projects

There are a variety of other relevant research studies currently underway in the fenland region, as well as in Yorkshire and Holland. The Institute of Hydrology and the British Geological Survey are conducting research for the National Rivers Authority Anglian region on an appropriate methodology for the rapid evaluation of the probable impact of new abstractions. As Coles (1995: 17) points out, this could well be adapted to predict the impacts on archaeological deposits in the fenland. At the late Bronze Age wooden platform and avenue site at Flag Fen, Peterborough (Pryor 1993), the Robens Institute of the University of Surrey is investigating the effects of adjacent sewage treatment on the preservation of the wood on site. In addition, a bunded freshwater lake was created at Flag Fen in 1986 over the bulk of the site in order to try to prevent further deterioration of this 3,000 year old wooden-built site. In a related project, Caple and Dungworth (1997) have examined the chemical changes occurring in simulated anoxic conditions such as those found at Flag Fen and elsewhere. In particular, they have suggested that the redox potential should be maintained between −100 and −400 mV to insure the maintenance of anoxic preservation environments.

At Sutton Common, Yorkshire, hydrological monitoring is being used to determine the best way of promoting long-term *in situ* preservation of the wooden remains at two Iron Age sites linked by a wooden causeway crossing a peat-infilled former channel (Parker Pearson and Sydes 1997; Van de Noort *et al.* in press). Recent land management practices at the site had led to a rapid acceleration in dewatering which had to be arrested to prevent final destruction of the organic record. To halt destruction of the organic record here, a co-operative approach to *in situ* preservation was taken. This involves a variety of public bodies acting together, buying the land, and re-engineering the drainage system of the area, with the effectiveness of this management scheme being monitored by high resolution hydrological monitoring including groundwater levels, redox conditions and micro-biological activity. In this case, it has been demonstrated that the stability of the burial environment is of prime importance, and that it is fluctuations that lead to rapid destruction.

A recent evaluation study of archaeological and organic remains carried out at 44–5 Parliament Street in York on medieval deposits (Carrott *et al.* 1996) has demonstrated the detrimental effects of recent building techniques on the preservation of the organic record (Kenward and Hall 2000). Dewatering during the construction of a recently demolished building combined with the down-profile movement of salts derived from an overlying concrete slab has caused recent deterioration in the preservation status of plants, parasites and insect remains. This is the first time that such a dramatic and recent deterioration in organic remains has been observed in twenty intensive years of archaeological work in York's city centre. Thus the extensive use of concrete rafts and slabs that were for so long favoured as an engineering solution to ensure the *in situ* preservation of urban archaeological remains could pose a very serious problem to continuing organic preservation in urban areas such as York. Without immediate monitoring of the designs for preservation, much of medieval York that is believed to be reasonably well preserved beneath basement and cellar level, could in fact be a fast-diminishing resource.

Finally, there is a very important monitoring programme currently in progress which is examining peat desiccation in the Limmen Heiloo area of north Holland (R. Exaltus pers. comm.). After one year with groundwater tables lowered by 0.5 m, the peat on the sand 'islands' or 'terpen' was exhibiting increased rates of bioturbation, about a 30 per cent increase in the void/air space, and receding levels of calcium carbonates. These changes will eventually affect the state of preservation of bone artefacts and artefact assemblages of the associated prehistoric sites, as well as the pollen/plant record and wooden remains.

Conclusion

It is only through this kind of data-gathering research that future management schemes may be more appropriately designed. Coles' (1995: 31–46, 77–92) recent survey of various management approaches to wetland conservation indicates the wide range of possible approaches. But without possessing sufficient predictive data as well as monitoring any *in situ* preservation scheme as it is implemented, it will remain difficult to be certain of the longevity and effectiveness of any management programme. Information is sadly lacking about the potential areas of land influenced by draw-down effects associated with water abstraction and large-scale gravel quarry operations, to say nothing of the continuing threat of drainage schemes and concreting over much of our urban environments. Moreover, hydrological data on the specific effects of dewatering on the various components of the archaeological record is essential. Only then will we be able to devise and implement effective management and preservation strategies to ensure the survival of at least some of this rapidly diminishing resource in the former wetlands of a region such as East Anglia.

Essential reading

Caple, C. and Dungworth, D. (1997) 'Investigations into waterlogged burial environments', in A. Sinclair, E. Slater and J. Gowlett (eds) *Archaeological Sciences 1995*, pp. 233–7, Oxford: Oxbow Monograph 64.

Coles, B. (1995) *Wetland Management: A Survey for English Heritage*, Exeter: Wetland Archaeological Research Project.

French, C., Davis, M. and Heathcote, J. (1999) 'Hydrological monitoring of an alluviated landscape in the lower Great Ouse valley, Cambridgeshire', *Environmental Archaeology* 4: 41–56.

Parker Pearson, M. and Sydes, R. (1997) 'The Iron Age enclosures and prehistoric landscape of Sutton Common, South Yorkshire', *Proceedings of the Prehistoric Society* 63: 221–59.

Van de Noort, R., Chapman, H.P. and Cheetham, J. (in press) '*In situ* preservation as a dynamic process; the example of Sutton Common, UK', *Antiquity*.

Ward, R.C. and Robinson, M. (1990) *Principles of Hydrology*, Chapters 5 and 6, London: McGraw-Hill.

12 Wyke Down and the upper Allen valley, Cranborne Chase, Dorset, England

Introduction

Combined palaeoenvironmental and geoarchaeological fieldwork focusing on the later Neolithic-earlier Bronze Age periods in the Wyke Down and upper Allen valley area of Cranborne Chase in Dorset (Figure 12.1) is producing new types of data (Allen 1998; French *et al.* 2000) with which to re-examine the land-use models put forward principally by Barrett and Bradley (Barrett *et al.* 1991a and b).

The Cranborne Chase landscape is a 'classic' example of the chalk downlands in southern England or the Wessex region (Figure 5.3), with dense concentrations of prehistoric monuments of all kinds present in close proximity and in different parts of the valley system. This area has been the focus of archaeological investigations by the 'fathers' of British field and scientific archaeology for the last two centuries, such as Colt Hoare (1812), Pitt-Rivers (1887, 1888, 1892, 1898) and Crawford and Keiller (1928). Moreover, many of the theories derived from fieldwork in this area are now central to the interpretative framework of British prehistory (e.g. Bradley 1978, 1984; Thomas 1991; Barrett 1994). But despite the significant amount of field archaeology done in Cranborne Chase and the importance of the area to British prehistory, it has never really been investigated from a palaeoenvironmental perspective until now.

Rationale behind the project

The project described below was designed to investigate recurrent signatures of land management practices in the geoarchaeological and ecological records of buried land surfaces in the chalk downland region of southern England, using the upper Allen valley of Cranborne Chase as its pilot testing area. The new data collected were to be used to develop our understanding of the interactions between prehistoric settlement and land-use, the monumental landscape and landscape/environmental change.

A principal emphasis of the project was to be the prospection for and analysis of buried palaeosols. Buried soils constitute the only readily available

Figure 12.1 Wyke Down/Allen valley, Dorset, survey area location map (H. Lewis after Barrett *et al.* 1991: fig. 1.1).

and widespread reservoirs of evidence for prehistoric land-use in the otherwise severely plough-denuded Wessex region. They also contain time-depth information in terms of landscape and land-use change, but this record has rarely been systematically exploited, especially in regard to site-specific, pre-monument land-use. Buried soils under monuments and associated colluvial/alluvial deposits were to be investigated using a combined approach of soil stratigraphic and micromorphological study with pollen and molluscan analyses, in order to document landscape changes in the later Neolithic and earlier Bronze Age. All of these methods have been used in previous research in the area (Barrett *et al.* 1991a and b; Cleal and Allen 1994; Allen *et al.* 1995; Cleal *et al.* 1995), but only very rarely have all three of them been combined (Macphail 1993; Cleal *et al.* 1994). Problems of interpretation, reworking and preservation, especially in the unique environments underneath monuments such as barrows in the chalk downlands (calcitic parent material with overlying weakly acidic barrow deposits), ensure that molluscan and soil pollen methods on their own can only partially address the history of landscape changes in the region. Previous soil micromorphological studies (e.g. Gebhardt 1992; Courty *et al.* 1989) suggest that it is possible through a pedogenic approach and by analogy with experimental results to identify the nature of prehistoric landscapes and land-use practices, as these are reflected in relict pedofeatures found in modern soil horizons. Furthermore, it is possible to examine these practices on both a site-specific and a wider regional scale over time. The project designers believe that only through the systematic comparison of the results of these methods can a well-defined and detailed history of the late Neolithic and earlier Bronze Age landscape in this region be developed.

Most of the existing detailed palaeoenvironmental work is based on the analysis of molluscan assemblages and, more rarely, on palynological data from ditch fills and buried soils from a number of monuments (e.g. on Cranborne Chase, Hambledon Hill, Wessex Linear Ditch project, King Barrow Ridge) (Barrett *et al.* 1991a and b; Entwhistle and Bowden 1991; Allen 1994, 1995, 1997a and b, 1998; Cleal and Allen 1994). This evidence has been coupled with more generalized colluvial sequences (eg. Strawberry Hill; Heytesbury) and with the regional pollen record in order to reconstruct sequences of early prehistoric land-use (Allen 1992, 1995). When specific monuments have been investigated (Cleal and Allen 1994; Allen *et al.* 1995), only rarely has micromorphological analysis of the buried palaeosols accompanied archaeological, molluscan and occasionally palynological studies (Fisher 1982, 1983, 1991; Macphail 1993; Scaife 1994). The free-standing sequences at each monument investigated require corroboration and integration with the wider archaeological and palaeoenvironmental record of the region, along with testing of previous palaeoenvironmental results through the application of finer sampling intervals and interpretation in the light of recent disciplinary/technological developments and ecological and experimental studies (Allen *et al.* 1993).

The present state of knowledge concerning the environmental evidence for land-use during the late Neolithic to the Middle Bronze Age in Wessex may be summarized as follows. The regional pollen record shows an increase in forest clearings over time, and a change from small, short-term clearings to larger and longer-term clearings by the second millennium BC (Kerney *et al.* 1964; Thorley 1981; Scaife 1982, 1988). The implied connection (inferred from a small amount of archaeological evidence, supplemented by the use of ethnographic analogy) is increasing human clearance of woodland and scrub vegetation, and greater maintenance of open areas for settlement and pastoral and arable use (Bradley 1978; Barrett 1994). Associated with this record is evidence indicative of a period of accelerated erosion and colluviation processes during the second millennium BC (Allen 1992). This is often cited also as evidence for the intensification of agricultural land-use, but a variety of factors may have been responsible for this erosion such as soil destabilization due to forest clearance, intensification of arable practices in general, 'evolutionary' technological changes in tillage implements, or even extensive abandonment or lack of management of much of this landscape, none of which has been addressed in detail across the landscape. The molluscan record is the most comprehensive (Kerney *et al.* 1964; Evans 1971; Bell 1983; Allen 1992, 1995, 1997, 1998; Green and Allen 1997), and suggests an increasing opening-up of woodland over these periods, with more frequent occurrence of grassland areas and disturbed, possibly tilled, land.

The importance of systematically examining buried soils in the chalk downland region for indicators of landscape and land-use changes lies in the fact that many past and current models of social practices in prehistoric southern England as a whole are based primarily on the archaeological remains of this area (Bradley 1978: Barrett *et al.* 1991a and b; Barrett 1994). Barrett (1994) for example, suggests that the fourth millennium BC was marked by long fallow systems in a partially cleared landscape, with extensive mixed agriculture practised by a mobile community. Long-term land-use and landscape perception changes, relating the agricultural system and the funerary monuments of the region to the development of land tenure, are said to have culminated in the evolution in the second millennium BC of a short fallow and more agrarian system, with traction-based tillage, perm-anent settlements and land division. Despite the long-standing popularity of models such as this, which invoke land-use and subsistence changes to explain the archaeological record in the region, very little systematic effort has been expended to document the proposed changes themselves (the evidence cited above comes mostly from excavation-driven projects). The project described here set out to examine a number of broadly contempor-aneous buried soils and colluvial/alluvial/riverine deposits in one area of the region, namely in the upper Allen valley, and to provide an opportunity to assess, test and/or refine such models on both site-specific and sub-regional scales in the light of new evidence.

The project is also an attempt to address the key interpretative problems associated with each technique when used in this chalk downland context. For example, to observe accurately the pedological effects of agricultural land-use in thin section through soil micromorphology is not always easy or straightforward (Macphail *et al.* 1990; Gebhardt 1992; Carter and Davidson 1998; Lewis 1998a; Macphail 1998; Usai 2001). The recognition and interpretation of true woodland molluscan faunas is also fraught with inter-pretative difficulties, especially when dealing with landscapes which may have been in a state of transition from woodland to open ground and/or which may have been subject to periods of decalcification (Cameron 1978; Evans 1991; Bell and Johnson in Bell *et al.* 1996). The interpretation of pollen assemblages from buried land surfaces and soils, especially from calcareous soils and sediments, may be affected by a variety of taphonomic problems (Dimbleby and Evans 1974; Crabtree 1996). Moreover, there is an apparent dearth of sub-regional pollen sequences for the chalklands of southern England as few suitable deposits with good preservation have been located. Only by repeatedly using the three methods in combination from similar contexts with fine sample resolution will these specialisms provide reliable results applicable to archaeological questions about this landscape. Thus the expected results of this three-fold approach will be of wide use to the whole archaeological community involved with the interpretation of past landscapes. Finally, the land-use model(s) developed through this research project will have a predictive value for the other chalk downland areas of the Wessex region, for example in the Stonehenge environs (Richards 1990; Cleal *et al.* 1995).

Specific aims

The specific aims of the project are two-fold and interlinked. First, to re-examine a selection of scheduled and unscheduled prehistoric monuments, namely a selection of Neolithic long barrows, Bronze Age round barrows of the Wyke Down group, the Neolithic Dorset cursus and the Iron Age Gussage Down field systems by targeted excavation to allow environmental sampling for new pollen, molluscan and soil micromorphological analyses. This will allow the establishment of chronologically controlled palaeo-environmental sequences to augment existing studies in the area (Allen 1995, 1997a and b; Green and Allen 1997; Allen and Green 1998). Second, the geomorphological survey of the upper part of the Allen valley will employ aerial photographic survey to facilitate geographical information system mapping of erosion versus aggradation zones in the landscape, plus making systematic augering transects followed up by sampling trenches (where appropriate) to extract pollen, soil and molluscan samples from zones of colluvial and alluvial aggradation, old land surfaces, and relict channel systems in the valley bottom. This will make possible the assessment of the processes of change and degradation in the landscape, and allow prospection for off-site buried landscapes containing new palaeoenvironmental data. All the results will be combined to produce new sub-regional palaeoenviron-mental sequences and new models of land-use change in the earlier to mid-Holocene, and to re-examine existing models based largely on prehistoric funerary monument distributions and applications of social theory (cf. Bradley 1978, 1998; Barrett 1994).

Field methodology

As a rule, the actual methodologies employed in a field project are defined in the specific design brief and are rarely available for others to see. In this instance, it is worthwhile setting out the methodological approach adopted for this project, as follows:

For the investigation of the monuments :

1   Select prehistoric monuments of major periods in different parts of the valley (i.e. on brow, upper slopes, lower slopes and valley bottom) for survey and sampling with all members of the project team.

2   For the most part the monuments are scheduled and therefore require scheduled monument consent before any work begins; prospective sites must be identified, and the project design and access to them discussed, first with the relevant English Heritage inspector and ancient monuments warden, the land owner, and then an application must be made to the Secretary of State for consent.

3   Once consent has been obtained, initial hand auger survey will be done to construct monument profiles, to confirm the presence/absence and thickness of buried soil survival beneath the mound and on the inner berm of the ring-ditch, and to ascertain the depth of infill deposits in the ring-ditch.

4   Conduct topographical survey and plan of each monument at a scale of 1:20.

5   Undertake magnetometer and resistivity survey of each monument to reveal structural components; this is occasionally augmented by ground-penetrating radar survey (see Pierce 2000).

6   Make a full photographic record of each monument being examined as they survive today.

7   Select areas for sample excavation on the basis of 1–6 above and in discussion with the English Heritage inspector and warden, and the land owner; sample excavation through ditches, banks and mounds of *c.* 1×2 m, 2×2 m and 2×3 m in size.

8   All excavated sections are thoroughly described, recorded at 1:10 and photographed.

9   Then four series of samples are taken for molluscan, soil micromorphological, plant macro-fossil and palynological analyses from the buried soil, ditch and bank/mound material, and if possible, samples for radiocarbon assay and optically stimulated luminescence (OSL).

10   Finally, all sample excavation trenches must be reinstated, with every effort made to follow the pre-existing contours.

11   During the course of the fieldwork and post-excavation analyses it is possible to acquire detailed information on the present condition of the monument and the sequence of past land-use history of the site with respect to its current scheduled status; this new information could aid in future management decisions taken by both the responsible national and county curators.

For off-site investigations, the following procedures were employed:

1   Obtain the land owner's permission for access.

2   Borehole transects were made by hand and power auger across the valley system, with *c.* 100 m between auger holes and the transects set at *c.* 500 m interval widths, with these intervals closed up in the valley bottom (Figure 12.2).

3   Aerial photographic mapping of the study area was done, delimiting zones of thin and thick soil cover with respect to known archaeological record (Figure 12.11).

4   An erosion assessment map for the region using data derived from 2 and 3 was produced (Figure 12.11).

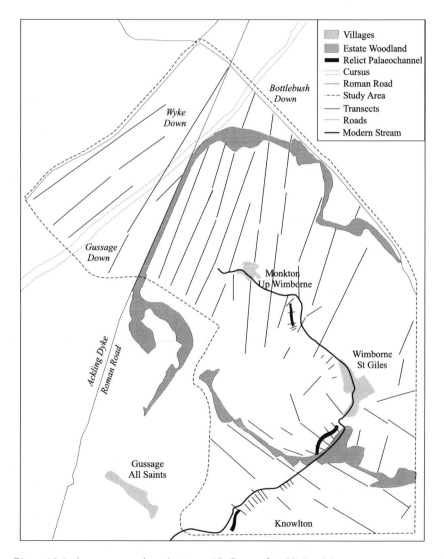

Figure 12.2 Auger survey location map (C. Begg after H. Lewis).

5   Relict meander loops in the river valley bottom were targeted for augering to recover palaeobotanical, molluscan and radiometric dating samples.

6   On the basis of 1 to 3, zones of colluvial aggradation or lynchet systems were identified for sample excavation using small trial trenches (1 × 2 m), again with the land owner's permission.

Results to date

Introduction

At the time of writing four Bronze Age barrows of the Wyke Down group had been investigated, a Neolithic enclosure at Monkton-up-Wimborne, the Dorset cursus on Wyke/Bottlebush Downs and a very late Upper Palaeolithic site at Deer Park Farm had been investigated (Figures 12.1 and 12.3). Each was damaged, either by antiquarian trenches and/or recent ploughing.

The conventional magnetometer and resistivity surveys of the main part of the Wyke Down barrow group as well as four individual barrows several large swathes of the Dorset cursus have been an indispensable prospection tool. These surveys have enabled the exact positioning of the sites as well as indicating possible structural aspects of the monuments prior to sample excavation (Figure 12.4) (GSB Prospection 1998, 1999, 2001; French *et al.* 2000).

The palaeoenvironmental data from the barrows

The four barrows of the Wyke Down group investigated exhibited different construction techniques in terms of numbers of ring-ditches, mound type and composition (French *et al.* 2000). But the palaeoenvironmental data recovered from ring-ditches, mounds and palaeosols were all very similar.

Samples for pollen analysis were taken from the palaeosols and the turf mound material for each barrow mound and analysed by Dr Rob Scaife. Given the calcareous subsoil and thin rendsina type profiles present, any pollen preservation would have been a bonus. As might be expected, pollen preservation was very poor overall. Nonetheless, the buried soil beneath barrow 34 produced pollen of bracken and ferns, as well as grasses, and might imply an herbaceous and grassland habitat. There are a couple indicators of former woodland present, namely *Polypodium vulgare* (polypody fern) and *Corylus avellana* (hazel). The possible palaeosol from beneath the flint cobble-stones below the turf mound of barrow 41 (Figure 12.5) produced relatively more pollen and suggests a cold and open herbaceous environment, possibly of the Loch Lomond stadial towards the end of the late glacial period.

A series of samples for land snail analysis were taken from the ditch, palaeosol and mound contexts of each barrow by Dr Mike Allen. Although there was variable shell survival, the molluscan record has provided a consistent picture of the contemporary environment during and after barrow

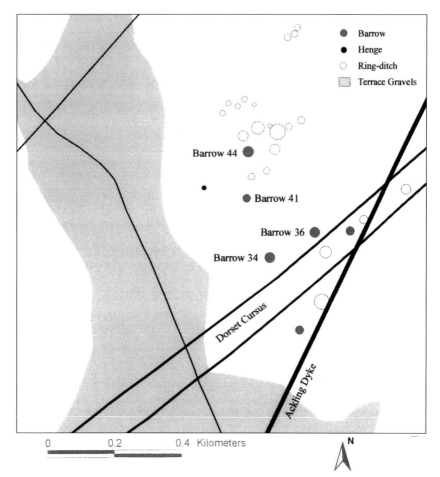

Figure 12.3 Wyke Down terrain model showing the Dorset cursus, henges and
           barrows with the terrace gravels in the valley bottom shaded
           (C. Begg after P. White).

construction. The palaeosol beneath barrow 41 exhibited the poorest
molluscan preservation of any context examined, exhibiting an impoverished
open-country fauna, possibly indicative of cold climate, periglacial type
conditions existing in late glacial times. This helps to corroborate both the
palynological and soil micromorphological evidence. There were also
relatively very low numbers of open-country snails in the fill of the ring-
ditch, dominated by *Vallonia costata*. It is likely that there has been some
decalcification of the ditch deposits subsequent to their infilling.

On the other hand, all the contexts in barrow 34 (Figure 12.6) exhibited
good preservation of molluscs. Each major context was consistently
dominated by the open-country species *Vallonia costata*, *V. excentrica*, *Helicella
itala* and *Vertigo pygmaea* (Figure 12.7). This is strongly indicative of well-

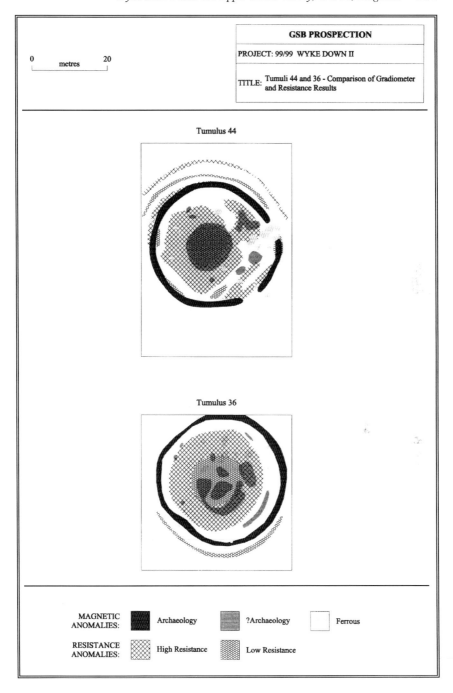

Figure 12.4 Combined magnetometer/resistivity surveys of barrows 36 and 44
(GSB Prospection).

Figure 12.5 Section through the mound, solifluction debris and palaeosol of barrow
41, Wyke Down.

Figure 12.6 Trench through barrow mound 34 with the thin turf and rendsina at the base of the profile, Wyke Down.

drained, close-cropped, grass sward being established by the earlier Bronze Age in this area (M. Allen pers. comm.). There is little evidence of woodland or shaded contexts existing in the near vicinity, but the secondary fill of the inner ditch did exhibit a more restricted range of open-country snails, with the lower secondary fill containing the only shade-loving species present (mainly *Carychium tridentatum* and *Punctum pygmaeum*). However, the presence of these species along with the catholic species *Trichia hispida* and *Cochlicopa* sp. probably reflects the establishment of longer (? ungrazed) grass on and around the barrow, or possibly in the ditch itself. These assemblages are mirrored to an extent by those in the outer ditch, although the diversity of shade-loving species of Clausiliidae may reflect changes in the wider landscape rather than on the barrow itself.

The palaeosols

The sample excavation through the mound of barrows 34, 36 and 44 revealed a turf and weathered subsoil horizon comprising what appears to be a thin (*c.* 10–15 cm), rendsina type of palaeosol profile (Ah, B/C, C) (Lewis 1998b) (Figures 12.5, 12.6 and 12.8). There was no indication of plough, ard nor spade marks visible, but in such a small area of excavation one cannot be categoric on this score. It contained no relict features of any B horizon material, is strongly earthworm reworked, but is not perfectly sorted with

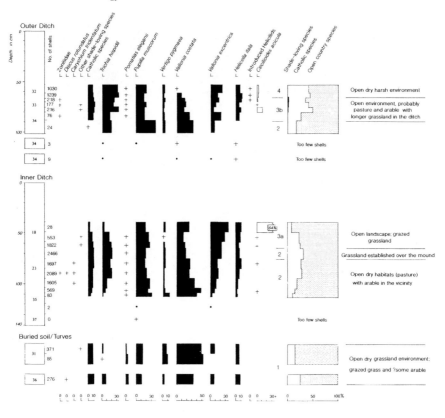

Figure 12.7 The molluscan assemblages from the turf mound and buried soil of barrow 34, and both ring-ditches (M. Allen and Liz James).

respect to its chalk fragment component. These features suggest that this was a grassland soil either with some early disturbance which has left no trace, or which saw some continued input of fine chalk through physical disturbance. Nonetheless, the implication is that the soil was already severely denuded and altered, and had become open grassland by the Bronze Age. In addition, Dr Allen suggests that the high silt component of the secondary fills of at least two of the ring-ditches (34 inner and 36) could be indicative of a local, aeolian component which could imply a very open, arable environment in the near vicinity in middle-later Bronze Age times (but see below). In addition, the turves that comprise the bulk of each barrow mound contain a significant clay content. This hints at an origin as part of an argillic brown earth type of soil, which is known from elsewhere in the valley (Fisher 1991; and see below).

The section beneath barrow 41 revealed a different story (Figures 12.5 and 12.9) (Lewis 1998b). Beneath the turf mound was an irregular horizon of large, compacted flint cobbles, probably some kind of late glacial drift or solifluction deposit. Almost no soil cover appears to have survived on these cobbles and beneath the turf core of the barrow mound except for a thin turf line, implying both poor soil development and severe truncation in pre-barrow times. Underlying this cobble horizon were a series of near-contiguous solution hollows with palaeosol material preserved within them exhibiting two horizons (Figure 12.5). The upper horizon was a reddish brown silty clay loam with a small, sub-angular blocky ped structure and the lower horizon was a dark brown silt clay loam. The observation that most of the clay is located in the pore space instead of being incorporated within the fine groundmass, causes 'alarm bells to ring'. Despite the interpretation that the translocation of clay and the inclusion of silt and organic matter particles creating a dusty aspect are generally related to soil disturbance (Macphail *et al.* 1987), this could be related to a number of other events. These include the deposition of drift or solifluction debris, pre-barrow land-use and/or erosion, barrow construction or even modern plough destruction of the mound above. In summary, the most likely interpretation is that this profile represents soil formation in an interstadial phase within the last glacial period and is a palaeo-argillic brown earth (after Fisher 1991: 16), with strong evidence of much more recent disturbance.

The observable horizon sequence found within the turves of the barrow 41 mound suggested that they originated from an argillic brown earth type of

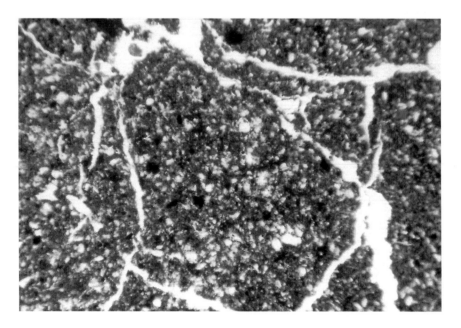

Figure 12.8 Photomicrograph of typical buried rendsina beneath the chalk central cairn in barrow 34 (in plane polarized light; frame width = 2.25 mm).

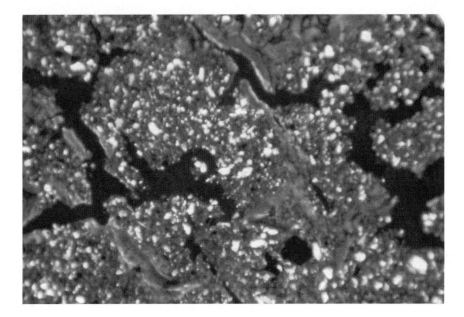

Figure 12.9 Photomicrograph of the clay-rich palaeosol beneath barrow 41 (in crossed polarized light; frame width=4.25 mm).

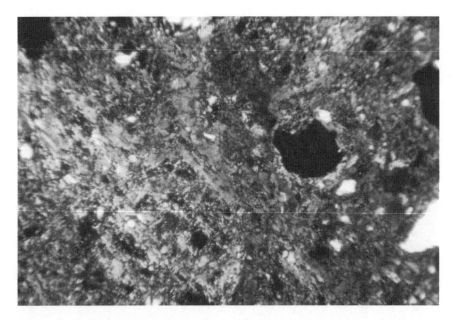

Figure 12.10 Photomicrograph of the argillic brown earth at Deer Park Farm (in crossed polarized light; frame width=2.25 mm).

profile (Lewis 1998b). The turves possess a thin (<3 cm) turf horizon (or Ah) developed on an horizon depleted of clay and organic matter (or an eluvial or Eb horizon). This sequence suggests that an argillic brown earth or former forest brown earth had once existed beneath the mound, and had been systematically truncated by turf cutting for barrow construction. Subsequently, the turves within the mound had been affected by the deposition and translocation of dusty and dirty clays within the pore space. This could be indicative of modern disturbance, and perhaps even localized wind-blow of fine material from adjacent ploughed fields. Even allowing for compression of the organic mat (see Macphail and Cruise 1996), there is only very thin turf development beneath the turves of the mound. This suggests that the pre-barrow soil had suffered severe truncation, removing most of the soil profile, and/or insufficient time and/or good management to allow the growth of a thick turf sward. This could be associated with repeated stripping of turf and soil for earlier monument construction in the vicinity (e.g. Wyke Down henges 1 and 2, or other barrows in the Wyke Down group), and/or the stripping and stacking of the turves from the very spot chosen for the building of barrow 41 at a slightly later date.

Earlier prehistoric sites in the study area that have also been investigated include a late Neolithic enclosure about 1 km to the northeast of the Wyke Down group on the brow of the chalk downland and a very late Upper Palaeolithic lithics assemblage with a thermoluminescence date of 10740±1120 BP about 5 km to the northeast at Deer Park Farm (Green *et al.* 1998). The Neolithic enclosure ditch at Monkton-up-Wimborne produced a rich snail fauna from its secondary and tertiary fills indicative of a landscape that was becoming rapidly open and the lenses of both turf and wind-blown silt suggesting a mixed pastoral/arable land-use. At Deer Park Farm, the lithics assemblage was associated with a well-developed argillic brown earth soil profile surviving beneath the modern soil profile (*ibid.*). The lower half of the *in situ* brown earth profile had survived, and exhibited a well-oriented clay component indicative of an argillic or Bt horizon (Figure 12.10) (after Avery 1980; McKeague 1983). The apparently 'absent' Eb and Ah horizons were probably incorporated in the modern ploughsoil through physical mixing processes. Interestingly, this palaeosol survives at the geological transition between the chalk downlands of Cranborne Chase and clays mixed with gravels of the Reading Bed Series where argillic brown earths are expected to be found (Fisher 1991: 16, fig. 2.1).

Other recent archaeological investigations at the Southern Henge of the Knowlton Circles by the University of Bournemouth have also revealed a palaeosol beneath a ploughed-out henge bank (Burrow and Gale 1995). Here, a 7 cm thick, dark brown and stone-free silty clay loam or probable turf horizon was developed over a 11 cm thick, calcareous, silty clay stony layer or the weathered A/C horizon. This is indicative of a typical rendsina profile already being developed by the later Neolithic or later third millennium BC. However, micromorphological analysis of this same profile suggests that this soil was once a poorly developed argillic brown earth which has suffered some pre-burial denudation and more recent disturbance through the impact of modern agriculture.

The Dorset cursus

Four sample sections were excavated through the northern and southern cursus ditch and bank on the *c.* 1 km stretch leading to the Bottlebush Down terminal (Figures 12.1 and 12.3). Unlike those sections excavated previously by Richard Bradley (Barrett *et al.* 1991: figs 2.12 and 2.13), these new sections revealed fills that were dominated by clean chalk rubble. Moreover, the surviving bank was much denuded in height and appeared to have been ploughed in pre-Roman times. Although the field investigation has only just been completed and the palaeoenvironmental samples have yet to be processed, it looks as if this length of cursus bank was deliberately slighted back into the ditch shortly after the cursus was constructed. This is in contrast to the other fill sequences observed further to the south in the same monument where the homogeneous organic silt loam and fine chalk rubble fills suggested a natural infilling over a lengthy time period. These observations in the northern sector of this Neolithic monument would suggest a complete change in its importance in the landscape within the later Neolithic, and possibly a complete realigning of the fields and boundaries in this part of the downland landscape. Moreover, the buried soil present beneath the cursus bank was also already a thin rendsina by the end of the fourth millennium BC, although there was a slightly greater organic component and better structure to the rendsinas observed beneath the Bronze Age barrows. The presence of this soil type mirrors the soil evidence from the near-contemporary Knowlton Southern ring henge further down-valley.

The off-site survey

The combined results of the aerial photographic and systematic augering surveys across the *c.* 8 by 4 km stretch of river valley are shown in Figure 12.11. The augering survey has revealed a few instances of relict argillic brown earths but much more commonly rendsina soil profiles (French *et al.* 2000). The rendsina-type soils appear to be widespread, with argillic brown earth survival in only a few zones. The latter's survival is often associated with tributary dry valleys and upper to mid-slopes currently under pasture in the southeastern sector of the study area.

The augering survey has also indicated a generally low level of colluvial deposition (thicknesses of less than 70 cm) and/or preservation within tributary dry valleys and the main valley and no alluvial deposition west of Wimborne St Giles (Figure 12.12). The zones of soil accumulation that have been identified by stereoscopic mapping and redrawn using AutoCAD Map (by Rog Palmer) are shown in Figure 12.11 as shaded zones and the probable zone from which this material has been derived is shown by the hatched

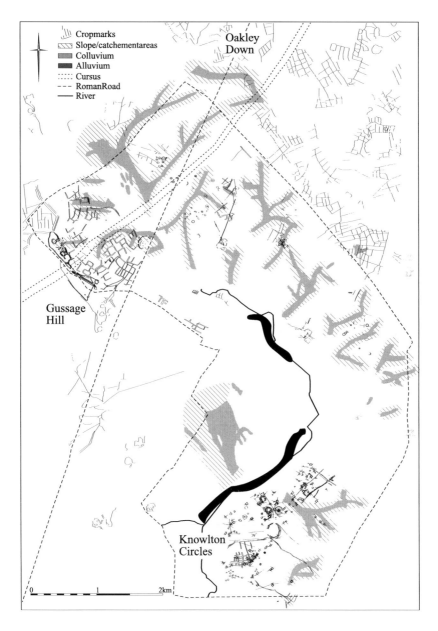

Figure 12.11 The location of the earlier and later Holocene palaeochannel systems
in the Allen valley (indicated by the linear alluviated zones in black),
as well as the colluviated dry valleys (shaded) exhibiting limited signs
of erosion and aggradation set against the aerial archaeological record
(R. Palmer; after Bowen 1990: fig. 1 and with permission of English
Heritage).

areas. Most of these erosion and accumulation zones have been tested and confirmed by the augering survey and test pits (Figure 12.12). These zones are also contrasted to the aerial photographic record of the archaeology in Figure 12.11 using information from Bowen (1990) and English Heritage (K. Stoertz pers. comm.), as well as new mapping by Rog Palmer. What is crucial to note is that the erosion/accumulation zones are concentrated in the now dry tributary valleys which bisect the downland slopes, and in localized parts of the river valley bottom. This in itself suggests that hillwash/ colluvial type erosion is localized and not necessarily universal across all areas of the chalk downland slopes. Unlike some other parts of the southern English chalklands (e.g. Sussex) (Allen 1992; Bell 1992) there is nothing like the same quantity of soil movement and accumulation in the upper Allen valley. But, as the tributary valleys and the upper 2.5 km of the Allen valley are now dry and only rarely contain even winterborne streams and the river just west of Wimborne St Giles has shrunk from a wide and deep river to very shallow and narrow stream since the earlier Holocene, so it appears that there has been extensive change in this hydrological system over at least the earlier Holocene.

Major discoveries of the augering survey have been the location and sampling of relict palaeochannel systems at three different loci in the study area (Figure 12.11). The first and probably earlier palaeochannel is situated between Wimborne St Giles and Monkton-up-Wimborne on the southern

Figure 12.12 Example of a thin colluvial accumulation over a brown earth in a dry valley, Monkton-up-Wimborne.

side of the modern floodplain of the River Allen (Figures 12.2 and 12.11). Here, still just visible in the field are two cut-off meanders of a relict river channel, up to 3 m deep and about 30 m wide, with a completely water-logged profile composed of a basal calcareous silt 'mud' with abundant included fine chalk fragments overlain by a sequence of well-preserved detrital and wood peats. The basal chalky silt mud could represent erosion of bare slopes under periglacial conditions at the end of the last glacial period. Palynological analysis of the basal peat and contact zone with the underlying chalky silt indicates evidence for an open and herbaceous plant-dominated landscape (Figure 12.13) and demonstrates that the fills of this channel are of late Devensian and early Holocene age that is, relating to the upper Palaeo-lithic and early Mesolithic periods. This is succeeded by the development of open scrub woodland dominated by juniper, birch and pine which suggests the beginnings of the climatic amelioration in the early Holocene. It is believed that the pollen sequence in the peat extends further into the earlier Holocene, but further analysis plus associated radiometric dating of the peat sediments is obviously necessary.

The second channel system lies just to the southwest of St Giles House, about 0.5 km south of Wimborne St Giles and 1 km to the north of the Knowlton henge complex (Figures 12.2 and 12.11). Here on the northwest side of the present River Allen lies a broad (*c.* 50–60 m), shallow (<1.8 m) meander over a distance of about half a kilometre. The infilling sequence is comprised of basal detrital reed peat and alternating horizons of calcareous silt, organic mud and brown silty clay loams, which together suggest variable inputs of eroded soil material accumulating under shallow water conditions. Initial palynological analysis of the basal peats and overlying colluvial/alluvial sequence indicates an open and mixed arable pastoral landscape, probably of later prehistoric or historic times, and relatively small amounts of soil movement into the active floodplain in more recent times. The palaeochannel deposits appear to be completely waterlogged today, although they may have suffered desiccation in the past which could cause problems for the preservation of pollen and its interpretation.

The third palaeochannel sequence was located in the floodplain immedi-ately to the west of the Knowlton henge complex (Figures 12.2 and 12.11). Here, a broad, double channel about 100 m across and up to 1.5 m deep was infilled with wood and detrital peats, with thin lenses of calcareous silt hillwash interrupting peat development. Although this is yet to be analysed for its palynological data, one may speculate that this could well be indicative of the uptake of land from woodland in the Neolithic and Bronze Age periods.

Nonetheless, it would appear that these discoveries are the only other glacial-Holocene peat sequences to have been found and analysed for the whole of the southern chalk downlands after one on the Isle of Wight (Scaife 1984, 1987) and another just east of Durrington Walls (Scaife 1994). As such, these new pollen data may hold the initial information necessary to build the first sub-regional vegetational sequences for the area.

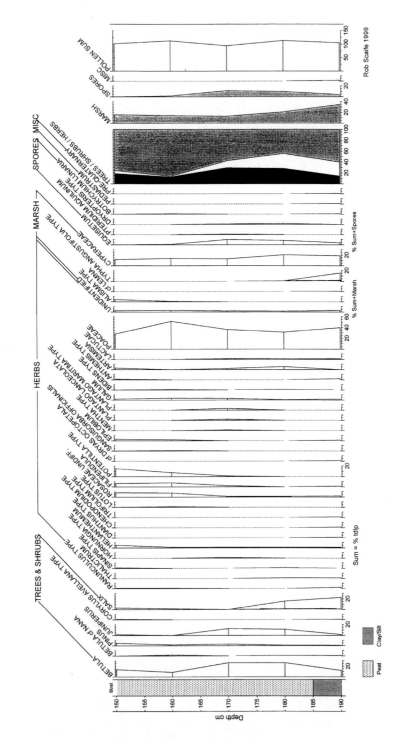

Figure 12.13 The late glacial/early Holocene pollen sequence from Wimborne St Giles (R. Scaife).

Some preliminary thoughts on landscape change in the upper Allen valley

It is now beginning to appear that a stable soil and slope system has been established in the upper Allen valley since at least the early second millennium BC, if not considerably earlier than this. There was also a considerable lessening in freshwater through-put in the valley system from at least the mid-Holocene. The soils were already mainly thin rendsinas under grass by the main period of barrow building on Wyke Down in the earlier-middle Bronze Age or the first half of the second millennium BC. But every indication from the turves in the cursus ditches and in the barrows is that argillic brown forest earths had previously existed on this slope, as was the case in the buried soil beneath the bank of the Southern Henge at Knowlton and at Deer Park Farm. However, these are not very well developed forest soils by any means. Indeed, Fisher (1991: 17) has suggested that argillic brown earth soils were probably once much more prevalent in the area than previously realized, naturally occurring on the more clay-rich subsoil outcrops such as the clay-with-flints, and perhaps even on the chalk downland itself which dominates the region. Thus, this initial work appears to begin to reinforce much of Fisher's (1991) model.

But there are several observations which are not satisfactorily explained by this model alone. The palaeosols surviving beneath all four barrows of the Wyke Down group that were investigated had apparently suffered several episodes of truncation and/or turf and soil stripping prior to barrow construction. Also, the palaeosol associated with the Knowlton Southern ring henge was already a thin rendsina by the late Neolithic, as was the surviving soil associated with the Dorset cursus banks. So, if there had been major change in soil type associated perhaps with wind-blow and sheetwash erosion caused by the disruption of once thicker forest brown earth soils, this may have occurred significantly earlier in prehistory. In particular, perhaps the major change in land use and associated soil type change occurred much earlier in the Neolithic period. Obviously this requires more proof based on further targeted investigation of earlier monuments in the same study area.

In addition, it is possible that the rendsina profiles beneath the cursus bank, henge and barrows may be exceptional and thin anyway, and rather unrepresentative. Why, for example, is the rendsina profile under each of the four barrows investigated less than 15 cm thick, even with a compression factor of one-third (see Macphail and Cruise 1996), while present day rendsina profiles in the adjacent fields are generally 25–32 cm thick? At the Southern Henge, Knowlton, the rendsina/relict argillic soil profile beneath the henge bank is somewhat thicker at 28 m, as is the truncated argillic brown earth profile at Deer Park Farm, but these are nowhere near the thickness of the soils that are postulated in the models of this area at say *c.* 45 cm thick. Perhaps because of repeated turf stripping to provide building materials for the numerous mounds, banks and roofs of monuments and structures that were constructed in these chalk downlands during the Neolithic and earlier Bronze Age, there has been severe denudation of certain parts of the earlier Holocene soils in this area of chalk downland. Going one step further, perhaps the climax soil development model is seriously flawed, and some areas of chalk downland never really developed thick forest brown earths in the first place as occurred on the clay-with-flints subsoil areas elsewhere in the same study area. Instead some areas, especially on the downland slopes, may have supported thin brown earths on chalk. This resulted from woodland development in the earlier Holocene being more patchy and less long-lived than envisaged, and as a result these areas were the first to be exploited from an early period in terms of woodland removal and both arable and pastoral use. These areas therefore had a greater propensity for forming thin brown earths which more easily developed into thin grassland soils and consequently became exploited as such during the Neolithic and Bronze Age periods.

An alternative impression and model that is now beginning to unfold is that there was much more a mosaic landscape of different soil types and associated vegetation present in the area from early in the Holocene (Table 12.1). This might be envisaged as argillic brown forest earths supporting stands of mature deciduous woodland on the clay-with-flints outcrops on the top of the down and in the base of tributary dry valleys running downslope across the downs, brown earths associated with more open woodland on the downland slopes and in the valley bottom, and a marshy floodplain zone with reeds and fen carr-like vegetation. As a result of the presence of these sub-environments, perhaps different areas within this landscape were treated and utilized differently to take account of this variation in the first place from the Mesolithic period onwards. This mosaic of different soil types and depths or the differential soil development model would go some way to explaining why there are variable soil types and survival depths in different areas of the chalk downland and beneath monuments. Thus this monumental landscape of the Neolithic and earlier Bronze Age may well have been selected for its inherent natural characteristics and then treated and maintained differently in terms of land exploitation and the built environment, resulting in different survivals as we discover and investigate them today.

Although wind and water erosion must have occurred sporadically depending on soil exposure, disturbance and locally extreme climatic events, they have not generated thick aggraded deposits in the any of the valley bottoms investigated. Rather there are thin colluvial and alluvial deposits never amounting to more than *c.* 50–70 cm of aggradation. This is unlike the situation observed elsewhere in the region (Allen 1992) and unlike many of the models proposed to explain soil loss (Catt 1978, 1979; Macphail 1992; Allen 1994). For example, a conservative estimate of soil depth loss in the Cranborne Chase area is 18 cm (Fisher 1991: 17), whereas Catt (1979) suggests as much as 1–4 m of loessic material may have eroded off this chalk

Table 12.1 Comparative examples of soil change and erosion sequences in the
Holocene in the upper Allen valley in southern England, the lower
Aguas valley of southern Spain, the Troina valley in north-central Sicily
and the Dhamar region of highland Yemen

Allen valley, Dorset, England	Aguas valley, S-E Spain	Troina, Sicily	Dhamar, Yemen
Soils:			
(argillic) brown earths developed in early Holocene; rendsinas developed subsequently	calcitic loams developed in colluvial marls in late 3rd millennium BC	organic sandy clay loams developed on calcitic loam colluvium by 3rd and 1st M BC	thick, humic soils with argillic horizons developed on calcitic loam colluvium by 3rd and 1st M BC
Erosion:			
major soil type change and disturbance prior to 3rd–2nd M BC; river constriction and infilling; slight colluvial aggradation on lower slopes of valley	extensive gullying, colluviation and terrace development in 2nd M BC, Roman period, 9–10th and and 15–20th centuries AD	change from river bed/boulder erosion to fine-grained overbank sediment; major smoothing of slopes with colluvium pre- and post-3rd–1st M BC; 3–4 phases of river incision, infilling and terrace formation	major periods of colluvial/alluvial aggradation before and after organic soils developed on slopes and in valley bottoms
Environmental factors:			
temperate; low relief; slow weathering substrate; locally extreme erosion events	steep slopes; unstable, easily saturated and highly mobile subsoils; recent instability through EC policies, tourism and dewatering	high, steep relief; rainy/snowy season; thunderstorms; volcanic activity; recent EC agricultural policies and rural abandonment	high, steep relief; rainy season; valley head dams by 1000 BC; recent dewatering

downland landscape in both late glacial/early post-glacial times under
periglacial conditions and again in the Holocene due to human activities.
Also, J. Boardman and D. Favis-Mortlock (pers. comm.) have run a soil erosion
model for the chalk downlands of Sussex with a loss of about 1 m of soil.
Although it is doubtful whether this much soil loss was ever involved in the

upper Allen valley, losses of up to 20–30 cm of soil could have occurred off the chalk subsoil areas, but with virtually no erosion off the heavier subsoils such as clay-with-flints and the Reading Beds areas of the study area. The only reasonable answer is that erosion of brown earth soils on chalk subsoils did not occur on such a grand scale as is often envisaged. Erosion was much more localized and less dramatic than conventionally thought, and it mainly occurred much earlier in the Holocene than the late Neolithic–Bronze Age. Also, there was a much greater through-put of water in the earlier Holocene as demonstrated by the discovery of the large relict palaeochannel systems, which may have flushed at least a proportion of the eroded soils through this part of the valley system to beyond our study area. Subsequent and intensifying land-use, coupled with wind and water erosion, has kept the soils exposed, thin and mono-horizonal from that period until the present day. This model is contrary to the mainstream of landscape interpretations for this area which would see the major periods of erosion and soil change occurring during and after the time the Wyke Down barrows were built, that is in the middle-later Bronze Age or the second half of the second millennium BC, associated with land-use intensification and the development of enclosed settlements and field systems (Bradley 1984, 1998; Barrett 1994).

Future work

It is essential to continue to investigate and analyse in detail the peat and sediment sequences present in relict river meanders between Wimborne St Giles and Knowlton. This will establish the subtleties of vegetational change in the mid- to later Holocene palaeobotanical record, and indicate periods and sources of erosion in the catchment. The difficulty of finding suitably well-preserved organic deposits is surmountable through systematic persistence and good field judgement.

The colluviated zones discovered by the augering survey in different parts of the slopes of the upper Allen valley must be targeted for trenching, especially for micromorphological and molluscan sampling and analyses. Also, the wealth of new and existing molluscan data should be re-examined using diversity indices as a measure of how localized is the snail data and what does it really represent in land-use and vegetation terms. So too a selection of prehistoric earthwork sites of different periods and in different parts of the valley system must be sample excavated to develop the time and sub-regional depth of picture that is just beginning to emerge. The suggestions put forward here regarding different stages of soil development occurring at similar times in different parts of this landscape with associated but different routes of exploitation must be tested. In particular, the question of the relative effects of deforestation, sheetwash and wind erosion, plus different human activities being responsible or not for denuding and altering soil types prior to the Bronze Age, can only be addressed through further sample excavations of a cross selection of on- and off-site locations in the valley system.

In addition to this work, the modern topography and aerial photographic record is being combined with the results of the valley augering survey to create both terrain and erosion assessment models. These will be used as comparative tools with which to evaluate the models of past erosion that are developed from this research project.

Essential reading

Barrett, J., Bradley, R. and Green, M. (1991) *Landscape, Monuments and Society: The Prehistory of Cranborne Chase*, Cambridge: Cambridge University Press.

Barrett, J., Bradley, R. and Hall, M. (1991) *Papers on the Prehistoric Archaeology of Cranborne Chase*, Oxford: Oxbow Monograph 22, Oxford.

French, C., Lewis, H., Allen, M. and Scaife, R. (2000) 'Palaeoenvironmental and archaeological investigations on Wyke Down and in the upper Allen valley, Cranborne Chase, Dorset: interim summary report for 1998–9', *Proceedings of the Dorset Natural History and Archaeological Society* 122: 53–71.

Green, M. (2000) *A Landscape Revealed: 10,000 years on a Chalk Downland Farm*, Stroud: Tempus.

13 The lower Aguas basin, southeastern Spain

Introduction and methodology

In the lower Aguas basin of semi-arid southeastern Spain (Figure 13.1) a large multi-disciplinary landscape project was carried out in 1995–6. It was funded by the European Commission and was under the direction of Professors Lull and Chapman (Castro *et al.* 1998, 1999). This project built on the Archaeomedes Project study of the Vera basin in the same area of southeastern Spain which investigated the nature and causes of desertification in southern Europe (Courty *et al.* 1994b; van der Leeuw 1997; Winder and van der Leeuw 1997). The main goal of the project was to examine the dynamics of past human settlement-landscape systems between 4000 BC and the present day as a crucial factor in the process of desertification and degradation of this part of the Mediterranean region.

As part of this larger project, this author undertook a geomorphological study of the lower Aguas valley in conjunction with Dr David Passmore and Prof. Tony Stevenson of the University of Newcastle-upon-Tyne and Dr Lothar Schulte (French *et al.* 1998). The main objectives were to document the successive phases of erosion and aggradation in the system during the Holocene, to investigate their morphology, depositional histories and chronology, and examine possible linkages between these events, human activity and geomorphic stability of the system (Thornes and Gilman 1983; Castro *et al.* 1998: 15; Brown 1999).

The main study focused on the tributary valleys directly associated with the Copper/Bronze Age sites of Gatas and Las Pilas and the lower Aguas valley from just upstream of Turre to the sea (Figure 13.1). The geomorphological survey involved aerial mapping and systematic field prospection of all the available gully systems in the study area. Key depositional sequences were described, photographed and sampled where appropriate for soil/sediment analyses such as bulk density and shear strength, micromorphological analyses and scanning electron microscopy. Samples for radiocarbon and optically stimulated luminescence (OSL) dating were also taken from key profiles to build the chronological control for the depositional sequences.

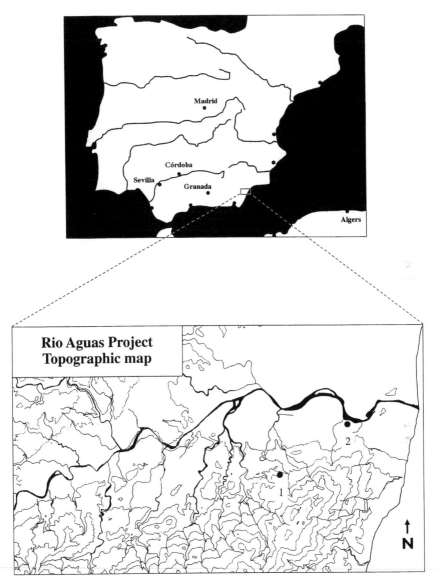

Figure 13.1 Location map of the lower Aguas valley, near Almeria, Spain (scale 1:50,000) (after Castro *et al.* 1998: map 1, by permission).

Results

In brief, the combined studies of the Archaeomedes (van der Leeuw 1997) and Aguas projects (Castro *et al.* 1998) suggested that the intermontane valleys cutting across and down through the slopes of the Sierra Cabrera mountain range and feeding into the River Aguas were already deeply incised with gullies or barrancos by the early Holocene (Figures 13.2 and 13.3). Since then and in contrast with the late Quaternary, these systems appear to have remained relatively quite stable, but punctuated by several main periods of erosion and aggradation. This type of sequence is known as punctuated equilibrium.

Subsequent landscape formation processes were dominated by more limited erosion and aggradation of slope and valley deposits, mainly occurring in the mid- to lower slopes, probably with much reworking of the same deposits and much material flushed through to the sea by brief but violent storm events. For example, the major part of the Barranco de Gatas below the site of Gatas contains colluvial deposits of about 1–1.5 m in thickness, and the terraces forming downslope in the Rambla Ancha are rarely more than 1 m in height above the previous terrace (Figures 13.3 and 13.5). In contrast in the Aguas floodplain itself, the vast bulk of the infilling and sediment aggradation occurred in pre-Roman times and again in the past 5–600 years, the latter probably associated with the advent of extensive terrace systems for agriculture on the valley slopes. For example, where the tributary stream Rambla Ancha meets the Aguas River, there is a *c.* 4 m thick accumulation of alluvial sediment interrupted by at least three phases of incipient soil formation (i.e. identified by episodes of organic accumulation) sealed beneath a Roman structure at Cortijo Cadima (Figure 13.4). In general, four major periods of erosion in the Holocene appear to have occurred in the earlier half of the second millennium BC (the late Argaric period), in the Roman period (0–400 AD), in the ninth and tenth centuries AD (Andalusian) and in the past 5–600 years.

Although the pollen record is rather scarce and poorly preserved in the region, there is sufficient evidence to suggest that the lower Aguas basin landscape has been severely modified since prehistoric times (Stevenson and Harrison 1992; Stevenson 1996; Rodriquez Ariza and Stevenson 1998). For example, the sequence obtained from an alluvial sequence in the Aguas valley floor at Cortijo del Campo near Las Pilas indicates a quite open environment dominated by Liguliflorae, Poaceae (grasses) and Chenopodiaceae (goosefoot, oraches) with a small amount of tree pollen of pine (*Pinus*) and olive (*Olea*) from the Chalcolithic period and throughout the Bronze Age (*c.* 3000–1000 cal BC). There are indications of weeds of cultivation and disturbed habitats being present, but very few shrubs. Also, it is clear that woodland fires were occurring which appear to be associated with higher frequencies of *Cistus* (Rosaceous shrub) pollen, an acknowledged pyrophyte. The lack of trees in the landscape is corroborated by other pollen cores from the immediate region where arboreal pollen, mainly of *Quercus ilex* type (oak), declines after 6000 BP and never recovers. Nonetheless, there is some evidence that the valley floor was repeatedly inundated, with marshy areas present. It is suggested that the modern vegetation is very similar to that occurring in the Roman and Andalusian periods. The modern pollen rain clearly reflects local differences in vegetation depending upon the location of

Figure 13.2 Typical gully section showing an immature buried soil beneath Holocene colluvium in the Barranco de Gatas.

Figure 13.3 Relict terraces and infilled channels in the lower reaches of the Rambla Ancha.

Figure 13.4 The intersection of Rambla Ancha and the Aguas River at the Roman
site of Cortijo Cadima illustrating the aggradation of overbank flood
deposits interrupted by standstill phases/incipient soil formation.

the sample sites on which mountain slope, but is characterized by *Pinus pinea*
type (pine), *Olea europaea* (olive), *Quercus coccifera* type (oak), *Myrtus communis*
type, a wide range of mattoral species, *Chenopodium album* type (fat hen),
Plantago lanceolata type (ribwort plantain) and relatively low frequencies of
grasses. In summary, this suggests an environment of abandoned agricultural
terraces, shrubby trees and grassy steppe-like vegetation.

In each case, it is suggested by Castro *et al.* (1998, 1999) that increased
erosion appears to be linked to the destruction of maquia (open scrub of olive
and pine) vegetation and expanding cultivation of cereal crops, in particular
barley. Moreover, from the Bronze Age, it appears that many more parts of the
valley system were beginning to be exploited on a greater and greater scale.

Implications

By the early Holocene, there was a general lack of well-developed soil cover
in the tributary valley systems and in the main Aguas valley itself. Not one
in situ or undisturbed buried soil was discovered despite extensive and
intensive field survey of all available exposed sections in the barrancos of the
lower Aguas system. The soils that are present beneath colluvial deposits
(Figures 13.2 and 13.5; Tables 12.1, 13.1–13.3) are themselves calcareous
silt loams developed in and from colluvial deposits on truncated surfaces.
These 'secondary' palaeosols are essentially calcitic soils being reworked in a

Figure 13.5 The profile on the edge of the modern Aguas floodplain showing three incipient buried soils sandwiched by colluvial marl material.

Table 13.1 Summary of the micromorphological characteristics, suggested interpretation and chronology of the Barranco de Gatas profiles, Aguas basin, southeastern Spain

Characteristics	Profile 2	Profile 3	Profile 4
Structure:	homogeneous, with vughy to intergrain channel	excremental within poorly developed blocky peds	successive laminae
Components:	amorphous $CaCO_3$, very abundant (35%) lenticular gypsum and abundant (20%) fine organics; clay slaking crusts in upper half	micro-sparite $CaCO_3$, minor amorphous of organic, calcitic $CaCO_3$ and minor (5%) lenticular gypsum	present day topsoil sand/silt with minor (5%) lenticular gypsum; excremental calcitic loam with minor (5%) gypsum; calcitic 'crust'; calcitic loam in excremental aggregates; laminated calcitic silt; gypsum and amorphous/micro-sparite $CaCO_3$ in excremental form; Profile 8: at base of Profile 4: alternating laminae of calcitic crusts and calcitic loam with abundant lenticular gypsum
Suggested interpretation:	secondary soil formation on eroded schist/marl bedrock; some anthropogenic activity; buried by debris flow	*in situ* soil formation on Neogene marl bedrock	terrace edge in barranco, with alternate wetting/drying and alternate stabilization/burial and erosion; all buried by later calcitic colluvium
Suggested chronology:	Neolithic to Bronze Age	early post-glacial to Neolithic	early post-glacial

Table 13.2 Summary of the micromorphological characteristics, suggested interpretation and chronology of the colluvial terrace units from the Rambla Ancha profiles, Aguas basin, southeastern Spain

Characteristics	Profile 1	Profile 2	Profile 3
Structure:	irregular blocky	excremental	excremental
Components:	micro-sparite $CaCO_3$; occasional (5-10%) to no lenticular gypsum in voids	micro-sparite and amorphous $CaCO_3$; minor (<5%) gypsum in voids & groundmass	micro-sparite $CaCO_3$ very rare (<1%) gypsum in voids and groundmass
Suggested interpretation:	calcitic alluvium with reworked eroded material derived from Barranco de Gatas soils	calcitic alluvium	calcitic alluvium derived from Neogene marl bedrock
Suggested chronology:	pre–late Neolithic	pre–late Neolithic	pre–late Neolithic
	Profile 4	Profile 5	Profile 6
Structure:	excremental, vughy heterogeneous mix of fabrics	heterogeneous mix of fabrics & excremental	homogeneous, vughy
Components:	amorphous and micro-sparite $CaCO_3$; very rare (<1%) gypsum in voids and ground-mass; occasional inclusion of organic/calcitic fabric similar to BG Profile 2; rare fragment of calcitic crust as in BG Profile 8	amorphous & micro-sparite $CaCO_3$; abundant (30%) gypsum in voids and groundmass; similar fabric inclusions as in Profile 4	micro-sparite $CaCO_3$; very rare (<1%) gypsum in groundmass
Suggested interpretation:	calcitic alluvium with reworked reworked material derived from Barranco de Gatas soils	calcitic alluvium	calcitic marl derived from Neogene marl bedrock
Suggested chronology:	post-Neolithic	post-Neolithic	late Quaternary

Table 13.3 Summary of the suggested interpretation and chronology of the Las Pilas profile, Aguas basin, southeastern Spain

Unit/depth (cm)	Interpretation	Chronology
I (355+)	compacted powdery gypsum	pre-Holocene
II (355-335)	redeposited marl from erosion upslope, with some influence of river erosion; associated with prolonged periods of high groundwater	early Holocene
III (335-255)	rapid deposition of Unit II type marl from upslope, with gypsum formation suggestive of alternating damp/hot conditions; first anthropogenic influence	post-Copper Age
IV (255-245)	erosional episode similar to upper part of Unit III, then exposed as a surface with immature soil development	post-Copper Age
V (245-215)	rapid, then slow accumulation of redeposited marl similar to Unit II and some eroded marl substrate; some anthropogenic influence	post-Copper Age
VI (215-150)	slow erosional episode similar to Unit IV; ? associated with terrace construction	recent event ?
VII and VIII (150-0)	erosion of recent terrace material	last 50 years

slow erosional dynamic. These thin, single-horizon soils are characterised by an absence of coarse component, abundant calcitic silty clay intercalations, abundant lenticular gypsum crystals in the void space and much reworking through biological activity (Figure 13.6; Tables 13.1–13.3). Today, these same soils can be adequately cultivated for cereals and will grow citrus fruit if well irrigated. The major destructive effects in this landscape are unpredictable flash flooding associated with torrential thunderstorms and the flattening out and enlargement of former small terraced field systems by bulldozer associated with European Community development incentives. The rare thunderstorms and flash floods can create deep incisions and new gullies literally overnight (Figure 13.7), metres deep and moving tonnes of material downslope. It has been demonstrated through shear and plasticity tests that the marly subsoils which dominate this system only require about 22–45 per cent saturation to move downslope as overland flow deposits, and the calcareous silt colluvial material requires quite similar saturation levels of about 27–46 per cent. Thus, localized but severe climatic moments could have been responsible for relatively large amounts of erosion over very short time periods. Moreover, once saturated and redeposited on a flat surface, the

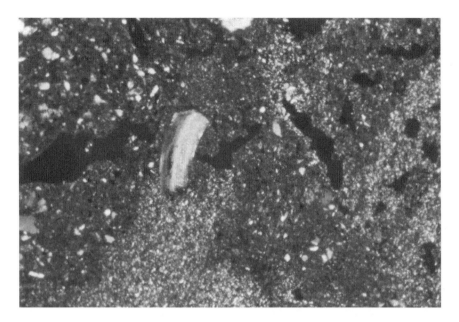

Figure 13.6 Photomicrograph of a typical Holocene colluvial soil in the Barranco de Gatas with an heterogeneous mixture of loam, calcitic loam and gypsum (in crossed polarized light; frame width=4 mm).

Figure 13.7 Modern gully head formation overnight by one year of thunderstorm events just upslope from Las Pilas.

upper surface of these sediments rapidly dries out and forms thin salt crusts which cause root starvation of crops. These crusts need to be physically broken up to be reincorporated into the ploughsoil. In many respects this associated effect of erosion is potentially more detrimental to arable agriculture and good crop growth than the actual mechanics of the erosion itself, and would have made arable agriculture precarious at the best of times.

Thus, having painted a picture of an occasionally highly unstable, dry, sparsely vegetated and rather marginal landscape, what are we left with? The calcium carbonate and gypsum-dominated and easily erodable soils of the Aguas system would have required husbanding as a resource to have enabled their evident exploitation since at least the Copper Age. Certainly, the extensive areas of poorly vegetated land with much bare earth would make the whole area prone to rainsplash and sheet erosion processes. Although it is not easily proved, to overcome the naturally rather poor soil and vegetation conditions present in this semi-arid environment, possibly the soil was treated very sympathetically in the past as an essential resource. This would mean sparse planting of cereal crops between other tree/fruit crops whose root systems helped to hold the soil system in place, and perhaps even some form of rudimentary irrigation and terrace wall retention of soils on hillslopes.

Although there is no firm archaeological evidence for terracing or irrigation prior to the past 500 years or so, some soil retention may have been practised through the use of a variety of 'organic' retaining boundaries such as slight banks, thorn/scrub trees and/or piles of field clearance stones. For example, Neolithic lithic scatter sites have been found on the lower slopes of the valley to the south of the confluence of the Rambla Ancha and the Aguas River just inland from Turre (R. Chapman pers. comm.). Despite some conflation, these are just the type of site that one would expect to be unrecognizable, either destroyed, transported or buried through erosion, but they are not. Moreover, taking deliberate advantage of the very localized micro-climatic conditions could have made the difference between near-desert and relatively lush land depending on the setting and orientation of individual valley systems. For example, in the Barranco de Gatas today, the north-facing slope remains green throughout the winter to spring months without irrigation as opposed to the year-round, bare, dry, pale yellowish brown of the opposing south-facing slope.

Finally the climatic record for southeastern Spain shows a trend of increasing aridity from the Neolithic to the Iron Age, but a further 41 per cent decrease in rainfall from then until the present day (Castro *et al.* 1998) and a steady decrease in rainfall from the late nineteenth to mid-twentieth centuries (Araus *et al.* 1997). This long-term desertification would suggest a gradually increasing sensitivity of this landscape to various forms of distur-bance since the Neolithic period. But this was a slow and gradual process, which was very occasionally punctuated by erosion and aggradation events, rather than the continuously violent landform manipulation, incision and destruction as was hitherto imagined to be the case.

Essential reading

Brown, A.G. (1999) 'Geomorphological techniques in Mediterranean landscape archaeology', in P. Leveau, F. Trement, K. Walsh and G. Barker (eds) *Environmental Reconstruction in Mediterranean Landscape Archaeology*, Vol. 2, pp. 45–54, Oxford: Oxbow.

Castro, P.V., Chapman, R.W., Gili, S., Lull, V., Mico, R., Rihuete, C., Risch, R. and Sanahuja, M. E. (eds) (1998) *Aguas Project: Palaeoclimatic Reconstruction and the Dynamics of Human Settlement and Land Use in the Area of the Middle Aguas (Almería), in the South-east of the Iberian Peninsula*, Luxembourg: European Commission.

Castro, P.V., Chapman, R.W., Gili, S., Lull, V., Mico, R., Rihuete, C., Risch, R. and Sanahuja, M. E. (1999) 'Agricultural production and social change in the Bronze Age of southeast Spain: the Gatas Project', *Antiquity* 73: 846–56.

French, C., Passmore, D. and Schulte, L. (1998) 'Geomorphological, erosion and edaphic processes', in P.V. Castro *et al.* (eds) *Aguas Project: Palaeoclimatic Reconstruction and the Dynamics of Human Settlement and Land Use in the Area of the Middle Aguas (Almeria), in the South-east of the Iberian Peninsula*, pp. 45–52, Luxembourg: European Commission.

Stevenson, A.C. and Harrison, R.J. (1992) 'Ancient forests in Spain: a model for land-use and dry forest management in south-west Spain from 4000BC to 1900AD', *Proceedings of the Prehistoric Society* 58: 227–47.

Thornes, J.B. and Gilman, A. (1983) 'Potential and actual erosion around archaeological sites in south-east Spain', *Catena Supplement* 4: 91–113.

van der Leeuw, S. E. (1997) *A DG-XII Research Programme to Understand the Natural and Anthropogenic Causes of Land Degradation and Desertification in the Mediterranean Basin*, Luxembourg: European Commission.

14 The Troina river valley, north-central Sicily

Introduction

The Troina Project is investigating the nature of human demography during prehistory in the highly eroded upland landscape around Troina in the Nebrodi mountain range of north-central Sicily (Figure 14.1). Although there are several models proposed regarding the nature of Neolithic-Copper-Bronze Age settlement and land-use history in the central uplands of Sicily (Cultraro 1997; Leighton 1999; Tusa 1999), very little concrete data exists in contrast to other regions and more lowland areas of the island. The collaborators in this study are Gianna Ayala of the University of Cambridge, Professor Diego Puglisi of Catania University and Dr Richard Bailey of the Oxford University Archaeological Research Laboratory, under the overall project direction of Drs Caroline Malone and Simon Stoddart (Malone *et al.* in press).

The geomorphological survey part of this project is an investigation of the Holocene soils and sedimentary history of a 10 km stretch of the Fiume di Sotta di Troina valley (Figures 14.2–14.4) (Ayala and French in press). The principal aim is to develop a three-dimensional chronosequence of major units of river incision, soil/sediment erosion, aggradation and terrace formation with respect to the human utilization of this landscape (French in press a). Through the use of aerial, terrain and deposit mapping, characterization analysis of the major sediment and soil types present and a programme of radiometric and luminescence dating, the intention is to document the erosion history of the landscape, and identify zones of stability versus instability and accumulation versus denudation. This information will then be used to address questions about the exploitation, sustainability and stability of this landscape, in particular from the third millennium BC onwards, and to allow models of landscape development and land-use change to be put forward.

Methodology

In terms of fieldwork, what is the actual approach on the ground? For the archaeological part of the project, there is a core 5 km sq area south of the

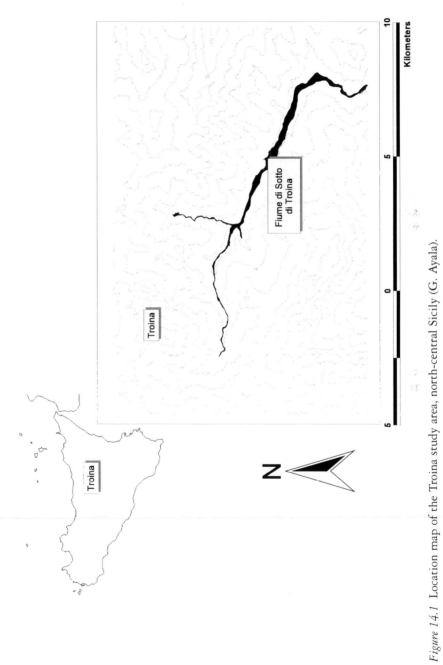

Figure 14.1 Location map of the Troina study area, north-central Sicily (G. Ayala).

town of Troina that has been totally fieldwalked at 10 m transect intervals, with artefacts collected and recorded by transect and field number. Concentrations of artefacts that may represent a site that are encountered were then subject to a total artefact pick-up on a 10 m grid basis. The artefacts are then cleaned and scanned for identification and numerical recording purposes. Beyond the core survey area, a series of ten *c.* 100 m wide transects aligned at right angles to the valley slopes were fieldwalked at 10 m intervals from watershed to watershed (north to south), with the same artefact collection policy as in the core area. Five new prehistoric sites were found in the 1999 survey season in addition to Casa Sollima in the core area.

To test each archaeological site discovered further, a combination of methods was used. These included augering transects to establish the stratigraphic context of the site, geophysical survey to investigate the nature and extent of each site, and test excavation for the retrieval of *in situ* dating material and soil sampling from the stratigraphic sequence. For example, geophysical survey has been conducted on the area of site 1135 just to the south of Peitralunga for evaluation purposes preparatory to future assessment excavation and this has revealed two substantial rectilinear structures reminiscent of the single example being excavated at Casa Sollima. At this latter site, these initial investigations have been followed by larger area excavations to tackle the structural and earthfast remains (Figure 14.7) (Malone and Stoddart 1999).

For the geoarchaeological survey part of the project, the research area has been defined by the extent of the archaeological surface survey, which in turn is delimited by the local administrative boundaries and access permissions. A full, vertical aerial survey that was taken in 1997 was made available to us by the Troina commune. This was used for the digital mapping of the relict channel meanders, and the identification and mapping of zones of soil/sediment erosion and accumulation. In the valley system, there was first a rapid field assessment by walking the whole length of the valley bottom to identify the locations of exposed profiles for recording and sampling. Second, the channel and gully systems were thoroughly fieldwalked, with every good soil/sediment exposure recorded by a combination of measured sketch, description and colour photograph. At the same time, samples for micromorphological and bulk soil analyses (i.e. particle size, organic content, magnetic susceptibility and trace elements) and OSL dating were taken as appropriate from horizons representative of the major fill units of the relict terrace and river systems along the length of the study area. These soil analyses are intended to characterize the sediments. In addition, the common minerogenic components in the major erosion units were identified by Professor Puglisi of the University of Catania to provide clues on the substrate source derivation of the sediments.

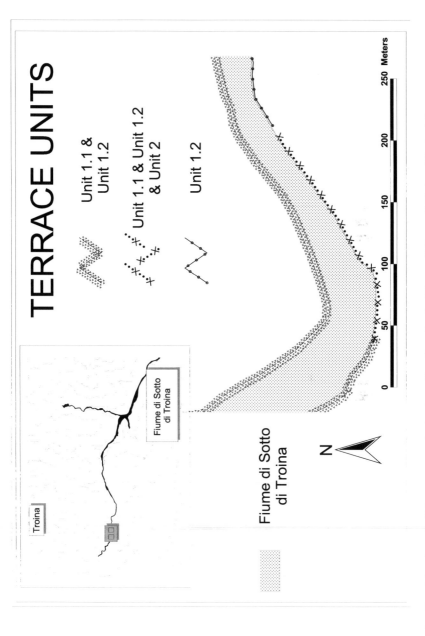

Figure 14.2 Provisional map of the terrace units in the valley floor in the Fiume di Sorta di Troina (G. Ayala).

Preliminary results and implications

As both field and laboratory work are still underway, some preliminary comments may be made regarding the formation of this landscape (Tables 12.1, 14.1 and 14.2). There is intense and extensive landscape alteration

Table 14.1 Summary of the main depositional units observed in the Fiume di Sotta di Troina, Sicily

Deposit unit number	Description	Interpretation
1.1	flysch stones/boulders; at base imbricated and above in all orientations; <1.5 m thick	cold periglacial conditions; erosion of bare bedrock prior to soil development; late Quaternary
1.2	flysch stones to sands to silty clay, fining upwards; exhibiting horizontal bedding and eroded bedrock outcrop material; <2 m thick	slope erosion and channel infill of exposed bedrock and subsoils from lower parts of valley system; variable flow; slight channel avulsion and braiding; early Holocene
4	flysch stones and silty clay soil in northern tributary valley and at river confluence in lower reach; <3 m thick	overland flow stone debris and soil aggrading on Unit 1.1/1.2; extensive disruption of hillslopes and colluviation, leading to major period of infilling of the lower 0.5 km of northern tributary valley; earlier prehistoric ?
5	silty clay loam with columnar to blocky ped structure; <1 m thick	soil erosion from hillslopes as colluvium; redeposited downstream as overbank alluvium on Unit 1.2 deposits
2	laminated and bedded sandy loam, silty clay, silt, fine to coarse sand, calcareous marl, weathered Reitano flysch deposits, with occasional gravel 'stringers'; <0.5m thick	erosion of most parts of valley system, colluviation, channel infill and overbank flooding; variable but slower water velocity and lower flow volumes; observed aggrading on Unit 1.2
3	modern channel cut into Units 1.2 and 2 channel infills and Unit 1.1 channel base	post-1960 hydraulic engineering of the river bed and valley base; recent incision into Units 1 and 2
6	flysch stones and silty clay soil at interface and just above present day water's edge	recent colluvial slumping at base of slope and current river bed; often being incised and removed by recent water flow

Table 14.2 Summary of the main features of soil change and erosion in the
Holocene from the soil profiles investigated in the Troina region, Sicily

---

Soils:

organic sandy clay loams developed on calcitic loam colluvium by 3rd and
1st M BC

evidence of continuing small additions of eroded fine material in the soils as
intercalated dusty clay

Erosion:

change from river bed/boulder erosion to fine-grained overbank sediment; major
smoothing of slope with colluvium pre- and post-3rd–1st M BC;

3–4 phases of river incision, infilling and terrace formation

Environmental factors:

high, steep relief; rainy/snowy season; thunderstorms; volcanic activity; recent
EC agricultural policies, dewatering and rural abandonment

---

around the late glacial/early Holocene transition involving channel avulsion
and colluvial aggradation leading to valley infilling. This first channel bed
unit is characterized by imbricated Reitano flysch boulders often exposed in
the base of the present river system and/or beneath later terrace deposits and
channel infills (Figure 14.3), and massive slump deposits of silty clay
colluvial material fingering onto the valley floor and infilling folds in the
slopes on either side (Figure 14.6). This accounts for the gently undulating,
quite smooth and non-dissected appearance of the valley sides today. Another
three sets of channel infilling and terrace make-up have been observed
consistently from the valley head for a distance of some 10 km downstream,
with the last phase being associated with dam construction in the 1960s
(Figures 14.4 and 14.5). The two intervening phases of incision and
aggradation have yet to be dated, but relevant profiles in two parts of the
valley system have been sampled for luminescence dating to address this
problem. The main difference between the sediments in terms of texture is
that they become increasingly finer up-profile, with overbank silty clay loam
material forming extensive alluvial terrace deposits in many places from
about the 3 km mark downstream (Figure 14.2). The second channel unit is
composed of alternating and bedded sands, gravels and silty clay loam
overbank flood sediment, and the third unit is composed of laminated fine
gravel and coarse/medium/fine sand with intermittent horizons of material
derived from different eroded subsoils in various parts of the valley system
(Figure 14.4). Whatever their date in the Holocene may be, this indicates
increased disturbance and movement down-slope of eroded soil material,
plus increasing exploitation and disturbance of soils and subsoils of more
varied and higher parts of the valley system over time.

Figure 14.3 Unit 1.1 imbricated boulders at the base of a channel fill forming a
          later terrace.

Figure 14.4 Unit 1.1 and 1.2 boulders and gravel exhibiting horizontal laminae
          with alluvial overbank material above.

Figure 14.5 Wide relict terrace just upstream of Pietralunga.

Figure 14.6 Modern colluvial slumping over slope, gully and terrace deposits.

All of this suggests that there are changing intensities and locales for the focus of erosion and accumulation recognizable in the archaeological and sedimentary records at different times in the Holocene. Initially in the earlier Holocene, incision and erosion appears to have been confined mainly within the active valley floor and lower slopes. The first major human impact in terms of established settlement structures occurred in the fourth and third millennia BC at about mid-slope levels, several hundred metres above the valley floor. This use of the mid-slope area does not seem to have liberated large amounts of eroded soil into the valley system, rather there is a slower aggradational dynamic and gradual river channel infilling, avulsion and terrace formation. The major change seems to have occurred with later prehistoric exploitation where most parts of the valley bottom and slopes are becoming more unstable and prone to erosion downslope as colluvial and alluvial material. This may well be associated with the suggested major expansion of agriculture into the uplands of Sicily during the late third and early second millennia BC postulated by several authors (Cultraro 1997; Leighton 1999; Tusa 1999). The increasing range and types of deposit suggest widespread devegetated and at least seasonally bare slopes, exposed soils and subsoils, as well as seasonally variable rainfall and river flow conditions. But our new fieldwork would suggest that much of the most dramatic incision and soil erosion off the slopes of the valleys sides that is visible today has probably occurred in the last ten to thirty years or so, and is associated with the amalgamation of smaller into larger fields and changeover from pasture to mechanized arable farming (Figure 14.6). Although these scenarios and hypotheses remain to be proven through more archaeological survey and radiometric/archaeomagnetic dating, the story appears to be quite consistent in this valley system.

The new survey work summarized here would nonetheless suggest that there was a lengthy period of relative stabilisation and soil formation which is associated with the establishment of late Neolithic and Bronze Age sites (six have been discovered to date) at the contour break just above mid-slope between about the 500–800 m OD contours (Figures 14.2 and 14.7). To date, the stratigraphic sequence from only one of these sites, Casa Sollima, has been examined micromorphologically. Here there is a palaeosol which is overlain by about 35–50 cm of coarse colluvial material (poorly sorted calcareous sandy/silt loam and flysch stones of all size grades) (Figure 14.8). The palaeosol has later Neolithic (or later third millennium BC) artefacts and settlement associated with it, and is characterized by an upper 'dark earth' horizon. This 'dark' horizon is mainly the result of abundant included fine charcoal. Nearby, there is an Hellenistic site, also characterized by a 'dark earth', which is in turn overlain by a further *c.* 60 cm of coarse, flysch derived, colluvial material.

The palaeosol associated with the later Neolithic site is a *c.* 40 cm thick sandy clay loam exhibiting three main horizons developed on Miocene flysch (Figure 14.9). Its lower horizon is a sandy clay loam which exhibits a well-

Figure 14.7 General view of the excavations at Casa Sollima (with the permission of C. Malone and S. Stoddart).

developed columnar structure with evidence of much intercalation of impure or silty clay within the groundmass and neo-formed calcite towards the base of the profile. Despite the development of soil structure, this soil material has the disorganized and unsorted aspect characteristic of hillwash or colluvium. The transition to the upper horizon is marked by an horizon of secondary calcite, possibly suggesting either a truncation zone and/or old land surface had existed at this level. The upper horizon is a similar sandy clay loam fabric similar to the lower horizon, but in this case contains abundant and very fragmentary organic matter (Figure 14.10). There is also evidence of within-soil mass-movement and intercalation of silt, clay and fine organic matter caused through rainsplash impact on a bare ground surface. These features suggest both the deliberate addition of organic matter derived from associated human occupation in the later Neolithic, and the slow aggradation and inclusion of eroded fine soil material from immediately upslope. This soil horizon is also probably of colluvial origin given its poorly sorted and disorganized aspect.

Thus, this sequence is showing at least four phases of colluvial aggradation followed by periods of stabilization in pre-Neolithic, late Neolithic, Hellenistic and recent times. The later two episodes of colluviation are considerably coarser than the earlier two, possibly suggesting more soil erosion initially, and then a much greater amount of bedrock and subsoil-derived material finding their way into the valley system associated with

Figure 14.8 The profile at Casa Sollima, near Troina, showing the buried palaeosol
beneath colluvial deposits with OSL sample containers in place.

deforestation, the uptake of land for agricultural purposes and general instability caused by extensive human exploitation.

Initial luminescence dates for Casa Sollima itself are beginning to corroborate these suggestions. Dates obtained from the hillwash material
covering the site suggest that this material was deposited in the mid-fifth
millennium BC, but this early date is more probably a result of earlier
material being reworked a short distance downhill sometime after the site
was in use in the mid-fourth millennium BC (Bailey and Rhodes 2001).

As a working model, when the Casa Sollima and river valley sequences are
considered together they suggest that lengthy periods of relative landscape
stability existed. But each major phase of stability was associated with a slow
aggradational dynamic, and these were occasionally violently interrupted by
major periods of erosion and aggradation. In addition, it is postulated that
the first period of accumulation of fine, soil-derived hillwash which has been
observed at Casa Sollima occurred due to the initial clearance (e.g. Figure

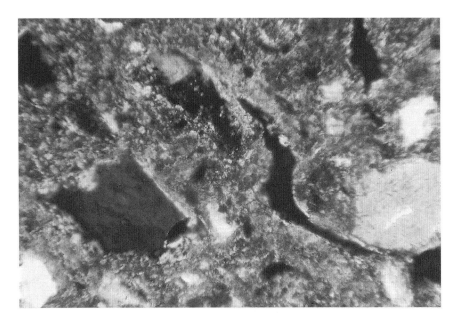

Figure 14.9 Photomicrograph of the lower part of the palaeosol or illuvial clay loam at Casa Sollima (in crossed polarized light; frame width=2 mm).

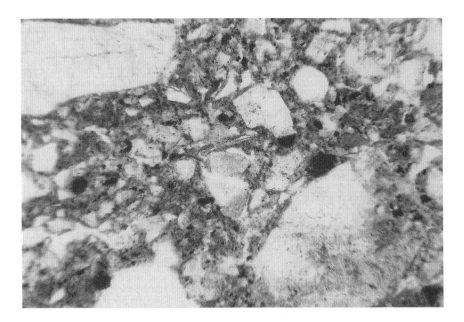

Figure 14.10 Photomicrograph of the upper part of the palaeosol, or organic loam at Casa Sollima (in plane polarized light; frame width=2 mm).

Figure 14.11 Present-day erosion of a woodland soil upslope, Idraci.

14.11) and uptake of land in the mid-slope area, possibly associated with the beginnings of agriculture in the area in the Neolithic or fourth millennium BC. The second period of fine aggradation may reflect the widening uptake of land for arable cultivation and the presence of much bare ground on the more gentle slopes in later prehistoric times (or third to first millennia BC). The later, much coarser colluvium may equate with periods of changed land-use such as the uptake of new land for cultivation, particularly in different parts of the valley system either higher up the valley sides and/or previously left as undisturbed, scrubby woodland or pasture, in Roman, medieval and modern times.

   Obviously much greater time and location precision is necessary to be really sure about the accuracy of the model. At this stage, it is not easy to reliably and directly relate the phases of stability and instability on the slopes with the observed phases of channel incision and aggradation in the valley bottom, nor to the large and thick zones of colluvial aggradation found in the side gully systems and at the base of the valley slopes that accumulated on the first and second terrace units. In particular, further relative and absolute dating of colluvial and alluvial deposits is required to address the time sequences of instability in different parts of the valley system. Nonetheless, the later prehistoric palaeosols formed in colluvium at Casa Sollima bear a remarkable resemblance micromorphologically to the over-bank flood deposits observed to have accumulated on the unit 2 and 3 channel infills/terrace deposits (Figure 14.12), and are certainly suggestive of

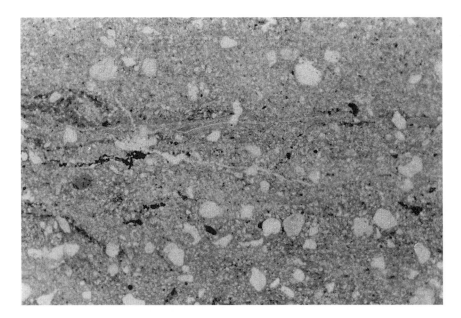

Figure 14.12 Photomicrograph of the fine overbank food deposits at profile L in the upper part of the Fiume di Sotta di Troina valley (in plane polarized light; frame width=4 mm).

quantities of eroded fine soil material getting into the river system from the slopes above in post-Neolithic times.

Essential reading

French, C.A.I. (in press a) 'Soil formation and erosion in Holocene valley landscapes: case studies from Cranborne Chase, southeastern Spain, Sicily and Yemen', in M. Bell and J. Boardman (eds) *Geoarchaeology: Landscape Changes over Archaeological Timescales*, Oxford: Oxbow.

Leighton, D. (1999) *Sicily before History*, London: Duckworth.

Malone, C. and Stoddart, S. (1999) 'A house in the Sicilian hills', *Antiquity* 74: 471–2.

15 The Dhamar region, Central Highlands, Yemen

Introduction

In apparent contrast to southern Spain and Sicily, new archaeological fieldwork in the semi-arid Central Highlands of Yemen in the Dhamar region (Figures 15.1 and 15.2) has revealed about 1,000 new archaeological

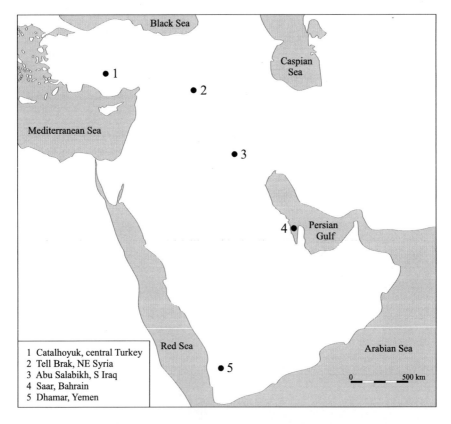

1 Catalhoyuk, central Turkey
2 Tell Brak, NE Syria
3 Abu Salabikh, S Iraq
4 Saar, Bahrain
5 Dhamar, Yemen

Figure 15.1 Location map of sites in the Near East which are mentioned in the text (1=Çatalhöyük, 2=Tell Brak, 3=Abu Salabikh, 4=Saar, and 5=Dhamar) (C. Begg).

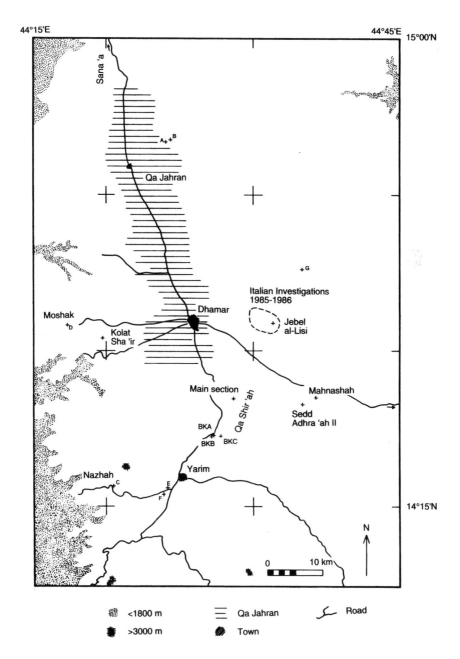

Figure 15.2 Location map of the Dhamar study region in Yemen (T. Wilkinson).

sites located from the highest volcanic mountainside position to high colluvially infilled tributary valleys and alluvially infilled basins between 2,000 and 3,000 m above sea level (Gibson and Wilkinson 1995). This is the first time in Yemen that a major survey has focused on a mountainous area rather than the desert fringes and foothills. In this case, geo-archaeological survey and a radiocarbon dating programme has been very much a part of the archaeological survey from the inception of the project. This is the only way that the relationship between the dense distribution of archaeological sites in the mountainous core of Yemen and the development of the evident, anthropogenically shaped landscape comprising suites of terraces, field systems and dams could be addressed. The geoarchaeological study set out briefly here aims to examine the erosion and infilling sequences that acted throughout the Holocene, to determine the impact of past agricultural activities, and to put forward models of landscape exploitation. This research is under the direction of Tony Wilkinson of the Oriental Institute, University of Chicago.

Preliminary results and implications

Fieldwork undertaken in six seasons since 1994 has led to the conclusion that the archaeological sites are associated with at least two major periods of stability and instability in the landscape (Gibson and Wilkinson 1995; Wilkinson 1997; Edens and Wilkinson 1998). The first major period of stability occurred in the sixth to third millennia BC, both preceded and followed by phases of colluviation and valley aggradation. Here, the period of stability is marked by the development of thick organic topsoils. The associated soil micromorphological and geo-chemical analyses aimed to investigate the conditions under which this soil formation took place, gain some ideas on the nature of prehistoric land-use in the region, test the models already put forward for landscape change and generally hone the land-use interpretations further. As in Sicily (see Chapter 14), this work is still in progress, so what follows are only preliminary observations.

The early to mid-Holocene, organic-rich topsoils investigated contained both a wind (aeolian) and water-borne (colluvial/alluvial) component, and exhibited an illuvial, clay-enriched, lower horizon (e.g. Sedd Adh Dra'ah) (Tables 12.1 and 15.1; Figures 15.3–15.5). This deposition and development had occurred by about 5000 cal BC (Wilkinson 1997: table 1). The combined presence of large amounts of organic matter in many forms in these former topsoils (Figure 15.3), subsequent partial humification and replacement with amorphous iron oxides and hydroxides, suggest that the soil profile was subject to intermittent, probably seasonal, wetting/drying cycles and associated organic accumulation. The very strongly iron-impregnated, upper part of the organic topsoil represents the zone of greatest water fluctuation and oxidation processes. There are several possibilities for how this occurred. Perhaps these features resulted from increased atmospheric humidity, or the presence of

Figure 15.3 Typical section of thick organic palaeosol buried by colluvial material at Sedd Adh Dra'ah, Dhamar region, Yemen (T. Wilkinson).

Table 15.1 Summary of the main micromorphological features of the stratigraphic sequences investigated in the Dhamar region, Yemen

Unit	Structure	Fabric	Features	Horizon
Ribat Amran:				
upper buried soil:				
	blocky peds; blocky microstructure	organic and calcitic silty clay	bioturbation; secondary iron and calcium carbonate	immature Ah
colluvium:				
	pellety to blocky	micritic calcium carbonate	overland flow; rapid wetting/drying	colluvial aggradation
lower buried soil:				
upper	columnar peds; vughy to blocky microstructure	very organic silt loam	oxidation; bioturbation; abundant illuvial coatings of voids	Ah and A1
middle	blocky peds to channel structure; small blocky microstructure	silty clay loam with very fine stone	strong hunification illuvial input to voids & groundmass	Bw
lower	columnar peds; vughy to small blocky micro-structure	organic silty clay	humification; illuvial input to groundmass; secondary calcium carbonate formation	Bckt
basal	dense; apedal	calcareous sandy clay loam on bedded fine stone swadi deposits	iron impregnated; secondary calcium carbonate	Bcks/C
Ghazwan:				
buried soil:				
upper	dense to weak, small blocky to micro-aggregated	organic, fine sandy clay	iron impregnated; minor calcium carbonate linings of voids	Ah
colluvium:				
	dense; apedal	calcitic silt loam with very fine stone		colluvial aggradation
buried soil:				
lower	small blocky peds with fissure microstructure	organic loam	oxidation; secondary iron and calcium carbonate; input; illuvial clay; groundmass material in voids	colluvial truncated Bt

Table 15.1 (Continued)

Unit	Structure	Fabric	Features	Horizon
Ad Dathiyah:				
buried soil:				
upper/ lower	weakly developed columnar blocky	sandy loam cemented with calcium carbonate	secondary iron and calcium carbonate; and illuvial pure clay	fine sediment exhibiting some soil formation, illuviation, organic accumulation and wetting/ drying or Bck
Beyt Nahami, Qa Jahran:				
buried soil:				
	blocky peds with small to large aggregated microstructure	heterogeneous mix of organic silty (clay) loam and micritic calcium carbonate	oxidation; illuvial clay; wetting/ drying	truncated and modern physically disturbed Bt
Beyt Mihras, Qa Jahran:				
basal ditch deposit:				
	8 fine laminae	variations of calcitic silt; micritic clay; micritic fine sand	horizontal; distinct boundaries	fine inwashings of calcium carbonate-rich fine sediments
Sedd Adh Dra'ah:				
transition to 'burnt' soil:				
	vughy microstructure	very organic sandy (clay) loam	all forms of organic matter; strong sesquioxide impregnation; thin dusty clay linings to voids and in groundmass	Ahs1; with illuvial and wet/dry influence
'burnt' soil:				
	blocky peds with pellety/vughy microstructure	very organic sandy loam	all forms of organic matter; strong sesquioxide impregnation;	Ahs2; subject to wet/dry conditions probable wind-blown component

Table 15.1 (Continued)

Unit	Structure	Fabric	Features	Horizon
buried soil:				
upper	irregular aggregates with pellety/vughy microstructure	organic sandy loam	all forms of organic matter; amorphous sesquioxide impregnation	Ahs3; subject to wet/dry conditions
lower	dense to aggregates with pellety to blocky microstructure	organic sandy clay loam	some organic matter; illuvial clay of all types; secondary iron and soil calcium carbonate	Bgt intermittent formation/ standing water on edge of wadi

standing water derived from localized flooding and run-off processes containing a colluvial fines component. Or just possibly, these features are a result of irrigation associated with the seasonal release of water held high up in the valley by damming. Certainly, substantial dams made of cut-stone can be observed blocking valley heads such as at Sedd Adh Dra'ah from about 1000 BC. Also, one palaeosol section at nearby Wadi Yana'im contained pollen suggestive of grass and scrubby vegetation interspersed with stands of trees, as well as pollen of *Sphagnum* moss, *Typha* (reedmace, bulrush) and *Calluna* (ling, heather) plus marsh-loving molluscan species which imply significantly increased valley floor moisture present by the mid-Holocene (Lentini 1988; Fedele 1990: 37; Wilkinson 1997: 852). Indeed, there was also a lens of peat present in the gully in the valley head at Sedd Adh Dra'ah, but unfortunately pollen did not survive in this deposit.

The mid-Holocene soil types and major characteristics appear to be relatively consistent in whatever part of the survey area that has been investigated. Essentially, well-structured cambic to argillic brown earth type soils had developed in the earlier half of the Holocene. These are not particularly well developed and have been subject to the input of organic matter and considerable post-depositional alteration through hydromorphism, bioturbation and occasionally the truncation of the upper part of the profile, which may well be associated with soil creep and overland flow erosion. There are variable amounts of clay and silty clay illuviation within the buried soil profiles, which in some cases are sufficiently well organized and oriented to suggest the formation of an argillic horizon of a brown forest earth type of soil (Figure 15.4).

The best-developed and thickest mid- to later Holcene buried soil discovered so far is that at Ribat Amram. Beneath the Himyarite construction levels, there is a palaeosol developed in the upper part of a calcareous silt and fine gravel colluvial deposit which is in turn developed on a thick (*c.* 90 cm)

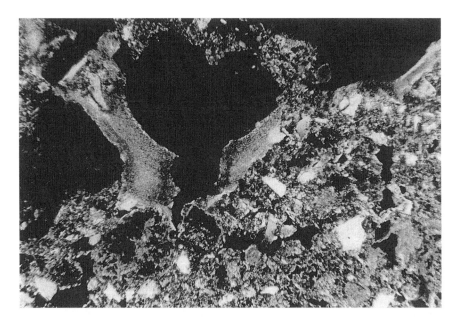

Figure 15.4 Photomicrograph of the base of the buried soil with oriented clay coatings (in crossed polarized light; frame width=4 mm).

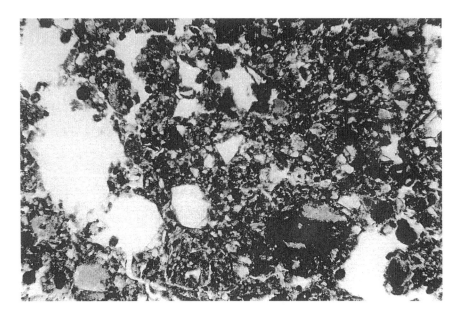

Figure 15.5 Photomicrograph of buried, thick, organic topsoil (in plane polarized light; frame width=4 mm).

palaeosol. The lower palaeosol exhibits micro-laminated clay features suggestive initially of former stability and possibly even woodland development. This was followed by considerable aggradation (with the accumulation of fine soil material which must be associated with soil disturbance and erosion), the formation of secondary calcareous deposits within the soil as a result of alternating periods of higher and lower groundwater tables (associated with evapo-transpiration leading to the formation of a calcic horizon), and the accumulation or deliberate addition of organic matter leading to the development of a thick organic A horizon (Figure 15.3 and 15.5).

The present day soil mapping of the Dhamar montane plains area (Acres 1982) has divided the soils into eight groups, of which the first two are most relevant. One group is composed of deep (50–100+ cm), well-drained soils without a calcic horizon formed in colluvium. They tend to be silty clays to sandy clay loams to clay loams, often have a buried dark horizon, and exhibit calcareous nodules and/or other forms of carbonate. These soils are classified as vertic and calcic cambisols. The second group is composed of deep (>50 cm), well-drained, non-saline soils with a calcic horizon within 100 cm of the surface. They are formed either in alluvial deposits or are buried by more recent alluvium, and are classified as calcic cambisols. In addition to the calcic (Bck) horizon, these soil groups can display either a cambic (Bw) horizon characterized on the basis of soil structure and colour mottling, and/or a clay-enriched or argillic (Bt) horizon. In summary, the past soil types bear remarkable similarities to the modern soil system, and their characteristic features are corroborated by micromorphological analysis.

Taking the modern soil (Acres 1982) and geoarchaeological surveys (Wilkinson 1997) into account, there are two major models of earlier Holocene soil development offered for the high montane plain Dhamar area. First, Acres (1982) has suggested that the dark horizons of the first soil group, or those buried horizons that contain a high organic content in the alluvial plain and valley locations, formed under grassland prior to alluviation. It is also suggested that these horizons indicate the climate was previously wetter than now. In addition, the strongly developed calcic horizons found in the main valleys and plains soils of the second group suggest that the groundwater tables were once much higher, in contrast to their well-drained nature today with groundwater tables at considerable depths.

Second, Wilkinson (1997: 852) states that although the high terrain and winter frost may have checked tree growth on basin floors, the presence of argillic soil horizons within buried palaeosols suggests that this landscape may have been more substantially wooded in the mid-Holocene prior to significant human habitation and disturbance than hitherto envisaged.

The present soil study appears to substantiate parts of both of these models, but offers a more complex series of pedogenic scenarios that may have occurred in the past. Crucial to this interpretation is the occurrence in combination of the aforementioned dark, organic rich upper soil horizons and lower horizons enriched with illuvial clay or argillic/Bt horizons. Together these features point to the existence of much more stable and well-drained conditions in the earlier Holocene, perhaps even to the presence of woodland. This system began to be disrupted by clearance quite early in the Holocene (by the fifth and third millennia BC) which led to some depletion of fines and organic status, as well as gradual aggradation and incorporation of eroded fine material (of either colluvial or alluvial origin) and within-soil mass movement of fine material (mainly impure silty clays). In some cases these combined events appeared to stop/start after a period of relative stability, often associated with either later third millennium BC or later first millennium BC dates and artefacts, before colluvial aggradation began or was resumed. It is in these relative standstill phases that the dark organic horizons may well have become better developed as they remained open and relatively stable under grassland conditions. Nonetheless, these soils were subject to the incorporation of organic matter through soil faunal mixing processes and to receiving minor amounts of fines in suspension in freshwater, perhaps on a seasonal basis and/or through lateral flushes on slopes (R.I. Macphail pers. comm.). It is also conceivable, but not very easily proved one way or the other, that these processes were human-enhanced through water control either by deliberate flooding or irrigation of these valley soils. This set of circumstances would appear to better explain the gradual development of the fine texture, thickness of and the dark, rich-brown colour of these soils, despite the now evident oxidation and breakdown of the organic components through soil faunal activity within these buried dark horizons. Whether partially wooded or grassland conditions existed or not, what the soils suggest is the former presence of thick, organic, moist and well-structured soils that were available by the mid-Holocene for human exploitation.

The one remaining problem is that it is impossible to be certain about the origin of the organic matter in these prehistoric soil profiles. For example, were the thick organic topsoils naturally developed under either woodland or even grassland, or has the organic component been enhanced through the deliberate addition of organic material by human agency, or is it due to high groundwater tables created by greater rainfall and run-off in the past and slower oxidation processes, or were the higher groundwater tables a result of deliberate damming and irrigation throughout prehistory, or is it due to some combination of any or all of these scenarios ?

Obviously, one of the major tasks ahead is to identify earlier prehistoric water and soil management through the discovery of new archaeological data and structures, to prospect for pollen sampling catchments that will provide the necessary detail on the Holocene vegetation within the survey area, and to collate these with the available climatic data from deep sea core evidence.

Essential reading

Edens, C. and Wilkinson, T.J. (1998) 'Southwest Arabia during the Holocene: Recent archaeological developments', *Journal of World Prehistory* 12: 55–119.

Gibson, M. and Wilkinson, T.J. (1995) 'The Dhamar Plain, Yemen: a preliminary study of the archaeological landscape', *Proceedings of the Seminar for Arabian Studies* 25: 159–83.

Wilkinson, T.J. (1997) 'Holocene environments of the High Plateau, Yemen: Recent geoarchaeological investigations', *Geoarchaeology* 12: 833–64.

16 The environs of Tell Brak, northeastern Syria

Introduction

Tell Brak is situated in an extensive area of alluvial and colluvial Quaternary silts and sandy silts derived from the calcareous mountains of southern Turkey at the confluence of Wadis Radd and Jaghjagh in the Khabur basin of northeastern Syria (Figure 15.1). It has a Mesopotamian steppe vegetation (Zohary 1973), with Mediterranean brown soils or calcic xerosols, or semi-arid soils with weak horizon development and a lower horizon of calcium carbonate enrichment (Courty 1994).

The immediate environs have been subject to limited geoarchaeological survey by Tony Wilkinson in 1991 and 1999, and by the present author and Wendy Matthews in 1993 (Wilkinson *et al.* 2001). This is a good example of disproportionate amounts of attention being paid to the archaeology and micromorphological interpretation of the tell itself (Matthews *et al.* 1997a; Oates *et al.* 1998), with relatively little attention focusing on the site's landscape setting and context throughout the major part of the Holocene. Other projects nearby have begun to redress this imbalance, such as Courty's work at Tell Leilan, for example, some 40 km to the northeast (Weiss *et al.* 1993; Courty 1994; Courty and Weiss 1997), and more detailed geomorphological work is now in progress for the Tell Brak area.

What follows is an account of what has been done so far to elucidate the landscape context, and a series of models and hypotheses to test by future work. The uppermost questions that should be borne in mind at this stage and in the future are: why is Tell Brak where it is?; were the floodplains of the river channels and wadis active on a seasonal or permanent basis and over what timeframe?; is it a rain-fed or irrigated floodplain system?; and was the area suitable for large-scale arable production sufficient to feed the inhabitants of Tell Brak? Similar questions have led to the comprehensive geomorphological survey currently being undertaken, for example, of the environs of the tell site of Çatalhöyük in central Turkey by Neil Roberts and his team (Roberts *et al.* 1996), and by Wilkinson (1994) investigating rain-fed, prehistoric farming communities in Syria, Iraq and Turkey.

Survey results

Field survey investigation of the Belediya pipe trench to the southeast of the main mound at Tell Brak revealed a thick buried soil sealed beneath about 80–100 cm of alluvial silty clay material (Figure 16.1). It consisted of two horizons, an upper, 15 cm thick, pale greyish brown silty clay loam, overlying a 85+ cm thick horizon of pale orangey brown silty clay loam. Both horizons exhibited an irregular to sub-angular blocky ped structure in the field. Two sets of spot samples were taken for micromorphological analysis from the upper part of this soil exposure, just beyond the point where the soil was overlain by fourth millennium BC occupation debris of the Middle Uruk period (i.e. mid-fourth millennium BC; J. Oates pers. comm.).

Both sets of samples exhibited similar features and are therefore described together. In the field and in thin section, the soil exhibits a poorly to moderately well-developed sub-angular blocky ped structure defined by interpedal channels. The soil is composed of a pale greyish to yellowish brown clay loam which is dominated by pure, non-laminated clay and irregular to sub-rounded aggregates of amorphous calcium carbonate. The predominant clay component is probably a result of repeated past flooding and the settling of fines out of suspension in still, relatively shallow water conditions associated with seasonal episodes of overbank flooding and alluviation. The calcium carbonate component has a similar derivation, formed from the drying out of base-rich flood- and groundwater.

Figure 16.1 The alluvial soil profile in the Belediya pipe trench immediately
southeast of Tell Brak.

There are a variety of other minor inclusions present. The rare aggregates of pure clay and silt and fine organic matter are suggestive of rolled aggregates carried in alluvial floodwaters. There are a few irregular zones of amorphous sesquioxide impregnation of the fine groundmass which are indicative of alternate wetting/drying conditions. Some of the void space is discontinuously infilled with sub-rounded to irregular aggregates of fine groundmass material similar to the main groundmass. These probably indicate disturbance and movement down profile between peds in dry episodes.

The buried soil profile should be seen as a standstill surface of a gradually accreting alluvial soil in an active floodplain. Although the alluvial events that deposited this material cannot be dated precisely, at least this alluvial aggradation and soil development had already occurred by the fourth millennium BC as it is overlain by Uruk period artefacts. There is some secondary disturbance of the profile causing the partial infilling of the void space with calcareous clay aggregates, which may well be associated with recent agricultural disturbance and the general drying out and cracking of the overlying alluvium and ploughsoil.

This alluvial complex appears to be confined to a narrow but deeply buried floodplain, with much of the alluviation occurring after the occupation of Brak and before more recent times. But, there is an extensive area beyond Tell Brak, some 2.5 km east and 3.5 km south, respectively, of gently undulating clay loam plain which is probably 'hiding' a series of relict river systems, terrace remnants and levee banks beneath alluvial deposits, all of which require investigation.

Conclusions

The alluvial soil/subsoil sequence observed to the southeast of Tell Brak is essentially situated within the Jaghjagh river floodplain. Its characteristics suggest long-term seasonal flooding and the gradual accretion of alluvial fines over a lengthy period (Figure 16.2). As the location of Tell Brak could be considered as marginal, both in terms of its intermediate position between two wadi systems and in terms of rain-fed agriculture today, it may have been located deliberately at this confluence of wadis for easy access to water for human consumption and either natural and/or human managed irrigation of adjacent fields.

There are several implications. First, given the evident thickness of the alluvial aggradation in the floodplain, it suggests that the Jaghjagh may have been a much larger and more active river and associated floodplain. Second, the silty clay alluvial soils would have been rich in nutrients, and seasonally renewed, and may have been one major factor responsible for the extensive utilization of the area in prehistoric times. Nonetheless, this soil type would have been rather difficult to use for arable farming, either 'rock hard' when dry or intractable when wet. It is only with the advent of mechanized farming practices that it generally becomes feasible to utilize

Figure 16.2 The Roman bridge footings within the present-day cut for the
          Jaghjagh showing the alternating alluvial and immature soil sequence,
          southeast of Tell Brak.

this type of 'heavy' soil easily for arable agriculture on a large scale. Third,
the thick and extensive alluvial aggradation which overlaps the outer edges
of the Tell Brak mound may mean that both the archaeological record and
old land surfaces are relatively well preserved around the periphery of the
mound. Moreover, there may be extensive buried landscapes surviving to the
south in the clay plain area. What is unknown is how stable the floodplain
was during the main fourth to third millennia BC use of the tell and how it
was exploited, and when were the major periods of alluvial aggradation in
this system? Also, is there any evidence in these sealed contexts of the
dramatic climatic change that is said by some researchers to have occurred
around the end of the third millennium BC in this region (Weiss *et al.* 1993;
Courty and Weiss 1997)? Thus, in future, more systematic investigation of
this vast alluviated valley and floodplain immediately adjacent to the site
may hold the key to deciphering past land-use and organization that
supported the community living on and around the tell.

As a working model to test, I would argue that the main period of alluviation beyond the wadi channels themselves is a post-Roman phenomenon. In
particular, there are Roman bridge footings across the Jaghjagh about a
kilometre downstream and to the southeast of the site. Here the footings are
about 3 m below the present-day ground surface and the thick alluvial
overburden is interrupted at least three times by a standstill phase and
incipient soil formation (Figure 16.2). This hints at there being an extensive

prehistoric land surface beneath which should contain clues as to its conditions of formation and burial, and whether it would have been sufficiently a tractable and well-drained soil for arable agriculture in the past and sustainable without irrigation. Obviously future geomorphological and associated palynological research must evaluate these hypotheses further, in particular to analyse and date the Jaghjagh profile as a priority. Also auger transect surveys must be conducted to map the palaeo-topography of the wider area in greater detail.

Essential reading

Courty, M.-A. (1994) 'Le cadre paléogéographique des occupations humaines dans le basin du Haut-Khabur (Syrie du Nord-Est): Premiers resultats', *Paléorient* 20: 21–59.

Courty, M.-A. and Weiss, H. (1997) 'The scenario of environmental degradation in the Tell Leilan region, NE Syria, during the late third millennium abrupt climate change', in H. Nuzhet Dalfes, G. Kukla and H. Weiss (eds) *Third Millennium BC Climate Change and Old World Collapse*, pp. 49–89, NATO ASI Series, Vol. I.

Oates, J., Oates, D. and McDonald, H. (1998) *Excavations at Tell Brak, Vol. 1: The Mitanni and Old Babylonian Periods*, Cambridge: British School of Archaeology in Iraq/McDonald Institute Monograph.

Wilkinson, T.J. (1994) 'The structure and dynamics of dry-farming states in upper Mesopotamia', *Current Anthropology* 35: 483–519.

Wilkinson, T.J., French, C. and Matthews, W. (2001) 'Geoarchaeology, landscape and the region'. in J. Oates, D. Oates and H. McDonald, *Excavations at Tell Brak, Vol. 2*, pp. 1–14, Cambridge: British School of Archaeology in Iraq/McDonald Institute Monograph.

17 The steppe at Botai, northeastern Kazakhstan

Introduction

During the archaeological expedition in the summer of 1995 to the Kokchetau region of northeastern Kazakhstan (Figure 17.1) led by Dr Marsha Levine and sponsored by the McDonald Institute for Archaeological Research, a field appraisal of the geomorphological and micromorphological potential of the archaeological site of Botai and its immediate environs was conducted by the writer (French 1995b). This included a brief geomorphological evaluation survey of the immediate vicinity of the site, description and photographic recording of exposed sections around the site and sampling the exposed palaeosols for micromorphological analysis.

This region of Central Asia supports a steppe biome, characterized by sparse vegetation, consisting mainly of short perennial grasses growing in small clumps or bunches with occasional stands of birch and pine woodland (Kislenko and Tatarintseva 1999). In general, plant ground cover is poor, and much bare soil is exposed. This type of environment has produced soils that are classified as chernozems (or black soil of the steppes) (Gerasimova *et al.* 1996: 136), that is they exhibit a thick, organic-rich A horizon and a weathered B (or Bw) horizon which retains large supplies of nutrients, and is often developed on loessic subsoils (Limbrey 1975: 196–8; Strahler and Strahler 1997).

The geoarchaeology of the site environs

The landscape at Botai today has a gently sloping aspect, cut by two major small valley systems (French 1995b). The smoothed slopes disguise a series of now infilled, small, north–south aligned, valley systems. The infills of these former valleys are exposed in the present day river cliff section, and these are seen to occur approximately every 200 m, ranging from 75–100 m in width, and at least 3–5 m in depth (Figure 17.2). These systems would have given the area a much more gently folded aspect in the past. Currently,

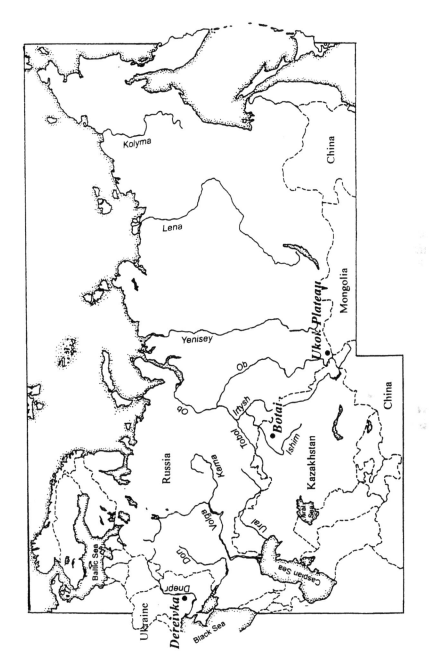

Figure 17.1 Location map of Botai, Kazakhstan (M. Kousoulakou).

an erosional phase is under way, manifested by active down-cutting of new gully systems and the enlargement of existing gullies.

These gully systems contain a consistent sedimentary sequence (Figure 17.2). Three main sedimentary units are distinguished, from oldest to most recent. Unit 1 is composed of multi-bedded coarse sands and fine gravels which suggest the erosion and redeposition of former river terrace deposits. Unit 2 is composed of pale orangey brown silt with fine gravel horizons which is indicative of wind and water deposition, such as would have occurred under cold periglacial conditions and before soil-forming processes began. Their accumulation may possibly be of late glacial/very early Holocene date, *c.* 12 000–10 000 years ago. As for the tertiary infills of the former valleys (or unit 3), these probably began to aggrade at some point after the occupation of Botai, as the site is also overlain by unit 3-type material. The unit 3 sediment is composed of organic, dark brown to black, silt loam soil. The nature of this deposit poses several questions relating to its provenance and mode of deposition. If it is colluvial material, it remains to be determined how it was initially formed and what generated its subsequent movement and redeposition. Moreover, the texture of the deposit strongly resembles the secondary and tertiary infills of the sunken floored dwellings of the Botai site itself (French and Kousoulakou in press). The complementary micromorphological analyses were used to examine these questions.

Figure 17.2 Typical erosion gully showing the loessic substrate, palaeosol and colluvium sequence.

The micromorphological analysis

The palaeosol was composed of an upper turf horizon over a weathered B horizon developed on an iron-rich, loessic silt subsoil (Figures 17.2–17.4; Table 17.1). The B horizon contained common textural pedofeatures of micro-laminated and non-laminated impure (or dusty) and pure clay. The laminar aspect of some of the clay indicates that there were successive episodes of disturbance, movement of fine soil in water and deposition down profile. In many respects this soil is much more typical of a rather poorly developed brown earth that would be commonly observed in northwestern Europe in river valley, flood-plain edge locations (Fedoroff 1968; Bullock and Murphy 1979; French 1990), rather than being a characteristic chernozem of the steppe.

This soil was overlain by heterogeneous, reworked soil material. It must have derived from upslope, where the soil surface had already been disturbed, perhaps truncated and the subsoil exposed. The agents that had caused the initial erosion could not be specifically recognized, but it is suggested that on sloping ground, sparsely covered by vegetation as is the case today in the area, soil could have easily been mobilized by rainsplash action and/or saturation through snow melt with consequent surface truncation induced by overland flow and gravity. However, common charcoal fragments indicative of settlement and/or limited-scale burning incorporated in the deposit might suggest some human involvement in the disturbance. Unfortunately it is impossible to be certain whether colluviation was intermittent or continuous and over what period of time.

Inferences about environmental conditions can also be made on the basis of other features. Post-depositional bioturbation by soil fauna and roots, decaying remains of which are preserved in voids, was evident throughout the profile. Abundant vermiforms co-existed with typical enchytraeid worm granular excrements, possibly indicating slight changes in the pH of the past micro-environment from calcareous to slightly acidic. In addition, the downward movement of calcium-rich solutions and capillary action account for the abundance of micrite in the groundmass throughout the profile. This calcium carbonate derives from the calcareous substrata of the region, and is typical of the soils developed in the region (Gerasimova *et al.* 1996). The oscillation in water content is related to the rate of evaporation, further implying the alternation of wet and dry periods which would be expected given the dry mid-latitude climate of the region with abrupt temperature changes. The rapid evaporation of soil moisture was also attested by the shrink-swell action observed in these clay-rich sediments and by the oxidation of iron.

This micromorphological glimpse of the palaeosols present at Botai has yielded information which contributes to our knowledge of the environmental context of the site. The sediments on whose upper surface the buried soils had developed probably originated in late glacial, cold climate condi-

Table 17.1 The summary micromorphological description of the buried soil profiles at Botai, Kazakhstan

Profile/sample	Fabric	Structure and texture	Major features
Buried soils:			
Profile 1	A	heterogeneous, sandy/silty clay loam with vughy to very fine crack microstructure	abundant micro-laminated pure to impure clay; minor organic component
	B	vughy and pellety microstructure; silty/sandy clay loam	dark brown, fine amorphous organic component; rare weathered bone fragments
	C	weakly developed columnar blocky peds; clay loam	frequent complete infillings of planar voids and fine intercalations of impure clay
Profile 2		50% pellety structure; 50% poorly to well developed, irregular blocky to columnar ped structure; clay loam	abundant non-laminated impure clay and amorphous iron in upper half; more abundant micrite in lower half

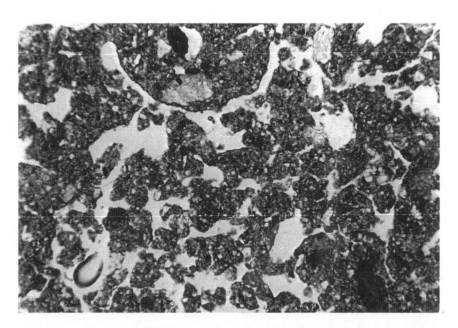

Figure 17.3 Photomicrograph of the turf comprising the upper part of the palaeosol (in plane polarized light; frame width=4 mm).

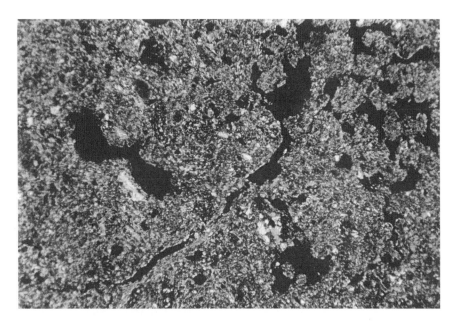

Figure 17.4 Photomicrograph of the illuvial B horizon of the palaeosol (in crossed polarized light; frame width=4 mm).

tions dominated by wind and water erosion. Thin brown earth type soils exhibiting some structural development and clay illuviation under stable conditions had begun to develop in the earlier part of the Holocene. But, these soils probably did not remain particularly stable for long, and soon became subject to erosion, the gradual intercalation of fine soil and even some truncation probably associated with disturbance of the vegetational cover, the saturation with water of bare soils and overland flow. There may have been some human involvement in the disruption of this environment, especially associated with the development of the site of Botai itself in the fourth millennium BC, but the nature and degree of human intervention is yet to be ascertained.

Model of landscape development

From the combined micromorphological analyses and geomorphological field survey evidence, it is possible to suggest the following model of landscape development at Botai. First a brown earth type soil had begun to form in the earlier Holocene. This soil exhibited some development with a blocky to columnar structure and clay illuviation, but its rather poor development suggests that it never supported a well-established woodland vegetation. This landscape became subject to disturbance, devegetation and soil erosion associated with rainsplash and overland flow which led to the partial infilling of small tributary valley systems with relatively small amounts of colluvial soil, effectively smoothing the contour of the slope at Botai. There may well have been a human input into triggering these processes through agri-cultural/pastoral/settlement activities, but these are not directly recognizable in the soil record. It is suggested that these events had begun to occur during and after the mid-fourth millennium BC settlement at Botai. This phase was followed by renewed erosion and soil movement which is still continuing today as a slow process along with river channel downcutting and avulsion.

This scenario is contrary to the 'accepted' view that a dominant coniferous woodland environment existed during the fourth millennium BC occupation of Botai. It is much more probable on the basis of the soil evidence that a combined open woodland and grassland environment existed at this time. Indeed, current thinking on the vegetational development of southeastern Europe and western Russia would echo this type of conclusion (Peterson 1983; Willis *et al.* 1998; Gardner 1999). These authors have suggested a forest steppe plant community in the late glacial, composed of open coni-ferous forest with patches of steppe-like grass and herb communities that rapidly became transformed into a more closed deciduous forest. This type of environment may well have persisted for some three millennia with discrete human activity causing subtle vegetation composition changes such as the reduction in oak and hazel about the fourth millennium BC, witnessed the greater opening up of this wooded environment and an increase in beech, hornbeam, herbs and grasses, along with minerogenic input into basins. Perhaps at Botai the earlier Holocene was characterized by a mixture of open coniferous woodland and steppe grass and herb communities, which with the occupation of the site led to an increasingly open and slightly unstable steppe environment which persists until the present day. Obviously without new palynological research at Botai and its immediate vicinity, these suggestions cannot be tested further.

Conclusion

Earlier Holocene soil development probably occurred under mixed open woodland and steppe-like conditions. This was later followed by erosion and colluvial processes probably from the mid-fourth millennium BC onwards. Woodland here may never have been as well developed as one might imagine from a northwestern European perspective, and once it became open steppe grassland it ostensibly remained so. Secondary evidence of pasture for horses and manure management was obtained from the analysis of the infilling material of the sunken floored dwelling. In order to test this model further, a systematic environmental survey of the archaeological site and its environs would be required, including for instance phosphate and magnetic susceptibility surveys, as well as detailed palynological studies.

Essential reading

Gerasimova, M.I., Gubin, S.V. and Shoba, S.A. (1996) *Soils of Russia and Adjacent Countries: Geography and Micromorphology*, Moscow-Wageningen.

Kislenko, A. and Tatarintseva, N. (1999) 'The Eastern Ural steppe at the end of the Stone Age', in M. Levine, Y. Rassamakin, A. Kislenko, N. Tatarintseva and C. Renfrew (eds) *Late Prehistoric Exploitation of the Eurasian steppe*, pp. 183–216, Cambridge: McDonald Institute Monograph.

Peterson, G.M. (1983) 'Recent pollen spectra and zonal vegetation in the western USSR', *Quaternary Science Reviews* 2: 281–321.

Willis, K., Braun, M., Sumegi, P. and Toth, A. (1998) 'Prehistoric land degradation in Hungary: Who, How and Why?', *Antiquity* 72: 101–13.

Conclusions

Whilst one cannot argue that major synchronous soil developmental events were linked in any way across different parts of Britain, Europe and the Near East, one can ask whether there are any common themes emerging from the geoarchaeological investigation of the different study areas summarized in the case study chapters.

Any attempt to answer this question might be seen as beyond generalization, but some comments are in order. Whatever the location and variation in circumstance, a major period of stability associated with extensive human land-use seems to have existed by the mid-Holocene or within earlier prehistoric times. The earlier Holocene had seen major and quite rapid changes in climate and the soil and vegetation complex which were essentially in place by the Neolithic period (or fifth to fourth millennia BC). From that time onwards and for a substantial period in many cases, there was often slow and gradual change. This change is often seen as detrimental and as a deterioration in state from the pre-existing situation. From my perspective, the soil/landscape system which we observe and discover may owe its development and survival to the inherent land factors of geology, soil and vegetation types in combination with much more sympathetic human land-use practices than are often envisaged. It involved learning to cope with new circumstances of soil and vegetation change and developing agricultural practices, many of which might not be recognized for several generations and therefore not always require immediate adaptation and acceptance. This might have had as much to do with factors such as the relatively small numbers of people involved as with any great environmental constraints; moreover the sublety of the environmental change was such that our analyses cannot easily detect the change until the transformation was already well advanced.

Subsequently throughout later prehistory and the historic periods, this system became disrupted in a variety of ways, as intensities, landscape parameters and timescales changed. The disruptions, essentially the product of woodland destruction, erosion and agricultural practices, are often believed to have been associated with climatic changes of variable intensities, frequencies and longevities. Some may have been abrupt and rapidly destabilizing, others may have been a series of smaller or punctuated events which led to longer-term change in aggregate, and some may have been slow and gradual over the long term. For example, there may be either gradual drying out of the system, such as in southern Europe and the Near East from the earlier Bronze Age on (from about 2200 cal BC), or increasing wetness such as in Britain in later prehistoric times (later second to first millennia BC), as well as changes in settlement type and pattern. These events were certainly exacerbated by greater land exploitation, a factor which may in turn may have been driven by other factors such as population increases and urbanization for example. In essence, wherever the archaeologist and geoarchaeologist works, they are dealing with part of a greater ecosystem. They must endeavour to decipher as many aspects of that system as possible, how they functioned, how they interacted, how human activity can force or hinder certain cause-and-effect relationships, and how climatic shifts can force changes and alter sequences either dramatically or more slowly over time. Any one factor or any combination of factors could upset the functioning of the system and tip the balance towards change as well as alter the intensity of change observed.

Within these greater, longer-term changes though, the nature and intensity of change was such as to preclude more than a few very broad generalizations regarding patterns of erosion linked to human land-use. Local variation was paramount, basin by basin, valley by valley, with each system's own life histories fully interlinked with every human and geographic factor that one could think of, and in any combination. A threshold must be reached, but that threshold will be reached and passed at different times, places and with various combinations of circumstances. One of the best examples is that every fen embayment in East Anglia has a slightly different palaeo-history despite being part of the same overall basin system.

What I hope has been presented is some insight into how valley landscape systems may be investigated and thought of from a geoarchaeological point of view. Obviously, it is a sub-set and personal view of some of the archaeological problems and topographies that may be encountered and explained using various methods of landscape reconstruction, but with a particular focus on the analysis of soils and sediments. This geoarchaeological approach uses a combination of conventional archaeological and geomorphological techniques in combination with the analysis of many other types of palaeo-environmental data. It could, but generally does not, use formulae the way a geographer might, but this is not to say that one should not delve deeper into the modelling of the data that is presented in an effort to analyse and present the data in different ways. I suspect that the increasing future use and development of various geographical information-based systems which allow one to superimpose several sets of related data will become a very productive avenue of interrogating new data and presenting new models.

Good project design is crucial at the outset. It must fit the scale of the target landscape and the questions being addressed. It goes almost without saying that it is no use deciding to sample only one site intensively when it is the decipherment of long-term change across the valley landscape that you are interested in investigating and diagnosing. Getting at the landscape context is often difficult and never as thorough as one might hope for because there are almost always logistical problems of accessibility, preservation, time and funding that may go against one. Ways round this include working in the same landscape repeatedly, and assembling a team of many different backgrounds and viewpoints to examine and combine each other's approaches to address similar problems and questions. Being flexible in one's research design and methodologies employed is also essential. For example at a practical level, if one cannot identify sufficient exposed sections to create one's catena sequence and cross-sections of the valley system, one may need a combination of data recovered by systematic augering or sample test stations cut by a machine to fill in the gaps.

It is extremely important to go into the field with an agenda and some very basic questions that one wishes to try to answer. But with this approach, one must remain flexible in terms of response and methodologies employed, and be willing to re-situate one's research agenda to tackle slightly different questions that appear to be more relevant at the time. Otherwise, it is easy to be side-tracked into examining many different things at once that cannot be easily related and without ever really getting very specific about any of them. This is where the present day strictures of project designs planned in great, costed, time-scheduled detail, necessary to procure the funding to do the work in the first place, can be detrimental to freedom and flexibility necessary in conducting good archaeological and geoarchaeological research.

I cannot stress enough how important it is to look beyond the site at its context and any important landscape feature in the vicinity. Many times I have gone on site to do a soil assessment and have asked the site excavator: have you seen the site from the air?, what is that bump in the field over there beyond the fenceline?; is that ridge and furrow cultivation?; what is off down the slope over there?, what is the nearest river doing? The response is: 'well, we are only working here and have no money nor time to look outside the development area.' Lifting one's head, observing and questioning one's surroundings on site are crucial to good archaeological landscape investigations and obtaining reliable interpretations.

It is essential to know extremely well whatever landscape that one is discovering and trying to decipher. One needs a good eye for this, something which cannot be learnt directly: the experience is only accumulated over time. Also, one needs to be able to think about and try to visualize in one's mind how the various parts of the landscape function and operate together as a system, both in two and three dimensions, in section and in plan simultaneously. Moreover, it is just as important to seek out local people who are intimate with the landscape in which one is engaged to give one an 'in' on all the other aspects that may be there, unrecognized by you, and central to the interpretation of that landscape. Either running one's own excavations or being involved with ongoing excavations and survey in the research area are excellent ways of beginning to familiarize oneself with the region, its archaeology, landforms, vegetation, subsoils and soil cover. There is nothing better than being on and in the ground to get a feel for the landscape and its variability at several different scales. Thus one really needs to be a jack of all disciplines to be a geoarchaeologist, or essentially what, until recently, would have been called a landscape archaeologist – you must be digger, surveyor, geographer, historian, archaeologist and palaeoenvironmentalist all rolled into one.

One of the central, important things that I hope comes out in this volume is that soils, soil science approaches and micromorphology are great tools of the trade but should not necessarily be used in isolation. Obviously much depends on local conditions of preservation in terms of what is preserved where, and how relevant some of the available data may be to the problem at hand. But a holistic approach, using as many different types and strands of evidence at as many different scales of resolution as possible, is the most desirable. As always in archaeological endeavour, much depends on funding resources, the people involved, the time available, as well as a certain degree of luck and having a nose for discovery.

Nonetheless, where micromorphology, both on its own and in combination with geomorphological and archaeological approaches, has shone is in its ability to investigate processes at a variety of scales in landscapes, on sites and even in individual contexts on archaeological sites. In particular, it can display and decipher relationships between things and events, both natural and linked with human activities. It is still a relatively young scientific application in geoarchaeology and archaeology, which means that there is still much testing to be done, both in the field, in the laboratory and under different sets of controlling variables. Moreover, it is often extremely difficult to relate the observed processes and changes directly to other events without resorting to inferential arguments and collaborative or ethnographic analogue data. This makes it sometimes a rather inexact science, and there is no getting away from this. And this is why it is essential that micromorphology is used as part of a multi-disciplinary approach to deciphering processes and events in landscapes and on sites, both in structures and in features, and on- and off-site.

It often pays not to be too sanguine to the archaeologists on the project team. In particular, one must not promise too much or imply that very specific and verifiable answers will necessarily be forthcoming. In order to achieve that, the resolution and reliability of different types of evidence need to be understood and the evidence weighted accordingly in the resultant interpretative story. Also, it is best not to be too much of a perfectionist in terms of what is produced at the end of the project, as the methods applied and their reliability may change for the better very quickly, thus in turn often adding to and altering the story one has produced. After all, it is the informed interpretative story over time, not just the factual scientific technical report, that makes the work interesting, relevant and important to archaeology and a wider public audience.

Glossary

Aeolian   Windblown

Agricutan   Illuviation coatings of very fine sand, silt, clay and fine organic matter occurring on the surface of certain types of soil voids which are thought to originate from agricultural disturbance; the term was coined by Jongerius (1970)

Allogenic   Externally forced change

Alluvium   Well-sorted, homogeneous, freshwater-borne sediment, generally composed of very fine sand, silt and clay-size material, entrained in and aggrading in a river valley floodplain situation

Ammonification   Process responsible for changing organic nitrogen compounds of dead organic matter to an inorganic form as ammonium salts

Anaerobic   Air excluded; iron reduced to the ferrous, more soluble form (Fe^{2+})

Anastomosing channel   Ladder-like river channel system, generally found in a cold, periglacial type of climate

Anoxic   Oxygen excluded

Ard   Single share wooden plough of Neolithic, Bronze and Iron Age periods

Argillic brown earth   or sol lessivé; well-structured, clay-enriched soil normally developed under woodland on well-drained, slightly acidic to calcareous subsoils/ substrates in the earlier Holocene

Autogenic   Internal change

Avulsion   Lateral movement and re-routing of stream/river channels across a floodplain

B horizon   Horizon of accumulation in a soil

Basic   or calcareous with a pH of >7

Basin mire   Freshwater peat accumulation in a basin with impeded drainage and fed by calcareous groundwater; e.g. East Anglian fens

Bioturbation   Mixing of the soil by the soil fauna

Blanket peat   Upland, acidic peat formed as a result of high rainfall and an impermeable subsoil

Braided channel   Multiple meandering river channel system in floodplain (or braid plain)

Brown earth   Well-structured, generally calcareous, soil exhibiting some weathering, and pedogenesis formed on well-drained, neutral to calcareous subsoils/substrates

Calcareous   or basic with a pH>7

Cambic B horizon   Weathered B horizon of a brown earth

Cambisol   Calcareous, clay/iron/calcium carbonate-enriched brown earth

Catena   Sequence of soil types on the same geology dependent on relief and drainage characteristics

Chelation Amino acids from root complex combine with iron, aluminium, silica and magnesium and move downprofile with a pH of <5 when they become redeposited

Chernozem Organic and clay-enriched brown earth of Russia and central Asia

Clastic Fine clay sediment

Coarse component Gravel and stone (>2 mm in diameter) component of a soil

Colluvium Loose, non-stratified, ill-sorted, heterogeneous mixture of sediment of various size grades derived from soil/subsoil erosion upslope and redeposited at the base of slopes

Conductivity Measure of the total solute content of aqueous environments

Consistency Handling properties of a soil along with cohesion/adhesion, strength and cementation

Coppicing Deliberate, managed removal of branches of trees, such as willow and alder, to just above the base of the trunk

Dendritic channel Channel system in the shape of an upturned bare oak tree's branches; e.g. the later Neolithic tidal channel system of the East Anglian fenland basin

Desertification Long-term aridification of an environment

Desiccation Drying-out

Dirty clay Illuvial clay containing abundant fine to very fine carbonized and amorphous organic matter

Dry valley Former stream valley, now dry, bissecting the slope; e.g. found in chalk downland landscapes of southern England

Dusty clay Illuvial clay containing micro-contrasted silt and fine organic matter

Dyke Drainage ditch in the East Anglian fens

Ecosystem Every interconnected aspect of the biosphere

Eluvial/eluviation Removal of silt/clay/fine organic matter from an upper soil horizon (Ea or Eb) by processes such as leaching and groundwater percolation

Fen Colloquial term for a low-lying/lowland peat bog or marsh such as the East Anglian fenlands

Fen-edge or 'skirtland' Seasonally wet margin of peat encroachment on the outer perimeter of a fen basin

Fen peat or basin peat See basin mire above

Fines Silt and clay component of a soil or sediment

Flysch A type of limestone bedrock found in the southern Mediterranean

Geoarchaeology Interlinked study of landforms, landscape change and human impact on the landscape through combined archaeological, geographical, geomorphological and soil science approaches

Geomorphology The study of landforms

Gleying Influence of groundwater leading to greater/lesser degree of waterlogging causing reduction of iron and manganese staining

Groundmass The main mineral and organic components of soil and their arrangement and relationships to each other

Gypsum Lenticular crystal composed of silica and oxygen (O_2)

Heath Lowland and acidic, heather and bracken-dominated landscape associated with poorly drained, acidic, sandy subsoils, podzols and peat, generally found in northwestern Europe

Humus Organic component of soils, as either plant tissue and/or amorphous matter; occurs in three types: mull (acidic), moder (neutral) and mor (basic)

Hydrolysis Reaction of disassociated hydrogen and hydroxide atoms of water with ions of mineral elements; it is measured by electrical conductivity

Hydromorphism formed under waterlogged conditions

Illuvial/illuviation Mobilization, removal and redeposition of fines (silt, clay and organic matter) towards the base of the soil profile, generally occurring in B horizons and leaving a depleted or eluvial horizon above

Leaching Removal of fines and nutrients of a soil or sediment through percolating groundwater

Lessivage Equates with eluvial/illuvial process of fines removal from upper soil horizons and their redeposition in a lower horizon; forms as clay skins (cutans or coatings) on channels, pores and structural surfaces in soils, and often follows the acidification of base-rich soils

Limpid clay Pure clay

Loam Soil term meaning the equal mix of sand, silt, clay and organic matter; gives optimum tilth and fertility for cultivation

Loess Wind-blown silt

Loss-on-ignition Method of determining the total organic content of a soil/sediment by burning off the organic content in a muffle furnace

Luminescence Dating method for pottery and soils/sediment horizons/surfaces

Magnetic susceptibility Measure of magnetic enhancement of the soil/sediment generally caused by burning

Maquia Open scrub of olive and pine trees, commonly found in countries around the fringe of the Mediterranean basin

Mere Freshwater lake in a lowland basin fen or bog

Micromorphology The study of soils/sediments in thin section

Microstructure Size, shape, organization and degree of development of a soil (comprising peds, pores, grains and aggregates) and their relationship to each other

Minerogenic Sand, silt and clay components of a soil or sediment

Mire Peat bog

Moder Organic horizon of a soil of neutral pH (6–7); characteristic of coniferous and deciduous woodland where the drainage is only moderate and there is high biological activity

Mor Organic horizon of a soil of acidic pH (<6); acidic humus; characteristic of soils under heath and coniferous forests with poor drainage

Mull Organic horizon of a soil of basic pH (>7); amorphous humus, well mixed with the soil; characteristic of base-rich soils with high faunal activity under deciduous forest on calcareous subsoils/substrates with good drainage

Nitrification The transformation of ammonium salts to nitrates by bacteria in soils

Oxidation Opposite of reduction; oxygen dominates soil system, leading to formation of iron oxides and hydroxides and destruction of organic component of the soil; ferrous iron (Fe 2+) becomes ferric (Fe 3+) resulting in the precipitation of iron, usually as an oxide

Palaeo-catena Sequence of buried soils on the same geological substrate which are dependent on variation in relief and drainage characteristics and the nature of burial

Palaeochannel Relict stream or river channel, usually of braided, meandering or anastomosing type

Palaeosol or buried soil, as found under either archaeological sites or monuments and under more recent drift deposits, and generally exhibiting soil characteristics no longer observed in the same locale today

Palynology Study of pollen to interpret past vegetational assemblages

Ped Unit of organization of a soil

Pedofeatures Discrete zones in soils distinguished from the groundmass and resulting from soil-forming processes

Plasticity Measure of the percent water saturation required to make a soil/sediment mobile

Podzol An acidic, leached and eluviated soil developed on acidic substrates with poor drainage characteristics, characterized by an eluviated lower A (or Ea) horizon and a spodic B horizon exhibiting either amorphous iron (Bs) or organic (Bh) accumulations or pans towards the base of the profile, and generally associated with acidic vegetation, thin blanket peat formation and impermeable and acidic subsoils/substrates

Podzolization Process of leaching leading to the formation of podzol (as above)

Pollarding The regular and deliberate chopping back of the upper story or crown of trees, especially alder and willow, as a form of woodland management and wood resource procurement

Ranker A weakly developed soil occurring on steep slopes

Raw soil Immature soil representing the first weathering and the beginnings of soil formation

Reave Linear boundary bank, normally referring to the later Bronze Age stone banks found on Dartmoor in southwest England which run parallel to but below the crest of the long axis of the moor

Redox potential Measure of electrical activity in the groundwater system which gives an indication of the presence of oxidizing or reducing conditions

Reduction Removal of oxygen and the formation of ferrous iron (Fe^{2+})

Rendsina Thin grassland soil developed on a calcareous parent material, generally composed of an amorphous, earthworm-reworked, organic A horizon over a weathered C horizon, which is maintained by soil faunal mixing, primarily by earthworms

Saltation Bouncing transport of wind-blown, generally silt-size material

Sediment Any inorganic/organic material ranging in size from a fine clay to coarse rock which has undergone weathering, transport and redeposition by various geographic agencies, which may or may not exhibit horizonation upon deposition

Sesquioxides Oxides and hydroxides of iron and aluminium

Shear strength Measure of the degree of saturation required to make a soil slump downhill in one event

Soil An inorganic/organic material developing through the weathering of earth's mantle by physical and chemical processes and geographic agents through time such that distinct horizonation occurs

Soil complex The whole ecosystem in the soil

Soil creep Slow downslope movement of saturated soil under gravity

Soil matrix The material finer than sand-sized material in a soil

Soil texture The relative proportions of sand, silt and clay in the soil

Solifluction Mass movement of unconsolidated sediment, gravel and stones under cold climate or periglacial conditions which is characterized by many different orientations of gravel/stone component

Spodic horizon A humic iron-enriched horizon found at the base of a podzol (or Bs horizon)

Tectonic Uplift and subsidence effects on landforms caused by volcanic eruptions and earth plate shifts

Terracette Linear erosion slumping of soil and turf on steeper slopes which look like shallow agricultural terraces

Textural pedofeatures Coatings/infillings of pure to intermixed clay, silt and organic matter formed by illuvial deposition of materials eluviated from upper layers

Translocation   The transport of material within a soil, either in suspension or solution

Truncation   Violent erosion or shearing of some or all of the soil profile downslope

Vermiforms   Worm-shaped pores in soils

Water table   The interface between the saturation zone and the capillary fringe in a soil/sediment/geological substrate sequence

Bibliography

Abdul-Kareem, A.W. and McRae, S.G. (1984) 'The effects of topsoil of long-term storage in stockpiles', *Plant and Soil* 76: 357–63.

Acres, B.D. (1982) *Yemen Arab Republic Montane Plains and Wadi Rima Project: Soil classification and correlation in the Montane Plains,* Project Record 72, Surbiton: Land Resources Development Centre.

Adderley, W.P., Simpson, I. and Davidson, D. (in press) 'Image analysis of soil thin sections - current uses and limits to future use', in M. Bell and J. Boardman (eds) *Landscape Changes over Archaeological Timescales,* Oxford: Oxbow.

Ahnert, F. (1998) *Introduction to Geomorphology,* London: Arnold.

Ainsley, C. (forthcoming) 'The faunal remains', in C. French and F. Pryor, *Archaeology and Environment of the Etton Landscape,* East Anglian Archaeology.

Aitken, M.J. (1985) *Thermoluminescence Dating,* London: Academic Press.

—— Michael, H.N., Betancourt, P.P. and Warren, P.M. (1988) 'The Thera eruption: continuing discusssion of the dating', *Archaeometry* 30: 165–82.

Allen, M.J. (1992) 'Products of erosion and the prehistoric land-use of the Wessex Chalk', in M. Bell and J. Boardman (eds) *Past and Present Soil Erosion,* pp. 37–52, Oxford: Oxbow Monograph 22.

—— (1994) 'The land-use history of the southern English chalklands with an evaluation of the Beaker period using colluvial data: colluvial deposits as environmental and cultural indicators', unpublished PhD thesis, University of Southampton.

—— (1995) 'Before Stonehenge, the environment sections', in R.M.J. Cleal *et al. Stonehenge in its landscape,* Archaeological Report 10, pp. 4–5, 34, 41–65, 116–17, 168–9 and 332–4, London: English Heritage.

—— (1997a) 'Landscape, land-use and farming', in R.J.C. Smith, F. Healy, M.J. Allen, E.L. Morris, I. Barnes, I and P. J. Woodward (eds), *Excavations Along the Route of the Dorchester By-pass, Dorset, 1986–8,* Wessex Archaeology Report 11, pp. 166–84, Salisbury.

—— (1997b) 'Environment and land-use: the economic development of the communities who built Stonehenge (an economy to support the stones)', in B.W. Cunliffe and A.C. Renfrew (eds) *Science and Stonehenge,* pp. 115–44, London: Proceedings of the British Academy 92.

—— (1998) 'A note on reconstructing the prehistoric landscape and environment in Cranborne Chase; the Allen valley', *Proceedings of the Dorset Natural History and Archaeological Society* 120: 39–44.

Allen, M.J. and Green, M. (1998) 'The Firtree Field Shaft: the date and archaeological and palaeo-environmental potential of a chalk swallowhole feature', *Proceedings of the Dorset Natural History and Archaeological Society* 120: 25–37.

Allen, M.J. and Macphail, R.I. (1987) 'Micromorphology and magnetic susceptibility studies: their combined role in interpreting archaeological soils and sediments', in N. Fedoroff, L.M. Bresson and M.-A. Court (eds) *Soil Micromorphology*, pp. 669–76, Paris.

Allen, M.J., Bloomfield, C., Macphail, R.I. and Wyles, S. (1993) 'A record of soil and molluscan changes resulting from landuse management at Butser Archaeological Farm: some preliminary results', *Butser Archaeological Yearbook* 1992/3.

Allen, M.J., Morris, M. and Clark, R.H. (1995) 'Food for the living: a reassessment of a Bronze Age barrow at Buckskin, Basingstoke, Hampshire', *Proceedings of the Prehistoric Society* 61: 157–89.

Araus, J.L., Buxo, R., Febrero, A., Gamalich, M.D., Martin, D., Molina, F., Rodriguez-Ariza, M.O. and Voltas, J. (1997) 'Identification of ancient irrigation practices based on carbon-isotope discrimination of plant seeds: a case study from the Southeast Iberian Peninsula', *Journal of Archaeological Science* 24: 729–40.

Archaeological Project Services (1996) *Preservation by Record: a proposal for archaeological excavation at Welland Bank Quarry*, unpublished report, Heckington.

Armour-Chelu, M.J. (1992) 'Vertebrate resource explanation, ecology and taphonomy in Neolithic Britain, with special references to sites of Links of Notland, Etton and Maiden Castle', unpublished PhD thesis, University College, London.

—— (1998) 'The faunal remains', in F. Pryor, *Excavations at Etton, Maxey, Cambridgeshire, 1982–88*, pp. 273–88, Archaeological Report 18, London: English Heritage.

Avery, B.W. (1980) *The Soil Classification of England and Wales*, Harpenden: Soil Survey Technical Monograph No. 14.

Avery, B.W. and Bascomb, C.L. (1974) *Soil Survey Laboratory Methods*, Harpenden: Soil Survey Technical Monograph No. 6.

Ayala, G. and French, C.A.I. (in press) 'Holocene landscape dynamics in a Sicilian upland valley', in A. Howard, D. Passmore and M. Macklin (eds) *The Alluvial Archaeology of North-west Europe and the Mediterranean*, Rotterdam: Balkema.

Bailey, R. and Rhodes, E. (2001) 'OSL Dating Report for the Troina Project', unpublished report, Research Laboratory for Archaeology and the History of Art, University of Oxford.

Balaam, N.D., Smith, K. and Wainwright, G.J. (1982) 'The Shaugh Moor Project: fourth report – environment, context and conclusion', *Proceedings of the Prehistoric Society* 48: 203–78.

Barham, A.J. and Macphail, R.I. (eds) (1995) *Archaeological Sediments and Soils: Analsyis, Interpretation and Management*, London: Archetype Books.

Barrett, J. (1994) *Fragments from Antiquity : An Archaeology of Social Life in Britain, 2900–1200BC*, Oxford: Blackwell.

Barrett, J., Bradley, R. and Green, M. (1991a), *Landscape, Monuments and Society: The Prehistory of Cranborne Chase*, Cambridge: Cambridge University Press.

Barrett, J, Bradley, R and Hall, M. (1991b) *Papers on the Prehistoric Archaeology of Cranborne Chase*, Oxford: Oxbow Monograph 11.

Bell, M.G. (1983) 'Valley sediments as evidence of prehistoric land-use on the South Downs', *Proceedings of the Prehistoric Society* 49, 119–50.

—— (1992) 'The prehistory of soil erosion', in M. Bell and J. Boardman (eds) *Past and Present Soil Erosion*, pp. 21–36, Oxford: Oxbow Monograph 22.

Bell, M.G. and Boardman, J. (eds) (1992) *Past and Present Soil Erosion*, Oxford: Oxbow Monograph 22.

Bell, M.G. and Johnson, S. (1996) 'Land molluscs', in M.G. Bell, P.J. Fowler and S.W. Hillson (eds) *The Experimental Earthwork Project 1960–1992*, pp. 140–2, Council for British Archaeology Research Report 100, York.

Bell, M. and Walker, M.J.C. (1992) *Late Quaternary Environmental Change: Physical and Human Perspectives*, London: Longman.

Bell, M., Fowler, P.J. and Hillson, S.W. (eds) (1996) *The Experimental Earthwork Project 1960–1992*, York: Council for British Archaeology Research Report 100.

Biddick, K. (1984) 'Animal bones from the Cat's Water subsite', in F. Pryor *Excavation at Fengate, Peterborough, England: The Fourth Report*, fiche pp. 245–75, Northampton/Toronto: Northamptonshire Archaeological Society Monograph 2/Royal Ontario Museum Archaeology Monograph 7.

Biddle, M. (1994) *What Future for British Archaeology?*, Opening address to the IFA Conference, Bradford, Oxford: Oxbow Lecture 1.

Binford, L.R. (1981) *Bones: Ancient Men and Modern Myths*, London: Academic Press.

Birkeland, P.W. (1974) *Pedology, Weathering and Geomorphological Research*, London: Oxford University Press.

Boardman, J. (1992) 'Current erosion on the South Downs: implications for the past', in M. Bell and J. Boardman (eds) *Past and Present Soil Erosion*, pp. 9–20, Oxford: Oxbow Monograph 22.

Boismier, W.A. (1997) *Modelling the Effects of Tillage Processes on Artefact Distributions in the Ploughzone*, Oxford: British Archaeological Reports 259.

Boivin, N. (2000) 'Life rhythms and floor sequences: excavating time in rural Rajasthan and Neolithic Catalhoyuk', *World Archaeology* 31: 367–88.

Bowden, M. (ed.) (1999) *Unravelling the Landscape*, Stroud: Tempus.

Bowen, H.C. (1990) *The Archaeology of Bokerley Dyke*, London: HMSO.

Bradley, R. (1978) *The Prehistoric Settlement of Britain*, London: Routledge, Kegan Paul.

Bradley, R. (1984) *The Social Foundations of Prehistoric Britain*, London: Longman.

—— (1998) *The Significance of Monuments: On the Shaping of Human Experience in Neolithic and Bronze Age Europe*, London: Routledge.

—— (2000) *An Archaeology of Natural Places*, London: Routledge.

Brandt, R., Groenman-van Waateringe, W. and van der Leeuw, S.E. (1987) *Assendelver Polders Papers 1*, Amsterdam.

Breunig-Madsen, H. and Holst, M.K. (1996) 'Genesis of iron pans in Bronze Age mounds in Denmark', *Journal of Danish Archaeology* 11: 80–6.

—— (1998) 'Recent studies on the formation of iron pans around the oaken coffins of the Bronze Age mounds in Denmark', *Journal of Archaeological Science* 25: 1103–10.

Brookes, I.A., Levine, L.D. and Dennell, R.W. (1982) 'Alluvial sequence in central west Iran and implications for archaeological survey', *Journal of Field Archaeology* 9: 285–300.

Brown, A.G. (1995) 'Holocene channel and floodplain change: A UK perspective', in A. Gurnell and G. Petts (eds) *Changing River Channels*, pp. 43–64, London: Wiley.

—— (1997) *Alluvial Geoarchaeology: Floodplain Archaeology and Environmental Change*, Cambridge: Cambridge University Press.

—— (1999) 'Geomorphological techniques in Mediterranean landscape archaeology', in P. Leveau, F. Trement, K. Walsh and G. Barker (eds) *Environmental Reconstruction in Mediterranean Landscape Archaeology*, vol. 2, pp. 45–54. Oxford: Oxbow.

Bull, I.D, Simpson, I.A., van Bergen, P.F. and Evershed, R.P. (1999) 'Muck 'n' molecules', *Antiquity* 73: 86–96.

Bullock, P. and Murphy, C.P. (1979) 'Evolution of a Paleo-Argillic Brown Earth (Paleudalf) from Oxfordshire', England, *Geoderma* 22: 225–52.

Bullock, P., Fedoroff, N., Stoops, G., Jongerius, A. and Tursina, T. (1985) *Handbook for Soil Thin Section Description*, Wolverhampton: Waine Research.

Bunting, B.T. (1967) *The Geography of Soil*, London: Hutchinson.

Burrough, P.A. (1986) *Principles of Geographical Information Systems for Land Resources Assessment*, Oxford: Monographs on Soil and Resources Survey No. 12.

Burrow, S. and Gale, J. (1995) 'Survey and excavation at Knowlton Rings', Woodland Parish, Dorset 1993–5, *Proceedings of the Dorset Archaeological and Natural History Society* 117: 131–2.

Burton, N. (1997) 'GIS in Archaeology: visualising the palaeo-environment', unpublished MPhil thesis, University of Cambridge.

Burton, R.G.O. (1981) *Soils in Cambridgeshire II*, Harpenden: Soil Survey Record No. 69.

Butler, S. (1992) 'X-radiography of archaeological soil and sediment profiles', *Journal of Archaeological Science* 19: 151–61.

Butzer, K.W. (1982) *Archaeology as Human Ecology*, Cambridge: Cambridge University Press.

Cameron, R.A.D. (1978) 'Interpreting buried land-snail assemblages from archaeological sites – problems and progress', in D.R. Brothwell, K.D. Thomas and J. Clutton-Brock (eds) *Research Problems in Zooarchaeology*, pp. 19–23, Institute of Archaeology Occasional Publication 3, London.

Canti, M.G. (1995) 'A mixed-method approach to geoarchaeological analysis', in A.J. Barham and R.I. Macphail (eds) *Archaeological Sediments and Soils: Analysis, Interpretation and Management*, pp. 183–90, London: Archtype Books.

Caple, C. (1993) 'Defining a reburial environment; research problems characterising waterlogged anoxic environments', in P. Hoffman (ed.) *Proceeedings of the 5th ICOM. Group on Wet Organic Archaeological Materials Conference, Portland, Maine*, pp. 407–21, Bremerhaven.

Caple, C. and Dungworth, D. (1997) 'Investigations into waterlogged burial environments', in A. Sinclair, E.A. Slater and J. Gowlett (eds) *Archaeological Science 1995*, pp. 233–40, Oxford: Oxbow.

Caple, C., Dungworth, D. and Clogg, P. (1997) 'Results of the characterisation of the anoxic waterlogged environments which preserve archaeological organic materials', in P. Hoffman (ed.) *Proceedings of the 6th ICOM. Group on Wet Organic Archaeological Materials Conference, York, 1996*, pp. 57–72, Bremerhaven.

Carrott, J., Hall, A., Issit, M., Kenward, H., Large, F., Milles, A. and Usai, R. (1996) 'Suspected accelerated *in situ* decay of delicate bioarchaeological remains: a case-study from medieval York', *Reports from the Environmental Archaeology Unit, York*, 96/15.

Carter, S. (1990) 'The stratification and taphonomy of shells in calcareous soils: implications for land snail analysis in archaeology', *Journal of Archaeological Science* 17: 495–507.

Carter, S.P. and Davidson, D.A. (1998) 'An evaluation of the contribution of soil micromorphology to the study of ancient arable agriculture', *Geoarchaeology* 13: 535–47.

—— (2000) 'A reply to Macphail's Comments on "An evaluation of the contribution of soil micromorphology to the study of ancient arable agriculture"', *Geoarchaeology* 15: 499–502.

Carver, M.O.H. (1998) *Sutton Hoo: Burial Ground of Kings?,* London: British Museum Press.

Castro, P.V., Chapman, R.W., Gili, S., Lull, V., Mico, R., Rihute, C., Risch, R. and Sanahuja, M.E. (eds) (1998), *Aguas Project: Palaeoclimatic Reconstruction and the Dynamics of Human Settlement and Land use in the Area of the Middle Aguas (Almería), in the South-east of the Iberian Peninsula*, Luxembourg: European Commission.

Castro, P.V., Chapman, R.W., Gili, S., Lull, V., Mico, R., Rihuete, C., Risch, R. and Sanahuja, M.E. (1999) 'Agricultural production and social change in the Bronze Age of southeast Spain: the Gatas Project', *Antiquity* 73: 846–56.

Catt, J.A. (1978) 'The contribution of loess to soils in lowland Britain', in S. Limbrey and J. G. Evans (eds) *The Effect of Man on the Landscape: The lowland zone*, pp. 12–20, London: Council for British Archaeology Research Report 21.

—— (1979) 'Soils and Quaternary Geology in Britain', *Journal of Soil Science* 30: 607–42.

Churchill, D.M. (1970) 'Post-Neolithic to Romano-British sedimentation in the southern Fenlands of Cambridgeshire and Norfolk', in C.W. Phillips (ed.), *The Fenland in Roman Times*, pp. 132–46, London: Royal Geographic Society Research Series No. 5.

Clark, J.G.D. (1933) 'Report on the Early Bronze Age site in south-eastern Fens', *Antiquaries Journal* 13: 266–96.

—— (1936) 'Report on a Late Bronze Age site in Mildenhall Fen', West Suffolk, *Antiquaries Journal* 16: 29–50.

Clark, J.G.D. and Godwin, H. (1940) 'A Late Bronze Age find near Stuntney, Isle of Ely', *Antiquaries Journal* 20: 52–71.

—— (1962) 'The Neolithic in the Cambridgeshire Fens', *Antiquity* 36: 10–23.

Clark, J.G.D, Godwin, H. and Clifford, M.H. (1935) 'Report on recent excavations at Peacock's Farm', Shippea Hill, Cambridgeshire, *Antiquaries Journal* 15: 284–319.

Clark, J.G.D., Higgs, E.S. and Longworth, I.H. (1960) 'Excavations at the Neolithic site at Hurst Fen, Mildenhall, Suffolk', *Proceedings of the Prehistoric Society* 26: 202–45.

Clarke, D.L. (ed.) (1977) *Spatial Archaeology*, London: Academic Press.

Cleal, R.M.J. and Allen, M.J. (1994) 'Investigation of tree-damaged barrows on King Barrow Ridge and Luxenborough Planation', *Wiltshire Archaeological and Natural History Magazine* 87: 54–84.

Cleal, R.M.J., Allen, M.J. and Newman, C. (1994) 'An archaeological and environmental study of the Neolithic and later prehistoric landscape of the Avon Valley between Durrington Walls and Earl's Farm Down', unpublished report, Salisbury: Wessex Archaeology.

Cleal, R.M.J., Walker, K.E. and Montague, R. (1995) *Stonehenge in its Landscape*, Archaeological Report 10, London: English Heritage.

Coles, B. (1995) *Wetland Management: A Survey for English Heritage*, Exeter: Wetland Archaeological Research Project Occasional Paper 9.

Collins, D.N. (1990) 'Glacial processes'. in A. Goudie (ed.) *Geomorphological Techniques*, 2nd edn, pp. 302–20, London: Unwin Hyman.

Colt Hoare, R. (1812) *The Ancient History of Wiltshire*, London: William Millar.

Cooke, R, Warren, A and Goudie, A. (1993) *Desert Geomorphology*, London: University College Press.

Coombs, D. (1992) 'Flag Fen platform and Fengate Power Station post alignment – the Metalwork', *Antiquity* 66: 504–17.

Corfield, M.C. (1993) 'Monitoring the condition of waterlogged archaeological sites', in P. Hoffman (ed.) *Proceedings of the 5th ICOM. Group on Wet Organic Archaeological Materials Conference, Portland, Maine*, pp. 423–36, Bremerhaven.

—— (1996) 'Preventative conservation for archaeological sites', in R. Asho and P. Smith (eds) *Archaeological Conservation and Its Consequences*, pp. 32–7, London: Preprints of the Contributions to the Copenhagen Congress.

Cornwall, I. (1958) *Soils for the Archaeologist*, London: Phoenix House.

Courty, M.-A. (1994) 'Le cadre paléogéographique des occupations humaines dans le bassin du Haut-Khabur (Syrie du Nord-Est): Premiers résultats', *Paléorient* 20: 21–59.

Courty, M.-A. and Weiss, H. (1997) 'The scenario of environmental degradation in the Tell Leilan region, NE Syria, during the late third millennium abrupt climate change', in H. Nuzhet Dalfes, G. Kukla and H. Weiss (eds) *Third Millennium BC Climate Change and Old World Collapse*, Nato A. S. I. Series, Vol. I, pp. 49–89.

Courty, M.-A., Fedoroff, N., Jones, M.K. and McGlade, J. (1994b) 'Environmental dynamics', in S.E. van der Leeuw (ed.) *Temporalities and Desertification in the Vera Basin, Southeast Spain, Archaeomedes Project*, Vol. 2, pp. 19–84, Brussels.

Courty, M.-A., Goldberg, P. and Macphail, R.I. (1989) *Soils and Micromorphology in Archaeology*, Cambridge: Cambridge University Press.

Courty, M.-A., Goldberg, P. and Macphail, R.I. (1994a) 'Ancient people-lifestyles and cultural patterns', in L. Wilding and Oleshko (eds) *Micromorphological Indicators of Anthropogenic Effects on Soils*, pp. 250–69, Acapulco: International Conference of Soil Science.

Crabtree, K. (1996) 'Lycopodium spores and pollen analysis of the old land surface', in M. Bell, P.J. Fowler and S.W. Hillson (eds) *The Experimental Earthwork Project 1960–1992*, pp. 127–31, York: Council for British Archaeology Research Report 100.

Crawford, O.G.S. and Keiller, A. (1928) *Wessex from the Air*, Oxford: Oxford University Press.

Crowther, D., French, C. and Pryor, F. (1985) 'Approaching the fens the flexible way', in C. Haselgrove, M. Millett and I. Smith (eds) *Archaeology from the Ploughsoil: Studies in the Collection and Interpretation of Field Survey Data*, pp. 59–76, Sheffield: University of Sheffield.

Crowther, J., Macphail, R.I. and Cruise, G.M. (1996) 'Short-term, post-burial change in a humic Rendzina soil, Overton Down experimental earthwork, Wiltshire, England', *Geoarchaeology* 11: 5–117.

Cullingford, R.A., Davidson, D.A. and Lewin, J. (eds) (1980) *Timescales in Geomorphology*, London: Wiley.

Cultraro, M. (1997) 'La civiltà di Castelluccio nella zona etnea', in A. Balistreri, E. Giannitrapani, F. Nicolletti, C. Picciotto, L. Titi and S. Tusa (eds) *Prima Sicilia. Alle origini della società siciliana*, pp. 353–57, Palermo: Ediprint.

Curtis, L.F., Courteney, F.M. and Trudgill, S. (1976) *Soils in the British Isles*, London: Longman.

Cuttler, R. (1998) *Land Off Third Drove, Fengate, Peterborough: An Archaeological Evaluation 1998, Preliminary Report*, Project No. 515, unpublished report, Birmingham University Field Archaeology Unit, University of Birmingham.

Dalrymple, J.B., Blong, R.J. and Conacher, A.J. (1968) 'A hypothetical nine unit landsurface model', *Zeitschrift für Geomorphologie* 12: 60–76.

Darby, H.C. (1940) *The Draining of the Fens*, Cambridge: Cambridge University Press.

Davidson, D.A. (1982) 'Soils and man in the past', in E.M. Bridges and D.A. Davidson (eds) *Principles and Applications of Soil Geography*, pp. 1–27, London: Longman.

Davidson, D.A., Carter, S.P. and Quine, T.A. (1992) 'An evaluation of micromophology as an aid to archaeological interpretation', *Geoarchaeology* 7: 55–65.

Davies, D.B., Eagle, D.J. and Finney, J.B. (1972) *Soil Management*, Ipswich: Farming Press.

Davis, M., Gdaniec, K., Brice, M and White, L. (1998) *Study of the Mitigation of Construction Impact on Archaeological Remains*, Cambridge/London: Cambridge Archaeological Unit/Hunting Technical Services Ltd.

de Coninck, F. and Righi, D. (1983) 'Podzolisation and the spodic horizon', in P. Bullock and C.P. Murphy (eds) *Soil Micromorphology*, pp. 389–417, Berkhamsted: A.B. Academic.

Department of Environment (D.O.E.) (1990) *Policy Planning Guidance 16: Archaeology and Planning*, London: Department of Environment.

Dettman, M.G. and Emerson, W.W. (1959) 'A modified permeability test for measuring the cohesion of soil crumbs', *Journal of Soil Science* 26: 215–16.

Dimbleby, D.W. (1962) *The Development of British Heathlands and Their Soils*, Oxford: Oxford Forestry Memoir 23.

—— (1972) 'The environment', in B. S. Bruce-Mitford *The Sutton Hoo Ship Burial*, pp. 48–65, London: British Museum.

—— (1985) *The Palynology of Archaeological Sites*, London: Academic Press.

Dimbleby, G.W (1965) 'Pollen analysis', in P.A.M. Keefe, J.J. Wymer and G.W. Dimbleby, 'A Mesolithic site on Iping Common, Sussex, England', *Proceedings of the Prehistoric Society* 31: 85–92.

Dimbleby, G.W. and Evans, J.G. (1974) 'Pollen and land snail analysis of calcareous soils', *Journal of Archaeological Science* 1: 117–33.

Downes, J. (1993) 'The distribution and significance of Bronze Age metalwork in the North Level', in C. French and F. Pryor (eds) *The Southwest Fen Dyke Survey Project, 1982–86*, pp. 21–30, Cambridge: East Anglian Archaeology 59.

Dugdale, R. (1990) 'Coastal processes', in A. Goudie (ed.) *Geomorphological Techniques*, 2nd edn, pp. 351–64, London: Unwin Hyman.

Edens, C. and Wilkinson, T.J. (1998) 'Southwest Arabia during the Holocene: Recent archaeological developments', *Journal of World Prehistory* 12: 55–119.

Edmonds, M. (1999) *Ancestral Geographies of the Neolithic: Landscapes, Monuments and Memory*, London: Routledge.

Edmonds, M., Evans, C. and Gibson, D, (1999) 'Assembly and collection – lithic complexes in the Cambridgeshire Fenlands', *Proceedings of the Prehistoric Society* 65: 47–82.

Entwhistle, R. and Bowden, M. (1991) 'Cranborne Chase: the molluscan evidence', in J. Barrett, R. Bradley and M. Hall (eds) *Papers on the Prehistoric Archaeology of Cranborne Chase*, pp. 20–48, Oxford: Oxbow Monograph 11.

Evans, C. (1992) 'Fengate: archaeological assessment', unpublished report, Cambridge Archaeological Unit Report No. 72, University of Cambridge.

—— and Hodder, I. (1984) 'Excavations at Haddenham', *Fenland Research* 1, 32–6.

—— (1985) 'Excavations at Haddenham', *Fenland Research* 2, 18–23.

—— (in press a) *The Emergence of a Fen Landscape, The Haddenham Project: Volume I*, Cambridge: McDonald Institute Monograph.

—— (in press b) *Marshland Communities and Cultural Landscape: The Haddenham Project: Volume II*, Cambridge: McDonald Institute Monograph.

Evans, C. and Knight, M. (1996) 'Barleycroft Farm, Bluntisham', unpublished report, Cambridge Archaeological Unit Report, University of Cambridge.

—— (1997a) 'The Barleycroft Paddock excavations, Cambridgeshire', unpublished report, Cambridge Archaeological Unit, University of Cambridge.

—— (1997b) 'The Over Lowland investigations, Cambridgeshire: Part I – The 1996 Evaluation', unpublished report, Cambridge Archaeological Unit, University of Cambridge.

Evans, C. and Pollard, J. (1995) 'The excavation of a ring-ditch and prehistoric fieldsystem at Barleycroft Farm, Bluntisham, Cambs., 1994', unpublished report, Cambridge Archaeological Unit, Barleycroft Farm/ARC Paper 2, University of Cambridge.

Evans, C. and Serjeantson, D. (1988) 'The backwater economy of a fen-edge community in the Iron Age: the upper Delphs, Haddenham', *Antiquity* 62: 360–70.

Evans, J. and O'Connor, T. (1999) *Environmental Archaeology: Principles and Methods*, Stroud: Sutton.

Evans, J.G. (1971) 'Habitat change on the calcareous soils of Britain: the impact of Neolithic man', in D.D.A. Simpson (ed.) *Economy and settlement in Neolithic and Early Bronze Age Britain and Europe*, pp. 27–74, Leicester: Leicester University Press.

—— (1972) *Land Snails in Archaeology*, London: Seminar Press.

—— (1991) 'An approach to the interpretation of dry-ground and wet-ground molluscan taxocenes from central-southern England', in D.R. Harris and K.D. Thomas (eds) *Modelling Ecological Change*, pp. 75–89, London: Archetype Publications Ltd.

Evans, J.G., Leighton, D. and French, C. (1978) 'Habitat change in two Late-glacial and Post-glacial sites in southern Britain', in S. Limbrey and J. G. Evans (eds) *The Effect of Man on the Landscape: The Lowland Zone*, pp. 63–74, London: Council for British Archaeology Research Report No. 21.

Evans, R. (1981) 'Assessments of soil erosion and peat wastage for parts of East Anglia, England: a Field Visit', in R.P.C. Morgan (ed.) *Soil conservation: problems and prospects*, pp. 521–30, New York: John Wiley.

—— (1992) 'Erosion in England and Wales – the present the key to the past', in M. G. Bell and J. Boardman (eds) *Past and Present Soil Erosion*, pp. 53–66, Oxford: Oxbow Monograph 22.

Evans, R. and Cook, S. (1986) 'Soil erosion in Britain', *SEESOIL* 3: 28–58.

Farmer, E.E. (1973) 'Relative detachability of soil particles by simulated rainfall', *Soil Science Society of America Proceedings* 37: 629–33.

Fedele, F.G. (1990) 'Man, land and climate: emerging interactions from the Holocene of the Yemen Highlands', in S. Bottema, G. Entjes-Nieborg and W. van Zeist (eds) *Man's Role in the Shaping of the Mediterranean Landscape*, pp. 31–42, Rotterdam: Balkema.

Fedoroff, N. (1968) 'Génèse et morphologie des sols à horizon B textural en France atlantique', *Science du Sols* 1: 29–65.

Ferring, C.R. (1994) 'The role of geoarchaeology in Paleoindian research', in R.

Bonnichen and D.G. Steele (eds) *Method and Theory for Investigating the Peopling of the Americas*, pp. 57–72, Corvallis, Oregon: Center for the Study of the First Americans.

Fisher, P.F. (1982) 'A review of lessivage and Neolithic cultivation in southern England', *Journal of Archaeological Science* 9: 299–304.

—— (1983) 'Pedogenesis within the archaeological landscape at South Lodge Camp, Wiltshire, England', *Geoderma* 29: 93–105.

—— (1991) 'The physical environment of Cranborne Chase', in J. Barrett, R. Bradley and M. Hall (eds) *Papers on the Prehistoric Archaeology of Cranborne Chase*, pp. 11–19, Oxford: Oxbow Monograph 11.

Fitzpatrick, E.A. (1971) *Pedology: A Systematic Approach to Soil Science*, Edinburgh: Oliver and Boyd.

—— (1984) *Micromorphology of Soils*, London: Chapman and Hall.

—— (1986) *An Introduction to Soil Science*, 2nd edn, Harlow: Longman.

—— (1993) *Soil Microscopy and Micromorphology*, Chichester: John Wiley and Sons.

Fleming, A. (1988) *The Dartmoor Reaves: Investigating Prehistoric Land Divisions*, London: Batsford.

French, C.A.I. (1980a) 'Sediment analysis of second millennium ditches', in F. Pryor *Excavation at Fengate, Peterborough, England: The Third Report*, pp. 190–202, Northampton/Toronto: Northamptonshire Archaeological Society Monograph 1/Royal Ontario Museum Archaeology Monograph 6.

—— (1980b) 'Analysis of molluscs from two second millennium ditches', in F. Pryor *Excavation at Fengate, Peterborough, England: The Third Report*, pp. 204–12, Northampton/Toronto: Northamptonshire Archaeological Society Monograph 1/Royal Ontario Museum Archaeology Monograph 6.

—— (1983) 'An environmental study of the soil, sediment and molluscan evidence associated with prehistoric monuments on river terrace gravels in north-west Cambridgeshire', unpublished PhD, University of London.

—— (1984) 'Molluscan fauna from two Iron Age ditches', in F. Pryor *Excavation at Fengate, Peterborough, England: The Fourth Report*, pp. M217–222, Northampton/Toronto: Northamptonshire Archaeological Society Monograph 2/Royal Ontario Museum Archaeology Monograph 7.

—— (1985a) 'Soil, sediment and molluscan analyses of excavated features', in F. Pryor and C. French *Archaeology and Environment in the Lower Welland Valley*, pp. 205–16, Cambridge: East Anglian Archaeology 27.

—— (1985b) 'Haddenham soils', *Fenland Research* 2, 23–5.

—— (1988a) 'Aspects of buried prehistoric soils in the lower Welland valley and fen margin north of Peterborough, Cambridgeshire', in W. Groenman-van Waateringe and M. Robinson (eds) *Man-made Soils*, pp. 115–28, Oxford: British Archaeological Reports S410.

—— (1988b) 'Further aspects of buried prehistoric soils in the fen margin northeast of Peterborough, Cambridgeshire', in P. Murphy and C.A.I. French (eds) *The Exploitation of Wetlands*, pp. 193–211, Oxford: British Archaeological Reports 186.

—— (1990) 'Neolithic soils, middens and alluvium in the lower Welland valley', *Oxford Journal of Archaeology* 9: 305–11.

—— (1991a) 'Fengate 1989: the soil micromorphological report', unpublished report, Fenland Archaeological Trust.

—— (1991b) 'Fengate, Cat's Water (1990): soil micromorphological analysis', unpublished report, Fenland Archaeological Trust.

—— (1992a) 'Alluviated fen-edge prehistoric landscapes in Cambridgeshire', England, in M. Bernardi (ed.) *Archaeologia Del Paesaggio*, pp. 709–731, Firenze.

—— (1992b) Fengate to Flag Fen: summary of the soil and sediment analyses, *Antiquity* 66: 458–61.

—— (1992c) 'Fengate 1992: soils assessment', unpublished report, Cambridge Archaeology Unit, University of Cambridge.

—— (1992d) 'Flag Fen: the soil micromorphological assessment', unpublished report, Fenland Archaeological Trust.

—— (1994a) 'Meadow Lane, St Ives, Cambridgeshire: soil/sediment assessment', unpublished report, Cambridge Archaeological Unit.

—— (1994b) *Excavation of the Deeping St Nicholas Barrow Complex, South Lincolnshire*, Heckington: Lincolnshire Archaeology and Heritage Report Series no. 1.

—— (1995a) 'Flag Fen Environs: soil micromorphology', unpublished report, Fenland Archaeological Trust.

—— (1995b) 'Botai, Kazakhstan: assessment of the geomorphological context and of the deposits within the sunken floored dwellings', unpublished report, Department of Archaeology, University of Cambridge.

—— (1996a) 'Broom Quarry, Southill, Bedfordshire, 1996: assessment of the buried soils', unpublished report, Cambridge Archaeological Unit, University of Cambridge.

—— (1996b) 'Molluscan analysis', in R.P.J. Jackson and T.W. Potter *Excavations at Stonea, Cambridgeshire, 1980–85*, pp. 639–54, London: British Museum Press.

—— (1997a) 'Sewage treatment works, Fengate, Peterborough: preliminary soil/ sediment assessment', unpublished report, Fenland Archaeological Trust.

—— (1997b) 'Fengate (MRP-96): micromorphological analysis of the buried soil', unpublished report, Cambridge Archaeological Unit.

—— (1997c) 'Land off Third Drove, Fengate, Peterborough: the micromorphological analysis', unpublished report, Birmingham University Field Archaeological Unit.

—— (1998a) 'Soils and sediments', in F. Pryor *Etton: Excavations at a Neolithic Causewayed Enclosure near Maxey, Cambridgeshire*, 1982–7, Archaeological Report 18, pp. 311–31, London: English Heritage.

—— (1998b) 'Land off Third Drove, Fengate, Peterborough: the micromorphological analysis', in R. Cuttler, 'Land off Third Drove, Fengate, Peterborough : an archaeological evaluation 1998, preliminary report', pp. 24–7, Project no. 515, unpublished report, Birmingham University Field Archaeology Unit, University of Birmingham.

—— (1998c) 'Deer Park Farm, Wimborne St Giles, Dorset: micromorphological analysis', unpublished report, Department of Archaeology, University of Cambridge.

—— (2000a) 'Dewatering, desiccation and erosion: an appraisal of water and peat fen in the Fenlands', in T. Lane, A. Crowson and J. Reeve (eds) *Fenland Management Project Excavations*, pp. 4–9, Heckington: Lincolnshire Archaeology and Heritage Report Series No. 4.

—— (2000b) 'Development of Fenland in prehistoric times', in T. Kirby and S. Oosthuizen (eds) *An Atlas of Cambridgeshire and Huntingdonshire History*, p. 4, Cambridge: Anglia Polytechnic University.

—— (2001a) 'The development of the Flag Fen and Fengate prehistoric landscape', in F Pryor *The Flag Fen Basin: Archaeology and Environment of a Fenland Landscape,* Chapter 17, pp. 400–4, Archaeological Reports, London: English Heritage.

—— (2001b) 'Soil micromorphological analyses', in F. Pryor *The Flag Fen Basin: Archaeology and Environment of a Fenland Landscape*, pp. 39–43, 53–8, 382–3, Appendices 1,2 & 5, Archaeological Reports, London: English Heritage.

—— (in press a) 'Soil formation and erosion in Holocene valley landscapes: case studies from Cranborne Chase, southeastern Spain, Sicily and Yemen', in M. Bell and J. Boardman (eds) *Geoarchaeology: Landscape Change over Archaeological Timescales*, Oxford: Oxbow.

—— (in press b) 'Soil micromorphology of the Haddenham sites', in C. Evans and I. Hodder *The Emergence of a Fen Landscape, The Haddenham Project: Volume I,* and *Marshland Communities and Cultural Landscape: The Haddenham Project: Volume II,* Cambridge: McDonald Institute Monograph.

—— (forthcoming a) 'The micromorphological analysis of the buried soils', in M.O.H. Carter *Excavations at Sutton Hoo.*

—— (forthcoming b) 'Soil micromorphology', in C. French and F. Pryor *Archaeology and Environment of the Etton Landscape*, East Anglian Archaeology.

French, C.A.I. and Davis, M.J. (1994) 'The long-term hydrological monitoring of relict landscapes at Willingham Gravel Quarry, Cambridgeshire: project design', unpublished report, Cambridge/London: English Heritage.

French, C.A.I. and Lewis, H. (2001) 'The Fengate Depot site: the micromorphological analysis', in F. Pryor, *The Flag Fen Basin: Archaeology and Environment in a Fenland Landscape*, pp. 20–2, Archaeological Reports, London: English Heritage.

French, C.A.I. and Heathcote, J. (in press) 'Holocene landscape change in the lower Great Ouse valley, Cambridgeshire, England', in A. Howard, D. Passmore and M. Macklin (eds) *Alluvial Archaeology in Northwest Europe and the Mediterranean*, Rotterdam: Balkema.

French, C.A.I. and Kousoulakou, M. (in press) 'Geomorphological and micromorphological investigations of palaeosols, valley sediments and a sunken floored dwelling at Botai, Kazakhstan', in M. Levine, C. Renfrew and K. Boyle (eds) *Prehistoric Steppe Adaptation and the Horse*, pp. 105–114, Cambridge: McDonald Institute Monograph.

French, C.A.I. and Marsh, P. (1999) 'Welland Bank Quarry, Lincolnshire, 1987: the soil micromorphological analysis of the dark earth and buried soil', unpublished report, Heckington: Archaeological Project Services.

French, C.A.I. and Pryor, F. (forthcoming) *Archaeology and Environment of the Etton Landscape*, East Anglian Archaeology.

—— (1992) 'Floodplain gravels: buried Neolithic and Bronze Age landscapes along the Fen margins', in M. Fulford and E. Nichols (eds) *Developing Landscapes in Lowland Britain: The Archaeology of the British Gravels: A Review*, pp. 63–77, London: Society of Antiquaries Occasional Paper 14.

—— (1993) *The South-west Fen Dyke Survey Project, 1982–86*, Cambridge: East Anglian Archaeology 59.

French, C.A.I. and Taylor, M. (1985) 'Desiccation, and destruction: the immediate effect of dewatering at Etton, Cambridgeshire', *Oxford Journal of Archaeology* 4: 139–56.

French, C.A.I. and Wait, G. (1988) *An Archaeological Survey of the Cambridgeshire River Gravels*, Cambridge: Fenland Archaeological Trust/Cambridgeshire County Council.

French, C.A.I., Davis, M. and Heathcote, J. (1999) 'Hydrological monitoring of an alluviated landscape in the lower Great Ouse valley, Cambridgeshire: interim results of the first three years', *Environmental Archaeology* 4: 41–56.

French, C.A.I., Lewis, H., Allen, M. and Scaife, R. (2000) 'Palaeoenvironmental and archaeological investigations on Wyke Down and in the upper Allen valley, Cranborne Chase, Dorset, England: interim summary report for 1998–9', *Proceedings of the Dorset Natural History and Archaeological Society* 122: 51–73.

French, C.A.I., Macklin, M. and Passmore, D. (1992) 'Archaeology and palaeo-channels in the Lower Welland and Nene valleys: alluvial archaeology at the fen-edge, eastern England', in S. Needham and M. Macklin (eds) *Alluvial Archaeology in Britain*, pp. 169–76, Oxford: Oxbow Monograph 27.

French, C.A.I., Passmore, D. and Schulte, L. (1998) 'Geomorphology and edaphic factors', in P.V. Castro, R.W. Chapman, S. Gili, V. Lull, R. Mico, C. Rihuete, R. Risch and M.E. Sanahuja (eds) *Aguas Project: Palaeoclimatic Reconstruction and the Dynamics of Human Settlement and Land Use in the Area of the Middle Agaus (Almería), in the South-east of the Iberian Penisula*, pp. 45–52, Luxembourg: European Commission.

Fryer, V. and Murphy, P. (1996) 'Macrofossils', in J. Pollard *Iron Age Riverside Pit Alignments at St Ives, Cambridgeshire, Proceedings of the Prehistoric Society* 62: 109.

Gallois, R.W. (1988) 'Geology of the country around Ely', *Memoir of the British Geological Survey*, Sheet 173, London: HMSO.

Gardiner, J. (1985) 'Intra-site patterning in the flint assemblage from the Dorset Cursus, 1984', *Proceedings of the Dorset Natural History and Archaeological Society* 105: 87–93.

—— (1991) 'The flint industries in the study area', in J. Barrett, R. Bradley and M. Hall (eds) *Papers on the Prehistoric Archaeology of Cranborne Chase*, pp. 59–69 and 110–11, Oxford: Oxbow Monograph 11.

—— (1998) 'Worked flint from barrows 34 and 41, Wyke Down, Dorset', unpublished report, University of Cambridge.

Gardner, A. (1999) 'The impact of Neolithic agriculture on the environments of South-East Europe', unpublished PhD, University of Cambridge.

Gdaniec, K. (1995) 'The post-excavation assessment report on the archaeology of the Anglian Water Isleham–Ely pipeline', Report 118, unpublished report, Cambridge Archaeological Unit, University of Cambridge.

—— (1997) 'Third Drove, Fengate, Peterborough (MRP-96): archaeological assessment', unpublished report, Cambridge Archaeological Unit, University of Cambridge.

Ge, T., Courty, M.-A., Matthews, W. and Wattez, J. (1993) 'Sedimentary formation processes of occupation surfaces', in P. Goldberg, D. T. Nash and M. D. Petraglia (eds) *Formation Processes in Archaeological Context*, Monographs in World Archaeology 17, pp. 149–64, Madison: Prehistory Press.

Gebhardt, A. (1990) 'Micromorphological analysis of soil structural modifications caused by different cultivation implements', in *L'Exploitation des Plantes en Prehistoire: Documents et Techniques*, Valbonnes: Actes de la Table Ronde CNRS, 1988.

—— (1992) 'Micromorphological analysis of soil structure modifications caused by different cultivation implements', in *Préhistoire de l'agriculture: Nouvelles approches expérimentales et ethnographiques*, pp. 373–81, Valbonnes: C.R.A. Monograph 6.

Gerasimova, M.I., Gubin, S.V. and Shoba, S.A. (1996) *Soils of Russia and Adjacent Countries: Geography and Micromorphology*, Moscow-Wageningen.

Gerrard, J. (1992) *Soil Geomorphology: An Integration of Pedology and Geomorphology*, London: Chapman and Hall.

Gibson, D. (1997) 'Fourth Drove, Cat's Water, Fengate, Peterborough: archaeological assessment', unpublished report, Cambridge Archaeological Unit, University of Cambridge.

Gibson, M. and Wilkinson, T.J. (1995) 'The Dhamar Plain, Yemen: a preliminary study of the archaeological landscape', *Proceedings of the Seminar for Arabian Studies* 25: 159–83.

Godwin, H. (1940) 'Studies of the post-glacial history of British vegetation. III. Fenland pollen diagrams. IV. Post-glacial changes of relative land and sea-level in the English Fenland', *Philosophical Transactions of the Royal Society London,* B 230: 239–303.

—— (1975) *History of the Britsh Flora*, 2nd edn, Cambridge: Cambridge University Press.

—— (1978) *Fenland: Its ancient past and uncertain future*, Cambridge: Cambridge University Press.

Godwin, H., Godwin, M.E. and Clifford, M.H. (1935) 'Controlling factors in the formation of fen deposits, as shown in peat investigations at Wood Fen, near Ely', *Journal of Ecology* 23: 509–35.

Goldberg, P. and Whitebread, I. (1993) 'Micromorphological studies of a bedouin tent floor', in P. Goldberg, D.T. Nash and M.D. Petraglia (eds) *Formation Processes in Archaeological Context*, Monographs in World Archaeology No. 17, pp. 165–88, Madison: Prehistory Press.

Goudie, A. (ed.) (1990) *Geomorphological Techniques*, 2nd edn, London: Unwin Hyman.

—— (1993a) *The Landforms of England and Wales*, Oxford: Blackwell Scientific.

—— (1993b) *The Human Impact on the Natural Environment,* Oxford: Blackwell Scientific.

Green, F.J. (1985) 'Evidence for domestic cereal use at Maxey', in F. Pryor and C. French (eds) *Archaeology and Environment in the Lower Welland Valley*, pp. 224–31, East Anglian Archaeology 27, Cambridge.

Green, M. (2000) *A Landscape Revealed: 10,000 Years on a Chalkland Farm*, Stroud: Tempus.

Green, M. and Allen, M.J. (1997) 'An early prehistoric shaft on Cranborne Chase', *Oxford Journal of Archaeology* 16: 121–32.

Green, M., Barton, R.N.E., Debenham, N. and French, C.A.I. (1998) 'A new late glacial open-air site at Deer Park Farm, Wimborne St Giles, Dorset', *Proceedings of the Dorset Natural History and Archaeological Society* 120: 85–8.

Greenland, D.J., Rimmer, D. and Payne, D. (1975) 'Determination of the Structural Stability class of English and Welsh soils using a water coherence test', *Journal of Soil Science* 26: 294–303.

G.S.B. Prospection (1998) 'Wyke Down, Gussage St Michael, Dorset', Bradford: Geophysical Survey Report 98/65.

—— (1999) 'Wyke Down II, Gussage St Michael, Dorset', Bradford: Geophysical Survey Report 99/99.

—— (2001) 'Bottlebush Down, Sixpenny Handley, Dorset', Bradford: Geophysical Survey Report 2001/87.

Gurney, D.A. (1980) 'Evidence of Bronze Age salt production at Northey, Peterborough', *Northamptonshire Archaeology* 15: 1–11.

Hall, D. (1981) 'Cambridgeshire Fenland; an intensive archaeological fieldwork survey', in R.T. Rowley (ed.) *The Evolution of Marshland Landscape*, pp. 52–73, Oxford.

—— (1987) *Fenland Project No. 2: The Cambridgeshire Survey, Peterborough to March*, Cambridge: East Anglian Archeology 35.

—— (1996) *The Fenland Project, Number 10: The Isle of Ely and Wisbech*, Cambridge: East Anglian Archaeology 78.

Hall, D. and Coles, J. (1994) *Fenland Survey : An Essay in Landscape and Persistence*, Archaeological Report 1, London: English Heritage.

Hall, D.N. (1982) *Medieval Fields*, Shire Archaeology No. 28, Princes Risboough.

Haselgrove, C., Millett, M. and Smith, I. (eds) (1985) *Archaeology from the Ploughsoil: Studies in the Collection and Interpretation of Field Survey Data*, Sheffield: University of Sheffield.

Hearne, C.M. and Birbeck, V. (1999) *A35 Bypass Tolpuddle to Puddleton Bypass DBFO, Dorset, 1996–8*, Salisbury: Wessex Archaeology Report No. 15.

Hesse, P.R. (1971) *A Textbook of Soil Chemical Analysis*, London: John Murray.

Hodge, R.D. and Arden-Clarke, C. (1986) *Soil Erosion in Britain*, Bristol: Soil Association.

Hodgson, J.M. (1974) *Soil Survey Field Handbook*, Harpenden: Soil Survey Technical Monographs No. 5.

Hogg, A.H.A. (1980) *Surveying for Archaeologists and Other Fieldworkers*, London: Croom Helm.

Holliday, V.T. (1997) *Paleoindian Geoarchaeology of the Southern High Plains*, Austin: University of Texas.

Horton, A., Lake, R.D., Bisson, G. and Coppack, B.C. (1974) *The Geology of Peterborough*, London: Institute of Geological Sciences Report No. 73/12.

Horton, R.E. (1945) 'Erosional development of streams and their drainage basins: a hydrophysical approach to quantitative morphology', *Bulletin of the Geological Society of America* 56: 275–370.

Howard, A.J. and Macklin, M.G. (1999) 'A generic geomorphological approach to archaeological interpretation and prospection in British river valleys: a guide for archaeologists investigating Holocene landscapes', *Antiquity* 73: 527–41.

Howard, A.J., Passmore, D. and Macklin, M. (ed.) (in press) *Alluvial Archaeology in Northwest Europe and the Mediterranean*, Rotterdam: Balkema.

Hunt, G. (in press) 'Waterlogged plant remains', in C. Evans and I. Hodder *Marshland Communities and Cultural Landscape: The Haddenham Project: Volume II*, Cambridge: McDonald Institute.

Hunter, F. and Carrie, J.A. (1956) 'Structural changes during bulk soil storage', *Journal of Soil Science* 7: 75–80.

Hunting Land and Environment Ltd. (1994) *Willingham Hydrological Monitoring Establishment of Monitoring Points: Final Report,* Hemel Hempstead: H.L.E. Report R930: HER-10.

Hunting Technical Services (1997) *Market Deeping Progress Report for the Period October 1995 to December 1996*, Hemel Hempstead: H. T. S. Report R1163: 305431.

Hutchinson, J.N. (1980) 'The record of peat wastage in the East Anglian fenlands at Holme Post, 1848–1978 AD', *Journal of Ecology* 68: 229–49.

Imeson, A.C., Kwaad, F.J.P.M. and Mucher, H.J. (1980) 'Hillslope processes and deposits in the forested areas of Luxembourg', in R.A. Cullingford, D.A. Davidson and J. Lewin (eds) *Timescales in Geomorphology*, pp. 31–42, New York: Wiley.

Jackson, M.L. (1958) *Soil Chemical Analysis*, Englewood Cliffs: Prentice-Hall Inc.

Jackson, R.P.J. and Potter, T.W. (1996) *Excavations at Stonea, Cambridgeshire, 1980–85*, London: British Museum.

Jelgersma, S. (1979) 'Sea level changes in the North Sea Basin', in E. Oele, R.T.E. Schuttenhelm and A.J. Wiggins (eds) *The Quaternary History of the North Sea*, Acta University of Uppsala Symposium Annum Quingentesimum Celebrantis 2, pp. 233–48, Uppsala.

Jennings, J.N. (1950) 'The origin of Fenland meres: Fenland homologues of the Norfolk Broads', *Geological Magazine* 87: 217–25.

Jenny, H. (1941) *Factors of Soil-formation: A system of quantitative pedology*, London: McGraw-Hill.

Johnston, A.E. (1973) 'The effects of ley and arable cropping systems on the amount of soil organic matter in the Rothamsted and Woburn ley arable experiments', *Report of the Rothamsted Experimental Station for 1972*, pp. 131–67, Rothamsted.

Jones, G. (in press a) 'Charred plant remains', in C. Evans and I. Hodder *The Emergence of a Fen Landscape: The Haddenham Project: Volume I*, Cambridge: McDonald Institute.

—— (in press b) 'Cereal processing, household space and crop husbandry', in C. Evans and I. Hodder *Marshland Communities and Cultural Landscape, The Haddenham Project : Volume II*, Cambridge: McDonald Institute.

Jongerius, A. (1970) 'Some morphological aspects of regrouping phenomena in Dutch soils', *Geoderma* 4: 311–31.

—— (1983) 'The role of micromorphology in agricultural research', in P. Bullock and C. P. Murphy (eds) *Soil Micromorphology*, pp. 111–38, Berkhamsted: A. B. Academic.

Juggins, S. (no date) 'Diatom analysis at Flag Fen', unpublished MSc thesis, University of London.

Keef, P.A.M., Wymer, J.J. and Dimbleby, G.W. (1965) 'A mesolithic site on Iping Common, Sussex, England', *Proceedings of the Prehistoric Society* 31: 85–92.

Keeley, H.C.M. (1982) 'Pedogenesis during the later prehistoric period in Britain', in A. F. Harding (ed.) *Climate Change in Later Pre-History*, pp.114–26, Edinburgh: Edinburgh University Press.

Keeley, H.C.M. and Macphail, R.I. (1982) 'Soils of the Saddlesborough reave area, Shaugh Moor', in N.D. Balaam, K. Smith and G.J. Wainwright, *The Shaugh Moor Project: fourth report – environment, context and conclusion*, *Proceedings of the Prehistoric Society* 48: 219–20.

Kenward, H. and Hall, A. (2000) 'Decay of delicate organic remains in shallow urban deposits: are we at a watershed?', *Antiquity* 74: 519–25.

Kerney, M.P., Chandler, E.H. and Brown, T.J. (1964) 'The Late-glacial and Post-glacial history of the Chalk escarpment near Brook', Kent, *Philosophical Transactions of the Royal Society* (B) 248: 135–204.

Kirkby, M.J. (1969a) 'Erosion by water on hillslopes', in R.J. Chorley (ed.) *Water, earth and man*, pp. 229–38, London: Methuen.

—— (1969b) 'Infiltration, throughflow and overland flow', in R.J. Chorley (ed.) *Water, earth and man*, pp. 215–227, London: Methuen.

Kislenko, A. and Tatarintseva, N. (1999) 'The Eastern Ural steppe at the end of the Stone Age', in M. Levine, Y. Rassamakin, A. Kislenko, N. Tatarintseva and C.

Renfrew (eds) *Late Prehistoric Exploitation of the Eurasian Steppe*, pp. 183–216, Cambridge: McDonald Institute Monograph.

Kooistra, M.J. (1987) 'The effects of compaction and deep tillage on soil structure in a Dutch sandy loam soil', in N. Fedoroff, L.M. Bresson and M.-A. Courty (eds) *Soil Micromorphology*, pp. 445–50, Plaisir: L'Association Française pour l'Étude du Sol.

Kubiena, W.L. (1953) *The Soils of Europe*, London: Thomas Murphy and Sons.

Kwaad, F.J.P.M. and Mucher, H.J. (1979) 'The evolution of soils and slope deposits in the Luxembourg Ardennes near Wiltz', *Geoderma* 17: 1–37.

Lambrick, G. (1992) 'Alluvial archaeology of the Holocene in the upper Thames basin 1971–1991: a review', in S. Needham and M. Macklin (eds) *Alluvial Archaeology in Britain*, pp. 209–28, Oxford: Oxbow Monograph 27.

Lambrick, G. and Robinson, M. (1979) *Iron Age and Roman riverside settlements at Farmoor, Oxfordshire*, Oxford: Council for British Archaeology Research Report 32.

Lane, T., Crowson, A. and Reeve, J. (2000) *Fenland Management Project: Salt Manufacture in the East Anglian Fenlands*, Heckington: Lincolnshire Archaeology and Heritage Report Series No. 4.

Lang, A. and Wagner, G.A. (1996) 'Infrared stimulated luminescence dating of archaeosediments', *Archaeometry* 38: 129–41.

Langbein, W.B. and Schumm, S.A. (1958) 'Yield of sediment in relation to mean annual precipitation', *Transactions of the American Geophysical Unit* 39: 1076–84.

Leighton, R. (1999) *Sicily before History*, London: Duckworth.

Lentini, A. (1988) 'Preliminary pollen analysis on paleosol horizon in the Yala area', in A. de Maigret (ed.) *The Sabaen Archaeological Complex in the Wadi Yala*, pp. 52–4, Rome: ISMEO.

Levine, M., Rassamakin, Y., Kislenko, A., Tatarintseva, N. and Renfrew, C. (eds) (1999) *Late Prehistoric Exploitation of the Eurasian Steppe*, Cambridge: McDonald Institute.

Lewin, J. (1990) 'River channels', in A. Goudie (ed.) *Geomorphological Techniques,* 2nd edn, pp. 280–301, London: Unwin Hyman.

Lewis, H.A. (1998a) 'The characterisation and interpretation of ancient tillage practices through soil micromorphology: a methodological study', unpublished PhD, University of Cambridge.

—— (1998b) 'Summary report on the buried soils and turf mounds from Wyke Down barrows 34 and 41', unpublished report, Department of Archaeology, University of Cambridge.

Limbrey, S. (1975) *Soil Science and Archaeology*, London: Academic Press.

Low, A. J. (1972) 'The effects of cultivation on the structure and other physical characteristics of grassland and arable soils (1945–1970)', *Journal of Soil Science* 23: 363–80.

Lyell, C. (1863) *Geological Evidences of the Antiquity of Man*, London: J. Murray.

McKeague, J.A. (1983) 'Clay skins and argillic horizons', in P. Bullock and C.P. Murphy (eds) *Soil Micromorphology*, pp. 367–88, Berkhamsted: A. B. Academic.

Mackereth, F.J.H. (1965) 'Chemical investigations of lake sediments and their interpretation', *Proceedings of the Royal Society of London* 161B: 295–309.

Macphail, R.I. (1986) 'Palaeosols in archaeology', in V. P. Wright (ed.) *Paleosols*, pp. 263–90, Oxford: Blackwell Scientific.

—— (1987) 'A review of soil science in archaeology in England', in H.C.M. Keeley (ed.) *Environmental Archaeology: A Regional Review,* Vol. II, pp. 332–77, London: English Heritage Occasional Paper 1.

—— (1992) 'Soil micromorphological evidence of ancient soil erosion', in M. Bell and J. Boardman (eds) *Past and Present Soil Erosion*, pp. 197–215, Oxford: Oxbow Monograph 22.

—— (1993) 'Soil micromorphology', in A. Whittle, A.J. Rouse and J.G. Evans 'A Neolithic downland monument in its environment: excavations at the Easton Down long barrow, Bishops Cannings, North Wiltshire', *Proceedings of the Prehistoric Society* 59: 197–239.

—— (1995) 'Warren Villas, Bedfordshire: soil micromorphology assessment', unpublished report, London: English Heritage.

—— (1998) 'A reply to Carter and Davidson's "An evaluation of the contribution of soil micromorphology to the study of ancient arable agriculture"', *Geoarchaeology* 13, 549–564.

Macphail, R.I. and Cruise, G.M. (1996) 'Soil micromorphology', in M. Bell, P.J. Fowler, and S. Hillson (eds) *The Experimental Earthwork Project 1960–1992*, pp. 95–107, York: Council for British Archaeology Research Report 100.

Macphail, R.I., Courty, M.-A. and Gebhardt, A. (1990) 'Soil micromorphological evidence of early agriculture in north west Europe', *World Archaeology* 22: 59–69.

Macphail, R.I., Romans, J.C.C. and Robertson, L. (1987) 'The application of soil micromorphology to the understanding of Holocene soil development in the British Isles, with special reference to early cultivation', in N. Fedoroff, L.M. Bresson and M.-A. Courty (eds) *Soil Micromorphology*, pp. 647–56, Plaisir: L'Association Française pour l'Étude du Sol.

Mahany, C. (1969) 'Fengate', *Current Archaeology* 17: 156–7.

Malone, C. and Stoddart, S. (1999) 'A house in the Sicilian hills', *Antiquity* 74: 471–2.

Malone, C., Puglisi, D. and Stoddart, S. (in press) 'La valorizzazione dei ritrovamenti preistorici di Troina, in *Atti del Primo Congresso di Preistoria e Prototoria Siciliana di Corleone*', Palermo.

Martin, E. and Murphy, P. (1988) 'West Row Fen, Suffolk: a Bronze Age fen-edge settlement site', *Antiquity* 62: 353–58.

Matthews, W. (1995) 'Micromorphological characterisation and interpretation of occupation deposits and microstratigraphic sequences at Abu Salabikh, Iraq', in A.J. Barham and R.I. Macphail (eds) *Archaeological Sediments and Soils: Analysis, Interpretation and Management*, pp. 41–76, London: Archetype Books.

Matthews, W., French, C., Lawrence, T., Cutler, D.F. and Jones, M.K. (1996) 'Multiple surfaces: the micromorphology', in I. Hodder (ed.) *On the Surface: Catalhoyuk 1993–5*, British Institute of Archaeology at Ankara Monograph No. 22, pp. 301–42, Cambridge: McDonald Institute.

—— (1997a) 'Microstratigraphic traces of site formation processes and human actvities', *World Archaeology* 29: 281–308.

—— (1997b) 'Activities inside the temple: the evidence of microstratigraphy', in H.E.W. Crawford, R. Killick and J. Moon *The Dilmun Temple at Saar*, pp. 31–46, London: Kegan Paul.

—— (1998) 'Microstratigraphy and micromorphology of depositional sequences', in D. Oates, J. Oates and H. McDonald *Excavation at Tell Brak Vol. 1: The Mitanni Palace and Old Babylonian periods*, pp. 135–40, Cambridge: British School of Archaeology in Iraq/McDonald Institute.

Mellars, P.A. (1976) 'Fire, ecology, animal populations and man: a study of some ecological relationships in prehistory', *Proceedings of the Prehsitoric Society* 42: 15–45.

Middleton, R., Wells, C.E. and Huckerby, E. (1995) *The Wetlands of North Lancashire*, Northwest Wetlands Survey 3, Lancaster: Lancaster University Archaeological Unit.

Milek, K.B. and French, C.A.I. (1996) 'The micromorphological analysis of a medieval occupational sequence and buried soils at Forehill, Ely, Cambridgeshire', unpublished report, Cambridge Archaeological Unit, University of Cambridge.

Milne, G. (1935) 'Some suggested units of classification particularly for East African soils', *Soil Research* 4: 183–98.

Ministry of Agriculture, Fisheries and Food (M.A.F.F.) (no date) *Data on Wind Erosion*, Mepal: Arthur Rickwood Experimental Husbandry Farm.

Mithen, S.J. (ed.) (2000) *Hunter-gatherer Landscape Archaeology: The Southern Hebrides Mesolithic Project 1988–98*, Vols. 1 and 2, Cambridge: McDonald Institute Monographs.

Mithen, S.J., Finlayson, B., Finlay, N. and Lake, M. (1992) 'Excavations at Bolsay Farm, a Mesolithic Settlement on Islay', *Cambridge Archaeological Journal* 2: 242–53.

Morgan, R.P.C. (1979) *Soil Erosion*, London: Longman.

Mortimer, R. (1997) 'Investigation of the archaeological landscape at Broom, Bedfordshire: the plant site phases 1 and 2', unpublished report, Cambridge Archaeological Unit Report No. 202, University of Cambridge.

—— (1986) *Soil Erosion and Conservation*, London: Longman.

Morton, A.G.T. (1995) 'Archaeological site formation: experiments in lake margin processes', unpublished PhD, University of Cambridge.

Moseley, M.P. (1973) 'Rainsplash and the convexity of badland divides', *Zeitschrift fur Geomorphologie, Supplementband* 18: 10–25.

Murphy, C.P. (1986) *Thin Section Preparation of Soils and Sediments*, Berkhamsted: A.B. Academic.

National Rivers Authority (N.R.A.) (1993) *Low Flows and Water Resources*, Bristol: National Rivers Authority.

Needham, S. and Macklin, M.G. (eds) *Alluvial Archaeology in Britain*, Oxford: Oxbow Monograph 27.

Neve, J. (1992) 'An interim report on the dendrochronology of Flag Fen and Fengate', *Antiquity* 66: 470–5.

Nye, S. and Scaife, R.G. (1998) 'Plant macro-fossil remains', in F. Pryor *Etton: Excavations at a Neolithic causewayed enclosure near Maxey, Cambridgeshire, 1982–7*, Archaeological Report No. 18, pp. 289–300, London: English Heritage.

Oates, D., Oates, J. and McDonald, H. (1998) *Excavations at Tell Brak, Vol. 1: The Mitanni and Old Babylonian periods*, Cambridge: McDonald Institute/British School of Archaeology in Iraq.

Odum, E.P. (1963) *Ecology: The Link between the Natural and Social Sciences*, 2nd edn, London: Holt Rinehart and Winston.

O'Neill, F.E. (1981) 'A Neolithic and Bronze Age barrow site at Orton Longueville, Cambs', unpublished report, Nene Valley Research Committee.

Palmer, R. (1994) 'Aerial photographic evidence for ring-ditches and barrows in the Little Duke Farm area', in C. French, *Excavations of the Deeping St Nicholas Barrow Complex, South Lincolnshire*, pp. 4–5, Heckington: Lincolnshire Archaeology and History Report No. 1.

Parker Pearson, M. and Sydes, R. (1997) 'The Iron Age enclosures and prehistoric landscape of Sutton Common, South Yorkshire', *Proceedings of the Prehistoric Society* 63: 221–59.

Passmore, D. and Macklin, M. (1993) 'Geochemical analysis of fine-grained late Holocene alluvial deposits at Barnack Quarry, Cambridgeshire', unpublished report, Cambridgeshire County Council Archaeological Field Unit.

Pearsall, W.H. (1950) *Mountains and Moorlands*, London: Collins.

Peglar, S. (in press) 'The Flandrian sequence in the Ouse channel core', in C. Evans and I. Hodder *The Emergence of a Fen Landscape: The Haddenham Project: Volume I*, Cambridge: McDonald Institute.

Peglar, S. and Waller, M. (1994) 'The Ouse channel, Haddenham', in M. Waller *Fenland Project, Number 9: Flandrian Environmental Change in Fenland*, pp. 174–9, Cambridge: East Anglian Archaeology 70.

Pennington, W. (1974) *The History of British Vegetation*, London: English Universities Press.

Perrin, R.M.S. and Hodge, C.A.H. (1965) 'Soils', in J. A. Steers (ed.) *The Cambridge Region*, pp. 68–84, Cambridge: British Association for the Advancement of Science.

Peterson, G.M. (1983) 'Recent pollen spectra and zonal vegetation in the western USSR', *Quaternary Science Reviews* 2: 281–321.

Pierce, C.W. (2000) 'Three dimensional geophysics and visualisation in archaeology', unpublished PhD thesis, University of Cambridge.

Pitt-Rivers, A.H.L. Fox (1887) *Excavations in Cranborne Chase, Vol. 1*, privately printed.

—— (1888) *Excavations in Cranborne Chase, Vol. 2*, privately printed.

—— (1892) *Excavations in Cranborne Chase, Vol. 3*, privately printed.

—— (1898) *Excavations in Cranborne Chase, Vol. 4*, privately printed.

Pollard, J. (1996) 'Iron Age riverside pit alignments at St Ives, Cambridgeshire', *Proceedings of the Prehistoric Society* 62: 93–115.

Potter, T.W. (1981) 'The Roman occupation of the Central Fenland', *Britannia* 12: 79–133.

Pryor, F.M.M. (1976) *Excavation at Fengate, Peterborough, England: The First Report*, Royal Ontario Museum Archaeology Monograph 4, Toronto.

—— (1978) *Excavation at Fengate, Peterborough, England: The Second Report*, Toronto: Royal Ontario Museum Archaeology Monograph 5.

—— (1980) *Excavation at Fengate, Peterborough, England: The Third Report*, Northampton/Toronto: Northamptonshire Archaeology Monograph 1/Royal Ontario Museum Archaeology Monograph 6.

—— (1984) *Excavation at Fengate, Peterborough, England: The Fourth Report*, Northampton/Toronto: Northamptonshire Archaeology Monograph 2/Royal Ontario Museum Archaeology Monograph 7.

—— (1992) 'Current research at Flag Fen', Peterborough, *Antiquity* 66: 439–547.

—— (1993) *Flag Fen*, London: Batsford.

—— (1996) 'Sheep, stockyards and field systems: Bronze Age livestock populations in the Fenlands of eastern England', *Antiquity* 70: 313–24.

—— (1998a) *Etton: Excavations at a Neolithic Causewayed Enclosure near Maxey, Cambridgeshire, 1982–7*, Archaeological Report No. 18, London: English Heritage.

—— (1998b) *Farmers in Prehistoric Britain*, Stroud: Tempus.

—— (2001) *The Flag Fen Basin: Archaeology and Environment of a Fenland Landscape*, Archaeological Reports, London: English Heritage.

Pryor, F.M.M. and French, C.A.I. (1985) *Archaeology and Environment in the Lower Welland Valley*, Cambridge: East Anglian Archaeology 27.

Pryor, F., French, C. and Taylor, M. (1985) 'An interim report on excavations at Etton, Maxey, Cambridgeshire, 1982–1984', *The Antiquaries Journal* 65: 275–311.

Pryor, F., French, C. and Taylor, M. (1986) 'Flag Fen, Fengate, Peterborough I: Discovery, reconnaissance and initial excavation (1982–85)', *Proceedings of the Prehistoric Society* 52: 1–24.

Purseglove, J. (1988) *Taming the Flood*, Oxford.

Raikes, R.L. (1984) *Water, Weather and Prehistory*, 2nd edn, New Jersey: Humanities Press.

Rapp, G. and Hill, C. (1998) *Geoarchaeology: The Earth Science Approach to Archaeological Interpretation*, London: Yale University Press.

Rees-Jones, J. and Tite, M.S. (1997) 'Optical dating results for British archaeological sediments', *Archaeometry* 39: 177–87.

Reynolds, P.J. (1979) *Iron Age Farm: The Butser Experiment*, London: British Museum.

Richards, J. (1990) *The Stonehenge Environs Project*, Archaeological Report No. 16, London: English Heritage.

Richardson, S.J. and Smith, J. (1977) 'Peat wastage in the East Anglian Fens', *Journal of Soil Science* 28: 485–9.

Roberts, N., Boyer, P. and Parish, R. (1996) 'Preliminary results of geoarchaeological investigations at Catalhoyuk', in I. Hodder (ed.) *On the surface : Catalhoyuk 1993–95*, pp. 19–40, Cambridge: McDonald Institute/British Institute of Archaeology at Ankara Monograph 22.

Robinson, M. (1992) 'The Coleoptera from Flag Fen', *Antiquity* 66: 467–9.

—— (1998) 'Chapter 14: Insect assemblages', in F. Pryor *Etton: Excavations at a Neolithic causewayed enclosure near Maxey, Cambridgeshire,1982–7*, Archaeological Report no. 18, pp. 337–48, London: English Heritage.

—— (2001) 'The Coleoptera', in F. Pryor *The Flag Fen Basin: Archaeology and Environment of a Fenland Landscape*, pp. 384–9, Archaeological Reports, London: English Heritage.

—— (forthcoming) 'The insect remains', in C. French and F. Pryor *Archaeology and Environment of the Etton Landscape*, East Anglian Archaeology.

Rodriquez Ariza, M.O. and Stevenson, A.C. (1998) 'Vegetation and its exploitation', in P.V. Castro *et al.* (eds) *Aguas Project: Palaeoclimatic Reconstruction and the Dynamics of Human Settlement and Land Use in the Area of the Middle Aguas (Almería), in the South-east of the Iberian Peninsula*, pp. 62–5, Luxembourg: European Commission.

Roose, E.J. (1970) 'Importance relative de l'érosion, du drainage oblique et vertical dans la pédogenèse actuelle d'un sol ferrallitique de moyenne Côte d'Ivoire', *Cah ORSTROM, ser Pedologie* 8: 469–82.

Royal Commission on Historical Monuments (1960) *A Matter of Time: An Archaeological Survey*, London: H.M.S.O.

Salway, P. (1967) 'Excavations at Hockwold-cum-Wilton, Norfolk, 1961–2', *Proceedings of the Cambridgeshire Antiquarian Society* 60: 39–80.

—— (1970) 'The Roman Fenland', in C.W. Phillips (ed.) *The Fenland in Roman Times*, pp. 1–21, London: Royal Geographical Society Research Series 5.

Scaife, R.G. (1982) 'Late Devensian and early Flandrian vegetation changes in southern England', in M. Bell and S. Limbrey (eds) *Archaeological Aspects of Woodland Ecology*, pp. 57–74, Oxford: British Archaeological Reports International Series 146.

—— (1984) 'Gallibury Down, Isle of Wight – pollen analysis of a Bronze Age downland palaeosol', *Ancient Monuments Laboratory Report* 4240, London.

—— (1987) 'Late Devensian and Flandrian vegetation of the Isle of Wight', in K. E. Barber (ed.) *Wessex and the Isle of Wight*, pp. 156–80, Cambridge: Quaternary Research Association Field Guide.

—— (1988) 'The Elm decline in the pollen record of South East England and its relationship to early agriculture', in M. Jones (ed.) *Archaeology and the Flora of the British Isles*, pp. 21–33, Oxford: Oxford University Archaeological Monograph 14.

—— (1992) 'Flag Fen: the vegetation environment', *Antiquity* 66: 462–6.

—— (1993) 'Pollen analysis at Crowtree Farm; Pollen analysis at Oakhurst Farm', in C. French and F. Pryor *The South-west Fen Dyke Survey Project 1982–86,* pp. 48–51 and pp. 54–9, Cambridge: East Anglian Archaeology 59.

—— (1994) 'Avon valley floodplain sediments: the pre-Roman vegetational history', in R.M.J. Cleal, M.J. Allen and C. Newman, 'An archaeological and environmental study of the Neolithic and Later Prehistoric landscape of the Avon valley between Durrington Walls and Earl's Farm Down', unpublished report, Wessex Archaeology.

—— (1996) 'Pollen analysis of the Bawsey Bronze Age barrow', in J. J. Wymer *Barrow excavations in Norfolk, 1984–88,* pp. 21–3, Dereham: East Anglian Archaeology 77.

—— (1998) 'Chapter 11: Pollen analyses', in F. Pryor *Etton: Excavations at a Neolithic Causewayed Enclosure near Maxey, Cambridgeshire, 1982–7*, Archaeological Report No. 18, pp. 301–10, London: English Heritage.

—— (2001) 'The vegetation and environment', in F. Pryor *The Flag Fen Basin: Archaeology and Environment of a Fenland Landscape,* pp. 351–81, Archaeological Reports, London: English Heritage.

—— (forthcoming) 'The pollen record from the palaeochannels', in C. French and F. Pryor *Archaeology and Environment of the Etton Landscape*, East Anglian Archaeology.

—— (forthcoming) 'The pollen analysis', in M. Carver *Excavations at Sutton Hoo*.

Scaife, R.G. and Macphail, R.I. (1983) 'Soils of the heathlands and chalklands', *Seesoil* 1: 70–99.

Schiffer, M.B. (1976) 'Archaeological context and systematic context', *American Antiquity* 37: 156–65.

—— (1983) 'Toward the identification of formation processes', *American Antiquity* 48: 675–706.

—— (1987) *Formation Processes of the Archaeological Record*, Albuquerque: University of New Mexico Press.

Seale, R.S. (1975) *Soils of the Ely District*, Harpenden: Memoir of the Soil Survey of England and Wales.

Serjeantson, D. (in press) 'The faunal remains', in C. Evans and I. Hodder *Marshland Communities and Cultural Landscape: The Haddenham Project: Volume II*, Cambridge: McDonald Institute.

Shackley, M.L. (1975) *Archaeological Sediments: A Survey of Analytical Methods*, London: Butterworths.

Sharples, N. (1991) *Maiden Castle: Excavations and Field Survey 1985–6,* Archaeological Report No. 19, London: English Heritage.

Sheals, J.G. (ed.) (1969) *The Soil Ecosystem*, London: The Systematics Association.

Shennan, I. (1982) 'Interpretation of Flandrian sea-level data from the Fenland', *Proceedings of the Geological Association* 83: 53–63.

—— (1986a) 'Flandrian sea-level changes in the Fenland I: the geographical setting and evidence of relative sea-level changes', *Journal of Quaternary Science* 1: 119–54.

—— (1986b) 'Flandrian sea-level changes in the Fenland II: tendencies of sea-level movement, altitudinal changes and local regional factors', *Journal of Quaternary Science* 1: 155–79.

Simms, J. (in press) 'Pollen analysis', in C. Evans and I. Hodder *Marshland Communities and Cultural Landscape: The Haddenham Project: Volume II*, Cambridge: McDonald Institute Monograph.

Simpson, G., Pryor, F., Neve, J. and Gurney, D. (1993) *The Fenland Project Number 7: Excavations in Peterborough and the Lower Welland Valley 1960–1969*, Peterborough: East Anglian Archaeology 61.

Simpson, I. and Milek, K. (1999) 'A reinterpretation of the great pit at Hofstaoir, Iceland, using sediment thin section micromorphology', *Geoarchaeology* 14: 511–30.

Simpson, I.A., Dockerill, S.J., Bull, I.D. and Evershed, R.P. (1998) 'Early anthropogenic soil formation at Tofts Ness, Sanday, Orkney', *Journal of Archaeological Science* 25: 729–46.

Simpson, I.A., Milek, K.B. and Guðmundsson, G. (1998) 'Archaeological sediments and site formation at Hofstaðir, Myvatn, Iceland', *Archaeologica Islandica* 1: 129–42.

Simpson, I.A., van Bergen, P. F., Perrett, V., Elhammali, M.M., Roberts, D.J. and Evershed, R.P. (1999) 'Lipid biomarkers of manuring practice in relict anthropogenic soils', *The Holocene* 9: 223–29.

Slager, S. and van de Wetering, H.T.J. (1977) 'Soil formation in archaeological pits and adjacent loess soils in Southern Germany', *Journal of Archaeological Science* 4: 259–67.

Smith, A.G., Whittle, A., Cloutman, E.W. and Morgan, L.A. (1989) 'Mesolithic and Neolithic activity and environmental impact on the South-east Fen-edge in Cambridgeshire', *Proceedings of the Prehistoric Society* 55: 207–49.

Smith, T.S. and Atkinson, K. (1975) *Techniques in Pedology*, London: Elek Science.

Soil Survey Staff (1975) *Soil Taxonomy*, Washington: United States Department of Agriculture Handbook No. 436.

Small, R.J. and Clark, M.J. (1982) *Slopes and Weathering*, Cambridge: Cambridge University Press.

Statham, I. (1979) *Earth Surface Sediment Transport*, Oxford: Clarendon.

—— (1990) 'Slope processes', in A. Goudie (ed.) *Geomorphological Techniques*, 2nd edn, pp. 225–59, London: Unwin Hyman.

Steila, D. (1976) *The Geography of Soils: Formation, Distribution and Management*, New Jersey: Prentice-Hall.

Stevens, C. (1997a) 'Bulk environmental samples', in C. Evans and M. Knight 'The Barleycroft Paddocks excavations, Cambridgeshire', pp. 108–19, unpublished report, Cambridge Archaeological Unit, University of Cambridge.

Stevenson, A.C. (1996) *A Short Synopsis of the Vegetation of the Vera Basin, Almeria*, unpublished manuscript, Aguas Project, Luxembourg: European Commission.

Stevenson, A.C. and Harrison, R.J. (1992) 'Ancient forests in Spain: A model for land-use and dry forest management in south-west Spain from 4000BC to 1900AD', *Proceedings of the Prehistoric Society* 58: 227–47.

Strahler, A.N. and Strahler, A. (1997) *Physical Geography: Science and Systems of the Human Environment,* Chichester: John Wiley and Sons.

Taylor, M. (1996) 'Worked wood', in J. Pollard, *Iron Age Riverside Pit Alignments at St Ives, Cambridgeshire, Proceedings of the Prehistoric Society* 62: 105–8.

—— (1998) 'Chapter 4: Wood and bark from the enclosure ditch', in F. Pryor, *Etton: Excavations at a Neolithic Causewayed Enclosure near Maxey, Cambridgeshire, 1982–7*, Archaeological Report No. 18, pp. 115–60, London: English Heritage.

Thomas, J. (1991) *Rethinking the Neolithic*, Cambridge: Cambridge University Press.

Thorley, A. (1981) 'Pollen analytical evidence relating to the vegetational history of the chalk', *Journal of Biogeography* 8: 93–106.

Thornes, J.B. and Gilman, P. (1983) 'Potential and actual erosion around archaeological sites in southeast Spain', *Catena Supplement* 4: 91–113.

Tusa, S. (1999) *La Sicilia nella preistoria*, 3rd edn, Palermo: Sellerio.

Usai, M.R. (2001) 'Textural pedofeatures and pre-Hadrian's Wall ploughed paleosols at Stanwix, Carlisle, U.K.', *Journal of Archaeological Science* 28: 541–53.

Valentine, K.W.G. and Dalrymple, J.B. (1975) 'The identification, lateral variation and chronology of two buried palaeocatenas at Woodhall Spa and West Runton, England', *Quaternary Research* 5: 551–90.

Van Andel, T.H. and Shackleton, J.C. (1982) 'Late Palaeolithic and Mesolithic coastlines of Greece and the Aegean', *Journal of Field Archaeology* 9: 445–54.

Van der Leeuw, S.E. (1997) *A DG-XII Research Programme to Understand the Natural and Anthropogenic Causes of Land Degradation and Desertification in the Mediterranean Basin*, Luxembourg: European Commission.

Van de Noort, R. and Davies, P. (1993) *Wetland Heritage: An Archaeological Assessment of the Humber Wetlands*, Kingston upon Hull: English Heritage.

Van de Noort, R., Chapman, H.P. and Cheetham, J. (in press) '*In situ* preservation as a dynamic process; the example of Sutton Common, UK', *Antiquity*.

Wainwright, G.J. and Longworth, I.H. (1971) *Durrington Walls: Excavations 1966–1968*, London: Research Report of the Society of Antiquaries London 29.

Wallace, G.E. (1995) 'Etton Landscape: the composition and environmental implications of a faunal assemblage found in a Grooved ware context', unpublished MPhil dissertation, University of Cambridge.

Waller, M. (1994) *The Fenland Project, Number 9: Flandrian Environmental Change in Fenland*, Cambridge: East Anglian Archaeology 70.

Waller, M., Cloutman, E., Alderton, A. and Peglar, S. (1994) 'South-central Fens', in M. Waller *The Fenland Project, Number 9: Flandrian Environmental Change in Fenland*, pp. 156–82, Cambridge: East Anglian Archaeology 70.

Ward, R.C. and Robinson, M. (1990) *Principles in Hydrology*, 3rd edn, London: McGraw Hill.

Waters, M.P. (1992) *Principles of Geoarchaeology: The North American Perspective*, Tucson: University of Arizona Press.

Weir, A.H., Catt, J.A. and Madgett, P.A. (1971) 'Postglacial soil formation in the loess of Pegwell Bay, Kent (England)', *Geoderma* 5: 131–49.

Weiss, H., Courty, M.-A., Wetterstrom, W., Guichard, F., Senior, L., Meadow, R. and Curnow, A. (1993) 'The genesis and collapse of third millennium north Mesopotamian civilisation', *Science* 261: 995–1004.

Wheeler, M. (1954) *Archaeology from the Earth*, Oxford: Clarendon.

Wilkinson, B., Broughton, W. and Parker-Sutton, J. (1969) 'Survey of wind erosion on sandy soils in the East Midlands', *Experimental Husbandry* 18: 53–9.

Wilkinson, T.J. (1994) 'The structure and dynamics of dry-farming states in upper Mesopotamia', *Current Anthropology* 35: 483–519.

—— (1997) 'Holocene environments of the High Plateau, Yemen: recent geoarchaeological investigations', *Geoarchaeology* 12: 833–64.

Wilkinson, T., French, C., Matthews, W. and Oates, J. (2001) 'Geoarchaeology, landscape and the region', in J. Oates, D. Oates and H. McDonald, *Tell Brak*

Volume 2, pp. 1–14, Cambridge: British School of Archaeology in Iraq/McDonald Institute.

Willis, K.J., Braun, M., Sumegi, P. and Toth, A. (1997) 'Does soil development cause vegetational change or vice versa? A temporal perspective from Hungary', *Ecology* 73: 730–40.

Willis, K.J., Braun, M., Sumegi, P. and Toth, A. (1998) 'Prehistoric land degradation in Hungary: Who, how and why?', *Antiquity* 72: 101–13.

Wilson, C.A. (2000) 'Processes of post-burial change in soils under archaeological monuments : a micromorphological study with particular reference to the processes of clay and iron redistribution', unpublished PhD thesis, University of Stirling.

Wilson, G. (1984) 'A report on the plant macrosossils from Fengate', in F. Pryor *Excavation at Fengate, Peterborough, England: The Fourth Report*, pp. M 242–4, Northampton/Toronto: Northamptonshire Archaeological Society Monograph 2/Royal Ontario Museum Archaeology Monograph 7.

Wiltshire, P. (1996) 'Palynological analysis', in J. Pollard *Iron Age riverside pit alignments at St Ives, Cambridgeshire, Proceedings of the Prehistoric Society* 62: 109.

—— (1997a) 'Pollen analysis', in C. Evans and M. Knight, 'The Barleycroft Paddocks excavations', pp. 101–7, Cambridge Archaeological Unit, University of Cambridge.

—— (1997b) 'Palynological assessment of soils and sediments', in C. Evans and M. Knight, 'The Over Lowland investigations, Cambridgeshire: Part I – the 1996 evaluation', pp. 76–82, unpublished report, Cambridge Archaeological Unit, University of Cambridge.

Winder, N.P. and van der Leeuw, S.E. (eds) (1997) *Environmental Perception and Policy Making: Cultural and Natural Heritage and the Preservation of Degradation-sensitive Environments in Southern Europe*, Luxembourg: European Commission.

Wolman, M.G. (1967) 'A cycle of sedimentation and erosion in urban river channels', *Geografiska Annales* 49–A: 385–95.

Wright, V.P. (ed.) (1986) *Paleosols: Their Recognition and Interpretation*, Oxford: Blackwell Scientific.

Yannouli, E. (1997) 'Faunal remains', in C. Evans and M. Knight, 'The Barleycroft Paddocks excavations', pp. 120–4, unpublished report, Cambridge Archaeological Unit, University of Cambridge.

Young, A. (1969) 'Present rate of land erosion', *Nature* 224: 851–2.

Zalaciewicz, J. A. (1986) 'Sedimentological evolution of the Fenland during the Flandrian: problems and prospects', *Fenland Research* 3: 45–9.

Zalaciewicz, J.A. and Wilmot, R.D. (1986) 'Conductivity mapping in facies analysis of the Holocene deposits of the Fenland', *Bulletin of the Geological Society of Norfolk* 36: 89–95.

Zohary, M. (1973) *Geobotanical Foundations of the Middle East*, Stuttgart: Fischer.

Index

Printed in Great Britain
by Amazon.co.uk, Ltd.,
Marston Gate.